GUNS OR BUTTER

R. H. BRUCE LOCKHART

GUNS
OR BUTTER

WAR COUNTRIES AND PEACE
COUNTRIES OF EUROPE REVISITED

PUTNAM

42 GREAT RUSSELL STREET
LONDON

First published October, 1938
Reprinted October, 1938
Reprinted October, 1938

PRINTED IN GREAT BRITAIN BY ROBERT MACLEHOSE AND CO. LTD.
THE UNIVERSITY PRESS, GLASGOW

CONTENTS

"GUNS WILL make us powerful; butter will only make us fat." FIELD MARSHAL GOERING

BOOK I

THE BENEFITS OF BUTTER

"LEAVING THE OLD, both worlds at once they view
That stand upon the threshold of the new."

CHAPTER ONE

WHEN A MAN has spent twenty-five years in foreign countries, he does not adapt himself readily to the restrictions of life in England. We all know the tragedy of the civil servant or soldier who, after a long period of pleasant foreign service, comes home to eke out an empty existence on a small pension in Cheltenham or Camberley. Still harder is the lot of the man who, by circumstances of chance or of his own folly, is forced to abandon a post abroad, which he likes, for one at home which is repugnant.

Until recently I belonged to this second category of returned exile. With the exception of three years in Malaya, my life from 1905 to 1929 had been lived in Central and Eastern Europe. Twelve of these years had been spent in the consular and diplomatic services of my country. Then, suffering from the post-war restlessness of my generation, I had abandoned government service for a post in a Central European bank which was sponsored by the Bank of England. My new work took me at more or less regular intervals to the different capitals of Central and South-Eastern Europe and, although I was no banker, the life was not unpleasant. After a few years of lofty endeavour the bank failed to realise its own expectations, and with the shrinkage of its business I found myself at a dead end. A chance meeting with Lord Beaverbrook brought me the offer of a journalistic post in Fleet Street under his aegis. I accepted it.

My change of occupation meant my withdrawal from Europe. Lord Beaverbrook is a generous but insistent taskmaster. I was nailed to my desk in London. From 1929 to 1937 my visits to Europe were few and of short duration. Journalism involved the abandonment of my active interest in foreign affairs, for the policy of my newspaper was isolationist and offered little scope for the display of my special knowledge of the smaller countries of Central Europe.

I am grateful to Lord Beaverbrook. His kindness and his hospitality were unstinted. At his house I met most of the political and public figures in Britain, and from him personally I absorbed some wisdom and much useful knowledge. But I was not happy. I chafed under the irksome restraints of an exacting profession. Moreover, I was not and never should be a good journalist. Few of Lord Beaverbrook's young men are born journalists. Fewer still would escape the anonymity of mediocrity, but for the fact that they are controlled, guided, and influenced by the master-mind of a man who, if the public did not regard him solely as a newspaper-proprietor, would be acknowledged as the most able journalist of his time. I felt that, if Fleet Street was an education, it ought not to be a permanency except for born journalists like Mr. James Agate, whose genius enables him to command a brilliant independence. After my first two years I wanted to abandon daily journalism. I longed to return to the European life which I knew and liked. Unfortunately, decision does not come so easily to middle-age as to youth, and for nearly seven years I drifted on the slack tide of postponement.

There are in the world's literature two prescriptive stories about journalism. The first is Daudet's story of *The Goat of M. Seguin*. It was written, you will remember, in reply to a letter from M. Pierre Gringoire, lyrical poet of Paris. Having spent ten years in the loyal service of Apollo, M. Gringoire is down-at-heels and often hungry. Nevertheless, he has refused a bread-and-butter job as a columnist on a Paris newspaper because he considers such work degrading. Daudet writes advising him to take the post, and to give point to his advice he tells the story of M. Seguin's goat.

M. Seguin is a small proprietor in Provence. The joy of his life are his goats. But he has no luck with them. Sooner or later they break the cord which attaches them to the picket in the enclosure behind his house. Then they climb the mountain to enjoy the wild grass which is so much sweeter than the grass of slavery. After a few hours of freedom they are devoured by the mountain wolf. Having lost six goats in this manner, M. Seguin buys a seventh. And this time he takes the precaution to buy a very young goat whose name is Blanquette. At first Blanquette seems happy, and M. Seguin, who loves her more than all his other goats, is enchanted.

"At last", he says, "I have found a goat who does not chafe under the restraints of captivity."

But M. Seguin is mistaken. Blanquette is bored. One day she, too, expresses a desire for the mountain, and to protect her against her own misguided judgment he locks her in the stable. Unfortunately, he leaves the window open. As soon as his back is turned, Blanquette skips over the ledge and trips her way up the mountain-side. There she spends the happiest day of her life. The grass is more luscious than the grass of the enclosure. She meets a young chamois and for an hour or two flirts with him deliciously. Then night falls, and Blanquette hears the howl of the wolf. From far away she catches the sound of M. Seguin's horn summoning her home. For a moment she thinks of going back. Then she remembers the cord and the picket in the enclosure, and resolutely she spurns a life of servitude. As she turns, she sees the glistening eyes of the wolf. All through the night she fights him with her horns. But with the dawn her strength fails, and in the morning the wolf eats her.

M. Daudet was a confirmed believer in economic "Safety first".

The other story, a true one, concerns Francis Carco, the popular French novelist and, in his youth, the closest friend of the painter Modigliani. Like Daudet's poet, like Modigliani himself, Carco could make no headway in the arts. Like many other young Frenchmen he preferred the breadless freedom of Montmartre and the Boulevard St. Michel to the monotony of routine. In those days he was a poet. The ideals of literature were not to be sacrificed on the altar of daily journalism. But one day not long before the Great War he suffered a momentary weakness from starvation and accepted a post as junior reporter on *L'Homme Libre*, the Paris newspaper of M. Clemenceau.

On his own confession he was an indifferent reporter. He took no interest in his newspaper. He was given small crime stories to report and reported them badly. On the anniversary of the theft of the "Mona Lisa" from the Louvre he was sent to interview the Paris Prefect of Police and was kicked out. He came back without a "story", without even an account of his ignominious exit. Obviously he would not have lasted long in English or American journalism.

Then, one day, there was a typical French political scandal. A French admiral had taken part officially in a religious manifestation at Athens on Good Friday, and Clemenceau, fiercely anti-clerical, had been demanding the officer's dismissal. In the hottest moment of the campaign it was discovered that the admiral had acted on official instructions. The Presidential decree authorising his participation in the manifestation had actually been published in the newspaper, *La Croix*. Here was bigger game for Clemenceau, and the "Tiger's" eyes shone with the light of battle. He wanted the number of *La Croix* immediately, and when he said "immediately" it meant that the whole staff would be tormented until he got what he wanted.

The editor rang his bell. All the reporters were out except Carco.

"Go at once to the office of *La Croix* and bring back the number with the famous decree," said the editor.

"What decree?" asked Carco.

The editor exploded.

"Don't you read the newspapers?"

"No."

"Don't you read your own newspaper?"

"No."

"Do you mean to say that you don't read Clemenceau?"

"No," stammered the unfortunate Carco.

There was a moment's silence while the editor wrestled with his collar. Then Georges Mandel, who was in the room, intervened:

"My young friend, you will read Clemenceau. . . . You will come to the editor every evening and you will give him a summary of Clemenceau's leader. Otherwise . . ."

There was no mistaking the threat in that silky voice, and for a week Carco carried out his instructions. Then his soul rebelled, and he walked out. He had nothing in his pocket except the manuscript of a half-finished novel. He went back to his garret. But from his window he saw the Seine flowing like a thread of silver between the dark walls of the *quais*. It was spring, and the trees were just turning green. He was free. He knew that he was "l'homme libre", and that the men whom he had left behind in the newspaper office were slaves.

To-day, Carco is one of the most successful French authors, a member of the Academie Goncourt and a best-seller in every country in which French is read. His story is the very antithesis to Daudet's cautionary tale, and, although I should not like anyone to take either my career or my character as a model, I would say this to British youth: "Live boldly and beware of the groove of routine. There are only two things in life that count. Make up your mind what you want to do and then, provided that you aim high, do it with all your might."

As for myself, my position in Fleet Street was much the same as that of Carco and of Daudet's poet. Indeed, if I was better paid, I was worse off. For I was much older and had heavier responsibilities. But Carco's courage appealed to me much more than Daudet's caution. During the later years of my journalistic career the two stories never left my mind. In direct connection with my own problem I discussed them with my relatives and with my friends. My father was on Daudet's side. My brother and Harold Nicolson were ardent Carcoists.

My final decision was influenced more by chance than by persuasion. Towards the end of 1936 I began to feel the strain of working in Fleet Street all day and writing books by night. Then an attack of influenza knocked me out and, feeling depressed, I determined to take medical advice. Close to my house lived Dr. David McMyn, one of the finest Rugby football forwards that ever played for Cambridge and Scotland. Although he was much younger than I, we had been friends for some years. He had his full share of brains and brawn. He had been Head of the school at Fettes and had done brilliantly at his hospital. Rosy-cheeked, broad-shouldered, and glowing with health, he had as sane an outlook on life as any man I knew. What was more important, he had acquired from first-hand observation a practical knowledge of the strain of Fleet Street. I sent for him. He sounded me all over and asked me a long list of questions. Then he smiled.

"You're all right," he said. "But do you remember the case of the man who shot himself in the taxi-cab a few minutes before his insurance policy would have lapsed in order that the insurance money might be available for his heirs and for his creditors? There was a case over it. The Court of Appeal gave its verdict in favour of the insurance company on the grounds of public policy."

I remembered the case.

"Well," said David, "if you asked me to-day to define the surest method of committing legalised suicide I should say unhesitatingly: 'lead the life that you are living. You can't go on writing books and doing daily journalism. One will have to go or you'll go. What are you going to do about it?'"

His bluntness brought me to the plunge. I had no hesitation over the choice. I went to Lord Beaverbrook. I told him that I wished to give up journalism in order to write books. He received me with great kindness. Whatever he may have thought of my chances of success, he wished me well. In these personal interviews Lord Beaverbrook's human side, always much nearer the surface than most people imagine, comes to the top, and his friendly words of encouragement almost made me regret my decision. But dominating every other emotion was the feeling that I was free—free to live my dream even if it failed to realise all its hopes, free to get away from London and to return to the Europe where my real interests lay.

I left Fleet Street—I hope for ever—in 1937.

B

CHAPTER TWO

AN AUTHOR, IF not wholly independent, can, at least, live and go where he likes. He is tied to no office. The area of his activities is as wide as the world itself. This mobility is perhaps the most pleasant attribute of an author's life.

I confess that at first I found my new freedom slightly bewildering. I wanted to travel again. Where was I to begin? Europe was a large field. Should I try to go back to Russia? The desire was there, but I was not sure of the nature of my reception. Once again chance, which has intervened so often in my life, brought opportunity to my door-step in the form of a message from Rex Leeper of the Foreign Office. Would I undertake a lecturing tour in the Balkans and Central Europe on behalf of the British Council, the new institution for the development of British cultural relations abroad? The Council, which receives a small Government subsidy, was supported by the Foreign Office. I should receive such official assistance as could properly be given.

I accepted at once. I had a preliminary and helpful talk with Sir Robert Vansittart, the brilliant descendant of a brilliant family which has given to Britain several famous public men. One, Nicholas Vansittart, was Chancellor of the Exchequer during the most difficult period of the Napoleonic wars. When he resigned, he left to his successor a surplus revenue of £2,000,000. This Nicholas Vansittart took a keen interest in foreign affairs, and had been employed on, at least, one important mission abroad.

Knowing the family history, I wondered if, in his turn, Sir Robert would be summoned to play a similar role in the affairs of Britain. If there were another war, his ability, his resolute courage, his immense capacity for work, and his wide knowledge of foreign affairs would make him one of the most indispensable men in the country. Attractive, witty, full of charm and a brilliant linguist, he excels in delicate negotiations with foreign diplomatists. I know only one minor failure in his public career. Many years ago he was best man at Sir Joseph Addison's wedding. At the crucial moment he dropped the ring down a grating in the church floor.

With Sir Robert's backing the arrangements for my journey were soon made, and early in 1937 I set out on a five weeks' tour which took me to all the capitals and sub-capitals of Central and South-Eastern Europe including Prague, Bratislava, Buda-pest, Zagreb, Belgrade, Sofia, Bucharest, Cluj, and Vienna. As far as the physical strain was concerned, it was a more hectic and more strenuous affair than even an American lecture contract. As a Scot I lectured rather cheekily on "An Englishman Looks At The World".

On the whole the tour was moderately successful. There was the inevitable *contretemps*. In Zagreb a Scot, who did not appreciate my humorous sallies at the expense of both Scots and English, walked out rather ostentatiously in the middle of my lecture. In Vienna where Herr Schuschnigg did not like the Beaverbrook Press and the British Minister did not think that I was a serious enough person to address a serious people like the Viennese, I was left to my own devices. On the other hand, the Hungarians, who had no reason to regard as a great friend anyone so closely connected with Slav countries as myself, received me with their habitual hospitality and kindness, and in Buda-pest I spoke from the Speaker's dais in the Delegations Hall in the Houses of Parliament.

From Countess Bethlen I heard a graphic account of her famous husband's escape from the Communists at the end of the war. At that time he was living on his estate in Transylvania. One day an armed band of Communists came to kill him. They ignored Countess Bethlen and the Hungarian servants and directed their questions to a Serbian prisoner of war who was still living on the estate. The Serb told the Communists that Count Bethlen had gone out to visit one of his farms. The Communists set out to look for him and after a vain search returned to threaten the Serb. This time they made him speak with a dozen rifles pointed at his breast. The Serb, however, stuck to his story, and because he was a Serb the Communists believed him and went away.

Count Bethlen was in the house the whole time. The Serb was then free and was leaving for Belgrade that evening. But he was grateful to the Bethlens. As a prisoner he had been struck down by the virulent Spanish "flu" which was claiming hundreds of victims in Hungary. "Of course," said Countess Bethlen simply, "I had nursed him myself."

I like this story. I see in it a hopeful augury for the appeasement of national hatreds, for it is a pleasant reflection that the one great European figure whom Hungary has produced since the war should owe not only his life but also his life's work to the courage and gratitude of a Serbian soldier.

In Rumania I enjoyed myself thoroughly and formed a new and much more favourable opinion of the Rumanians. Transylvania, where keen Rumanian anglers took me to mountain trout streams which one day I mean to fish, must appeal to every Scot, and to-day it takes its place beside Slovenia in my heart as a land where I could make a second home. I liked the sturdy Transylvanian peasants with their picturesque home-spun clothes and their neat, wooden houses. I was fascinated by the erudition and simplicity of the intelligentsia, and at Cluj, the little capital of the province, I danced the "hora" with sober and earnest university professors.

Bulgaria gave me my first introduction to that attractive personality, King Boris. In all these countries I met the leading politicians and public figures, and I was almost overwhelmed by the welcome and hospitality of my old friends in Czechoslovakia and Yugoslavia.

On my return to London I wrote a long report for the Foreign Office. My conclusions, if not optimistic, were in one respect favourable. What impressed me most was the immense material progress which had been made during the eight years of my absence. Backward provinces like Slovakia had been transformed. Villages like Belgrade had become modern cities. Everywhere I saw new schools, new roads, new hospitals and other standing stones which betokened a giant stride forward in the material welfare of community life. I felt that, if left to themselves, these small countries could solve all their difficulties by themselves. In spite of all that has happened during the last twelve months, I believe firmly that but for the conditional "if" this conclusion would have proved true.

I had enjoyed my tour, but it had been very exhausting. I therefore made a silent vow that never again would I go lecturing.

I soon changed my mind. In the autumn of 1937 I received an invitation from the various Anglo-Scandinavian Societies to visit Norway, Sweden, and Denmark, and once again I allowed the travel restlessness in my blood to over-ride any minor considerations of fatigue. At the request and with the assistance of the British Council, Holland was added to my list of countries.

I was glad to have this opportunity of re-visiting the Netherlands. I have a profound sympathy with the small countries of Europe, and my affection for Holland is of long standing. I like the Dutch people. I admire them for their courage, for their outstanding ability, and for their inexhaustible capacity for hard work. And the Hague is perhaps my favourite capital. Its neat squares, its woods and parks with the deer feeding tranquilly on the rich green grass, and the absence of even the vestige of a slum give to it an atmosphere of solidity and peacefulness which is not to be found in any other capital in Europe. I like the true democracy of its bicycles. Boys and girls, with their arms stretched across to rest on each other's shoulder, do their wooing on bicycles. Privates and generals ride to work on bicycles. House removals are carried out on bicycles. The police ride bicycles with a special slot below the handle-bars for their swords. Everywhere are parking places for bicycles. Even one of the arcades forming the wings of the Queen's Palace has a stand for bicycles. And the Palace has a street number like the smallest house in the Noordeinde.

I yield readily to the routine influence of the Hague. I feel pleasantly subdued in the quiet but expensive respectability of the Hotel des Indes. I enjoy the gentle conversation with M. Rey, its erudite Monagasque proprietor who knows so much and whose discretion is so irksome. I like the half-empty restaurant, because it gives me an opportunity to watch Herr Mannheimer, once the partner of the great Berlin banking house of Mendelssohn and to-day the most powerful Jewish exile in the world. He is the mystery man of Europe. Nobody knows the extent of his fortune. But he is or has been the banker of the French Government. His wealth does not seem to have brought him happiness. The Hague is justly famed for the excellence of its food. But Herr Mannheimer dines off a bottle of mineral water and a tiny sole. His health is not good. He looks frail. He walks slowly as though the burden of his cares was too heavy for his shoulders.

I know, too, no more pleasant emotion than to stroll down the Voorhout to the Mauritshuis and then, after admiring and envying the serene tranquillity of Vermeer's Rotterdamsche Vaart, to walk through the Binnenhof and from the other side watch the winter sun shedding its pale rays on the placid waters of the Vijver lake.

I must qualify this eulogy of the Hague by the statement that to the stranger the city may seem cold and friendless, for the Dutch are as reserved and as difficult to know as the English. Fortunately, I have the advantage of knowing some influential Dutchmen. And for such knowledge of the Hague as I possess I am indebted to Dr. van Karnebeek, the former Dutch Foreign Minister and to-day the Queen's Commissioner for South Holland. He is one of the cleverest and shrewdest diplomatists that I have ever met, and, as he is still a young man as Dutch and British politicians go, his voice is likely to be heard again in the counsels of Europe. Whenever I go to the Hague, he spares no pains not only to initiate me into the mysteries of Dutch politics but also to show and to explain to me the beauties and the engineering marvels of the Dutch countryside. With him I visited the poorer quarters of the Hague and of Scheveningen with its model harbour and garden city for the fisher-folk. When I thought of Edinburgh and Glasgow, I felt ashamed.

Among his many other activities Dr. van Karnebeek has been Burgomaster of the Hague and in this capacity has been mainly responsible for the intensive campaign of slum clearance. The Dutch do not say much. But they are very thorough, and since the war they have done a great work of insurance against revolution by providing housing amenities for the working classes. "Give the woman a home" has been their motto, and the Dutch woman has made the excellent home provided for her spotlessly clean.

With Dr. van Karnebeek, I paid some years ago my first visit to the Peace Palace. It is to my mind rather a grim and forbidding building, affording food for reflection both to the idealist and to the cynic. Like the League of Nations building in Geneva, it has been furnished and equipped by contributions in kind from nearly every country in the world. Britain's gift is in the big meeting room, where sit the fifteen judges of the Permanent Court of International Justice, and takes the form of stained glass windows representing war and peace. The cynically minded may see something sinister in the fact that Germany's contribution is outside the Palace. She gave the massive wrought-iron gates which not only guard the entrance, but also create the effect that Peace and anyone else would have some difficulty in forcing their way in.

The Palace, given by the late Andrew Carnegie, was opened in 1913, and the first President was Dr. van Karnebeek's father. The first Hague Peace Conference, however, was summoned in 1899, the meetings being held in the Huis ten Bosch, the charming Barok palace in the Hague wood. Neither since 1899 nor since 1913 has the Hague institution been able to do very much for the maintenance of peace. Perhaps the first delegates were not attuned to the idea. At any rate the only positive instruction given to the French delegates at the first Conference was to oppose as guilefully as possible the adoption of any resolution recommending obligatory arbitration in international conflicts. There were, too, among the delegates of other countries certain men who were later to acquire notoriety for actions which were the reverse of peaceful. Turkhan Pasha, the Turkish delegate, is remembered to-day as one of the fiercest executants of the sanguinary vengeances of Abdul Hamid. One of the Serbian delegates was Colonel Mašin who later achieved an unenviable fame for the active part which he played in the murder of King Alexander and Queen Draga. I found the Palace depressing. Subsequent visits and added knowledge of its history have not altered this first impression.

If I owe a debt of gratitude to Dr. van Karnebeek, I confess frankly that the chief attraction of my visits to the Hague were my meetings with Dr. Colijn, Holland's Prime Minister and a man who takes a very high place among the few outstanding post-war statesmen of Europe. Tall with dome-shaped head, pink cheeks, powerful shoulders, and attractive forceful hands, he is of peasant stock and belongs to the same type of Dutchmen who during the long struggle against Spain let in the famous dykes, built with so much toil and labour, in order to save their country. He was brought up on the Bible and knows it to-day as well as Lord Baldwin knows his Horace. His father who was very short-sighted knew it even better. He used to read the lessons in church. One day he forgot his glasses, but he went through the chapter without a mistake. He knew it off by heart.

To-day, Dr. Colijn is in his seventieth year, but his health and energy are amazing. He still smokes about twenty cigars a day, and I should back him to walk Mr. Hore Belisha or Mr. Eden off his feet. He is a stickler for punctuality and, because he knows how to live by the clock, he succeeds in giving the impression that he has time for everybody and everything. He is a great reader and prefers English history and English memoirs to any other form of literature. He is also a splendid conversationalist, and I would rather hear him talk for two hours in a small company than listen to the finest Parliamentary speech ever made.

Dr. Colijn has had a remarkable career. It began in the Dutch East Indies where his outstanding abilities soon attracted the attention of van Heutz, Holland's greatest Governor-General. With van Heutz's encouragement he built roads and hacked new towns out of the Sumatra jungle. He also found time to take an active and important part in the war against the Achinese. He lived dangerously and had many narrow escapes from a violent death. Perhaps the narrowest escape was when he was sent on the Governor-General's yacht to settle a disturbance in Flores. On his way the yacht was wrecked on the rocks off the island of Soembawa. In order to obtain help for the others Colijn stripped and swam ashore through the shark-infested sea. He knew that somewhere on the island there was a Dutch military post, but he had little idea where it was situated. Making himself a hat and a suit of banana-leaves, he wandered for four days through the jungle. At last, half-starved and with his banana-leaf suit in strips, he saw a clearing with a row of neat huts. It was the Dutch outpost, and he strode forward joyfully. His relief soon changed to embarrassment when he found that the Dutch officers were out somewhere on duty and that only the commandant's wife was at home. The lady, however, soon put him at his ease, although she had some difficulty in finding a suit large enough to fit him.

Then Colijn came back to Holland and went into home politics. He became Minister of Marine at the age of forty-two, and the Dutch newspapers claimed him as the youngest

Minister of Marine in the world. A few days later he received through the British Naval Attaché in the Hague a message from Mr. Winston Churchill to the effect that in Britain there was a First Lord of the Admiralty who was three years Colijn's junior.

From that moment dates Dr. Colijn's friendship with Mr. Churchill who to-day has no greater admirer than the Dutch Prime Minister. In particular, Dr. Colijn admires Mr. Churchill's Marlborough which, in his opinion, contains the best analysis of the Dutch character ever written by a foreigner. "The finest pen in Europe" is the Colijn verdict on Mr. Churchill, and he is not given to flattery.

I had had the pleasure of meeting Dr. Colijn on previous visits to the Hague and of hearing him talk until late into the night. On this occasion he came to my lecture and asked me to luncheon the next day. We were only six, and the other guests were the Minister of Foreign Affairs, the Minister for the Colonies, the Head of the Dutch Military Intelligence, and Sir Hubert Montgomery, the British Minister. The food was excellent, and the meal lasted nearly as long as one of Christopher Morley's functions at the Three-Hours-for-Luncheon Club in New York. Dr. Colijn was in his best form. Like all Dutchmen he is intensely interested in the East, and he and I had a common bond in our personal knowledge of the Malay Archipelago. His conversation covered the whole range of world politics, and his comments were always shrewd and sometimes outspoken. I should commit a breach of confidence in repeating them, but I think I may safely say that he is opposed to all extremes, dislikes and mistrusts ideological divisions, has no belief in political "lecturing", and is strongly in favour of an understanding between Britain, France and Germany. I hope that I may quote a story that he told and also one of his political comments.

On a certain occasion he asked Signor Mussolini who would succeed him. The Duce began to explain. The establishment of Fascism, he said, was like building a factory. Four stages were necessary. First, you had to lay the foundations and build the factory. Then you had to obtain the best machinery. Thirdly, you had to engage the best fitters and set the machinery up and keep it in running order. Finally, all that was required was a man to pull the lever.

"I'm at the third stage now," said Signor Mussolini. "I hope to live long enough to inaugurate the fourth stage. Then the question of the succession is simple."

"Very good," said Dr. Colijn, "but what about possible improvements in other countries and the deterioration of your own machinery."

"True," said Mussolini. "Every system is subject to this disadvantage, for nothing in life can stand still. It is up to the future generation of Italians to see that the quality of the machinery is not impaired."

Dr. Colijn's other comment was in reply to a question which I put to him:

"What would you do," I asked, "if you were given full dictatorial powers to settle the affairs of Europe? Could you establish peace and order within reasonable time?"

"Yes," he replied without hesitation, "I could. And I'd do it in this way. I should establish an economic federation out of the states of the old Austro-Hungarian Monarchy. I should go a long way to satisfy Germany's prestige requirements including the return of her colonies. And then I should make economic arrangements between the Great Powers for the production and distribution of raw materials similar to those Britain and the Netherlands have made for tin and rubber."

There was wisdom in his words, but now the dream of a Danubian Federation has been shattered.

Where Dr. Colijn is concerned, I am a hero-worshipper. He is cast in a big mould. He is a man full of understanding, magnanimous in all things, afraid of nothing. More than any other living European statesman he personifies all the virtues of commonsense, and when his commonsense tells him that he is right he can be firm as rock. In English eyes he has only one "fault". He is not an Englishman. Yet he has a warm affection for England and often flies over to London for a quiet talk with his friends. He travels unheralded and unaccompanied. He is a man wholly without conceit. He has a natural dislike of modern publicity.

I feel that we have much to learn from the Dutch. They have their failings. The existence of too many political parties is one weakness, and, when Colijn goes, as one day go he must, there may be difficulties. But the Dutch constitution has many good points, some of which we might well copy. For instance, Dutch Ministers, with the exception of the Prime Minister, rarely have to appear in Parliament and can therefore devote almost their full time to the work of their departments. Moreover, Holland, situated half-way between Britain and Germany, has a civilisation which in some respects is higher than our own, and, although the Dutch prize their neutrality above all other assets, there is little doubt where their sympathies lie. They have given to us many distinguished soldiers and statesmen: Bentincks, Keppels, and Vansittarts, and they are more like us than any other race, more like us even than are the Norwegians.

I shall never forget my first night in the Hague many years ago. I was alone and wanted to go to a theatre. My choice hesitated between Lohengrin at the Opera House and what I felt would be an insipid cabaret. In my indecision I sought the advice of the hall-porter at the Hotel des Indes.

"Take the cabaret," he said without hesitation. "This country has too much fog, and drinks too much gin to produce good singers."

The Dutch have many interests in common with us. Acre for acre, they possess the richest colonial empire in the world. They are obsessed by the conviction that one day the white races will have to face the yellow, and they therefore desire a united Europe. But, above all, they want Britain to be strong. They know both Britain and Germany intimately and regard such knowledge as an essential part of their education. They understand the faults and virtues of both countries. As they also see very clearly the causes of misunderstanding, the Hague is or should be an all-important diplomatic crow's-nest.

Yet the Dutch feel—and perhaps rightly—that we regard the Hague as a kind of diplomatic Sleepy Hollow. They would like us to know them better. Conscious of their great past, they remember that Holland was the first country to establish an embassy in London. To-day, they find it a little galling for the Dutch Minister in London to have to take a back seat to the Polish Ambassador, the Chilian Ambassador, the Portuguese Ambassador and all the other new ambassadors who have been created since the war. They believe that the prestige of a country is not to be measured solely by its area and by the size of its population. From a British point of view the importance of Holland's geographical position should make us sympathise with the Dutch attitude.

I left the Hague on St. Andrew's Day for Groningen, where the British Naval Brigade was interned during the Great War and where I had to give another lecture. I made the first part of my way by motor-car and between Gouda and Amsterdam drove through the little town of Breukelen. It will live in history. It gave its name to the great city which New Yorkers now call Brooklyn.

At Groningen my kind hosts took me by car to the extreme northern point of Holland in order to show me the famous "polder", which have been formed from land reclaimed from the ocean and protected by dykes. Some of the dykes were over a hundred years old. Others were new, enclosing land won back only recently from the cold North Sea. This new land, green and divided by narrow drains into long strips five or six yards wide, is extraordinarily rich, and hundreds of sheep were already feeding there. But what interested me most was a vast corn-growing district a little farther inland. Here I saw the unmistakable signs of prosperity. Nowhere in Europe have I seen such well-built farms and villages. But there were no big land-owners. The land belongs to the farmers. They have been there for centuries. They are a hard, strong race in which the family unit is everything and family discipline the supreme law. My host, a local banker, gave me some striking figures regarding their wealth. Yet I saw no evidence of the luxury which, in other countries, riches bring in their train. Here the animal came before the man. The farm-houses were well-built and architecturally attractive. But the huge barns dwarfed them. They were connected with the house by a narrow neck to enable the farmer to attend a sick cow by night without having to dress and go out into the open. The houses face North. The barns are on the sunny side.

Breukelen was a monument to the past greatness of Holland. The "polder" country was merely one reminder of the virility of a people who, although small in number, still rank culturally and commercially among the great races of the world.

CHAPTER THREE

I HAD NOT been in Scandinavia since the late autumn of 1918, when I passed through after the combined efforts of Scandinavian and Dutch diplomacy had effected my release from my Russian prison. In 1938 my way to Oslo, which was the starting point of my lecture-tour, took me through Denmark and the South-West corner of Sweden. At Helsingör, where I crossed the ferry, I had my first view of the famous Kroneberg Castle with its Hamlet platform. Helsingör is the Elsinore of Shakespeare and Thomas Campbell, and is a favourite shrine for British tourists. Here, two years ago, Mr. Lawrence Olivier and Miss Vivien Leigh, supported by a cast of English players, gave an historical performance of *Hamlet* in the castle courtyard. The Danes were delighted, and there was no more appreciative member of the large audience than Baroness Karen Blixen, the author of *Seven Gothic Tales* and *Out of Africa*. The Baroness, who writes better English than any foreigner since Joseph Conrad, and whose books have had very large sales in Denmark and in the United States, is a Dane. She is an enthusiastic Anglophil, and at Helsingör she suffered for her enthusiasm. At the first performance she arrived in a low-necked gown. But rain fell throughout the performance, and she was soaked to the skin. The next night the rain continued, and she armed herself against it with a pair of old ski-ing trousers, heavy boots, and three sweaters. She arrived at the castle to find that the outdoor performance had been abandoned. The play was given in the local hotel. The hall was hot and crowded. Everyone, including Lady Diana Cooper, was in brilliant and appropriate evening dress. The unfortunate Baroness was nearly suffocated. No wonder that the Danes like England. Their own climate is unpleasantly like ours.

I travelled through Scandinavia very comfortably. My carriage was new and spotlessly clean. The food in the dining-car was excellent, and not for the first time I wondered why British hotel-managers do not send a delegation of their chefs to Scandinavia to learn how to make *hors-d'œuvres*.

Half-an-hour before Oslo I had my first *contretemps*. At a wayside station a Norwegian journalist boarded the train and sought an interview. Scandinavia remembered that I had been exchanged for Litvinoff and that our trains had passed in the night at Oslo. Moreover, both Norway and Sweden are afraid lest their territory and their waters may become a battle-ground in the event of a war between Russia and Germany. From every Swede and Norwegian that I met I heard rumours of strange foreign aeroplanes which had been seen flying over Scandinavian territory, presumably in order to prospect the ground. My journalist wanted me to talk about Russia. He sought information on other points, including Britain's attitude towards Germany's request for the return of her lost colonies.

I sheered him off these delicate subjects by asking him questions about Norwegian politics. He was a young man, intelligent, quick-witted, and, like nearly all young Norwegians, thoroughly at home in the English language. He belonged to a generation which has no personal memories of the Great War. Realising that I was adamant in my determination not to give a political interview, he talked about Norway's attitude towards the European situation. That attitude was much the same as Holland's. Everyone in Norway wanted Britain and Germany to come to terms; everyone wanted Britain to be strong.

I was to hear this wish reiterated by nearly every politician not only in Scandinavia, but also in every other European country. The young journalist supplemented his wish with a comment which sticks in my memory. The Scandinavians, he told me, were like people warming their hands at a fire in a frozen world. The fire was Britain. If the fire went out, they would perish. And the great snowfield outside confirmed the appropriateness of the simile.

Oslo itself was deep in snow, but this was the only cold thing about it. I thought that I had scaled the highest peak of hospitality in the Slav countries, but I had not taken Norway and Sweden into my calculation. For the best part of a week I was fêted and feasted as I have been nowhere else in the world. Oslo looked and was prosperous. The Norwegians have a saying: "the land is poor, but the sea is rich." And the shipbuilders had been doing well. When they have money, they spend it royally. They are men of the world, jovial and open-hearted, but with a strong reserve of English phlegm in their character. They take their ups and downs with philosophic indifference.

What impressed me most about the people was the universal interest in things of the mind. Norway spends more money on books per head of population than any other country in the world except Denmark, and authors, artists and composers are honoured above all other men. Only a few years ago 120,000 sets of Björnson's collected works were sold in twelve months. In Oslo everyone is interested in pictures and buys them, and in order to encourage art both the state and private enterprise are lavish in their orders for frescos to decorate new buildings. Some of the finest frescos that I saw were on the walls of schools and factories. As a result of this stimulus Norway is the one country in Europe which has an original school of painting, in the sense that it owes nothing to Paris. The theatre is excellent and dramatic criticism good. Every second Norwegian that I met seemed to be a budding Shaw. Indeed, Mr. Shaw would be the first to admit that he owes something to Ibsen and Björnson, and Björnson's *Regent* must surely have inspired the Shavian *Apple-cart*.

There are other foreigners, less gifted than Mr. Shaw, who owe a debt to the great Norwegian dramatists. I remember Bulgakoff, the former Moscow Art Theatre producer, telling me his experiences in New York after his escape from Russia. Soon after his arrival he was sent for by Mr. Lee Schu-

c

bert. The American impressario received him as a medieval baron used to receive the lowest of his serfs. He was condescendingly polite about the Moscow Art Theatre. "But," he said, "it's no good for the States. What else can you do besides Russian stuff?"

Bulgakoff replied that he would like to produce Ibsen.

"Ibsen?" said Schubert. "Who the hell is Ibsen? Nobody's ever heard of him in New York."

Bulgakoff, however, had his way. Ibsen was produced in revival, and out of the proceeds of the success Mr. Lee Schubert bought two new houses.

Between meals I found, or rather made, time to indulge my passion for sight-seeing. Since my last visit Oslo had grown out of nearly all recognition, and I had some difficulty in finding my way. Nevertheless, I succeeded in discovering some old landmarks: the National Theatre with its statues of Ibsen and Björnson, and the café in the Carl Johann Gate where the Norwegian writers and artists of the classical period used to meet daily. The two statues looked rather comic. The snow had given a mantle to the great men, so that they looked like Cambridge graduates in white rabbit hoods. The café has been enlarged and renovated, and now bears little resemblance to its former Bohemian appearance. But a huge fresco, with Björnson in the centre and Ibsen, stick-in-hand and top-hatted, coming round the corner, commemorates the café's association with all that was best in Norwegian art and literature.

These old gentlemen of the classical period were not afraid of alcohol. Indeed, strong drink played havoc with many a Norwegian writer during the eighties and the nineties. Since the war, times and habits have changed and, although no one would call Norway a teetotal country, the average alcoholic consumption of the modern Norwegian would have seemed like teetotalism to his grandfather.

Another return to the past was my climb up the mountain slope to Holmkollen and Wetakollen, where I had stayed more than twenty years ago. From here the view over the fjords is unsurpassed. Hither comes all Oslo to ski, reaching its destination in fifteen minutes by a mountain railway which starts from a tube station in the centre of the city. From the terrace of a wooden bungalow, with a large cup of coffee and a glass of "acquavit" before me, I was able to admire and to envy the prowess of this sturdy race of athletes. The girls were just as proficient as the young men, and it is as much to the national pastime of ski-ing as to their natural virility as a race that the Norwegians owe their robust health and splendid physique.

My official duties were not light. In Oslo I gave two lectures, and after the second I was entertained at supper by the Anglo-Norwegian Society. Dr. Grieg, a grand-nephew of the composer, was in the chair, and the chief speech was made by M. Hambro, the Speaker of the Storthing and the leader of the Norwegian Conservative Party. He is, I think, the wittiest after-dinner speaker that I know. Certainly he made the best speech in English that I have ever heard delivered by a foreigner. It was long without seeming long; it was made without notes, and I believe that it was unprepared.

I sat next him. His private conversation was even better than his public oratory, and for the rest of the evening he kept me in fits of laughter. Although he is not a banker, he is a relation of the English Hambros.

Curiously enough, like many banking families, the Hambros are of Jewish origin, having come from the Rhineland to Scandinavia some two hundred years ago. Among his many activities the Norwegian Hambro includes his chairmanship of the Committee which collects the subscriptions to the League of Nations. He gave me an account of his method of persuading the bad payers to make good their arrears. It may be fairly described as a judicious mixture of flattery and legitimate blackmail. Mexico, for instance, was a troublesome customer, being not only short in her contributions, but also wanting to pay in francs instead of in gold. "Well, well," said M. Hambro to the Mexican delegate. "I'm afraid we'll now have to cancel the League Conference on Hygiene which we intended to hold in Mexico City." Mexico paid up.

Dr. Grieg was interesting, not so much for his relationship to the famous composer as for his Scottish connections, of which he is very proud. His speech was devoted to an account of the Grieg ancestry. The family left Scotland after the "Forty-Five" and, as its members became more and more Norwegian, the name was changed, more by accident than design, from Greig, the original Scottish name, to Grieg.

A Scot is sure of a specially warm welcome in Scandinavia, for Scotland has given many useful citizens both to Norway and to Sweden. Indeed, Dr. Grieg ended his speech by claiming me as a relation, for he, too, has Macgregor blood in his veins. He was not the only descendant of a great Norwegian that I met during my stay in Oslo. At the Book Exhibition I was introduced to "young" Björnson, the son of the famous writer. He is now an old man with white hair. But he is still known as "Little Björnson".

It was pleasant to be in a country where the possibility of war and the horrors of Europe were not the only topic of conversation. It is true that, if pressed to talk on politics, people expressed a healthy anxiety not to be drawn into any war. True it is that there were some Norwegians, mainly army officers, who admired and mildly advocated Nazi-ism, for even in the best-run democracy there are always certain elements who, being disciplined themselves, desire to impose discipline on others. But in the main the Norwegians were just ordinary folk interested in the ordinary things which make life pleasant. They had an amazingly high standard of civilisation. They had a warm admiration for, and would fit naturally into, the Anglo-Saxon conception of life.

I left Oslo on a Sunday morning. As my train did not start until eleven, I went out to have a last look at the town. It was like a city of the dead. The streets were deserted. Just beyond the National Theatre I saw a few belated stragglers, mostly housemaids and hotel-porters, scurrying with skis on their backs down the steps to the tube-station. All Oslo was on the mountain-slopes.

CHAPTER FOUR

FROM OSLO I went to Stockholm and, on my arrival, I had again to face the batteries of the camera-men and the fusillade of the journalists. But here the journalists were less exacting than those in Oslo, for the Swedes are more formal than the Norwegians, although just as hospitable and just as friendly. And they are infinitely richer. Indeed, it is not too much to say that they are now the most prosperous people in the world. Much of the prosperity is the result of European re-armament. Sweden sells to all countries: iron ore in huge quantities to Germany and anti-aircraft guns to Britain.

In Stockholm I stayed in the Grand Hotel, and there in the Moorish Hall, where during the war I had sat with Coleridge Kennard and Clifford Sharp while they pointed out the German spies and agents, my publishers gave me a public dinner of welcome. The gathering included the Swedish Foreign Office official who had conducted the negotiations for my exchange for Litvinoff, several prominent Swedish writers, and the Minister for Social Welfare, who made the speech to propose my health.

Throughout my stay in Sweden I found the Swedish rule of toasting—the famous "skold"—a little difficult to follow. If you are the chief guest, you are not allowed to drink until you have been officially welcomed and "skolded" by your host. Then at the end of the dinner you are expected to return thanks in a short speech and drink your host's health. The custom is formal and serious, but very pleasant. It is also very old. M. Carl Laurin, the well-known Swedish art historian, told me that its seriousness comes from the fact that in the Middle Ages it was a kind of grace beginning with the words: "In the name of the Father, the Son, and the Holy Ghost."

The Minister for Social Welfare was a Socialist, more intelligent, better educated, and less radical than the average

British trade union leader. I enjoyed my talk with him. The level of his conversation, which covered a wide range of subjects, was very high, and he had the Balfourian capacity for seeing every side of a problem. I rated him as an apostle of gradualness. Certainly there was nothing doctrinaire about his Socialism and nothing Marxist in his attitude towards King Gustav, who was the first European monarch to set the fashion in democratic kingship. The Minister told me that at the opening of every Swedish Parliament the Socialist Party tables a Republican resolution. Nobody pays any attention to it. If ever Sweden became a republic, King Gustav would be the first president, and he would be elected by the Socialist vote.

King Gustav has another democratic trait which must win him favour in Anglo-Saxon countries. He was the first Continental monarch to introduce sport into politics. Swedes may not yet appreciate such ultra-Baldwinesque sentiments as the statement made this spring by a former secretary of the Marylebone Cricket Club: "If Hitler and Mussolini had played cricket, there would be no trouble in Europe." But they can laugh at King Gustav's jokes about his tennis. The jokes and the stories are legion. They date back to the days of the King's tennis partnerships with the late Mlle. Lenglen, when the brilliant French lady player would say to him petulantly, "Keep to the left, sir," and the King would smile and answer good-humouredly: "Ah, yes, that's what my Ministers are always telling me."

As far as home politics are concerned, Sweden has done a wonderful work. She has a model social legislation. Stockholm's working-class is the best-housed of any working-class in Europe or America, and throughout the whole country social hygiene has been developed to a higher point than anywhere else in the world.

The Minister was less optimistic about external affairs. The Swedish Socialists, he told me, had been disillusioned by recent events in Russia. They were worried about Britain, whom they regarded as the main pillar of European peace.

They wanted us to be strong. During the war Sweden's sympathies had been divided. Then the people were pro-Ally, but the aristocracy and most of the bourgeoisie were pro-German. To-day, although Sweden was the special propaganda interest of General Goering, whose first wife was a Swede, there had been a revulsion, and the vast majority of the people now leaned both by inclination and by cultural instinct towards the Western democracies. Youth, which in Sweden as in other countries wanted a director's job before it had served its apprenticeship, had shown some sympathy with Nazi-ism. But the movement was not serious and had been quickly quashed.

I had also a long and interesting talk with Gustav Hellström, one of Sweden's most brilliant novelists and critics. A long residence in London has given him a perfect command of the English language, and he has also lived in Moscow. Incidentally, everyone in Sweden seemed to want to talk about Russia, who has always been the traditional enemy. In recent years the fear has declined, but the tradition remains. Hellström himself had certainly no fears. His view, and I share it, is that Russia is so intent on her own internal development that she will go to almost any lengths to avoid war. He made one good point. Whatever we might think of Russian methods, we owed something to Stalin. He had ousted Trotsky. If Trotsky had succeeded Lenin, we should have had a world-war long ago.

Mr. Hellström also told me an amusing story of a diplomatic reception given by Litvinoff to a Swedish delegation in Moscow. The bulky Commissar began by asking the Swedes if they would like to put some questions to him. Then, without waiting for a reply, he harangued them for twenty minutes, telling them that the Swedes were fools. They ought to back Russia. Otherwise Germany would swallow them. The whole speech, delivered in a loud rasping voice, was made in the presence of the German military attaché!

I remembered Stockholm, where in 1918 I was twice held up for a week or more on my way to and from Russia, much better than Oslo, and the memory only whetted my appetite for sight-seeing. I spent most of my afternoons in the "Town Between the Bridges", visiting the Old Storkyrkan and the Riddarholmskyrkan, which is Stockholm's Westminster. Here are the mausoleums of Charles XII, Gustavus Adolphus and Bernadotte. Here, too, are the shields and coats-of-arms of the Knights of the Seraphim. It was curious to see among them the arms of men like Poincaré, Fallières and Loubet, who had certainly never been knights in their own country.

I also visited the famous Town Hall. Indeed, I was taken there twice. As a town hall it is unique in its grandeur. The exterior is simple in design and is dominated by the great rectangular tower which stands over three hundred feet above the level of the ground. The site is superb, and the terrace commands a view down the water of a part of Stockholm which in the sunset looks like the Kremlin. Inside, the great halls and council rooms are magnificently furnished and decorated with mosaics, tapestries, and yards of mural paintings, the most striking of which is an allegorical fresco representing the ages of man from the cradle to the grave.

Undoubtedly, the Town Hall is a stupendous achievement. Moreover, it has given employment and encouragement to scores of Swedish sculptors, craftsmen and painters, including the King's brother, Prince Eugene. But because every Swede insists on your calling it a stupendous achievement, I found it a little disappointing. To my mind its most attractive feature is the stone statue of Birger Jarl, the founder of Stockholm, on the terrace outside the main building. There the great warrior, clothed in his coat-of-mail, lies in a massive stone four-poster, his eyes gazing down the water at the city which he founded. More adequately than any other monument in Stockholm the statue seems to express the silent strength and splendid virility of the Swedish race.

The pulse of a modern city is to be found in its streets and shops, and in Stockholm I neglected neither the well-laid-out streets, already festooned for Christmas, nor the splendidly-built and splendidly-lit shops. I visited the great store of P. U. Bergstrom, called by Swedes "Pub" for short, and was shown the department in which Greta Garbo once sold hats. Two streets away Jenny Lind was born. The singer is already represented in the Town Hall as an allegorical figure with a nightingale, but the goddess of the films has not yet achieved this honour.

I also spent many pleasant hours in the bookshops, which are the biggest and carry the largest stocks of any bookshops that I have seen. In one bookstore I ran into M. Martin du Gard, then in Stockholm to receive his Nobel prize, but Viscount Cecil who had been awarded the Peace prize was unable to make the journey to Stockholm, and the good Swedes mourned his absence. I tried to remember the names of previous Peace prize winners and found the effort difficult. How many would be remembered in a hundred years time? Lord Cecil, because of his passionate integrity, stood the best chance. Yet in the German newspapers there were sarcastic comments that he had done more harm to peace than any man of his time. Probably there were cynics in Britain who held the same view.

On prize-giving day I dined in the Operakällaren with a group of Swedish writers, and celebrated the occasion in claret, for the Swedes are great claret-drinkers and are now France's best customers.

In 1918 I lunched in the same restaurant with Ludwig Nobel, a son of the founder of the prizes. Ludwig's job was the Russian end of the Nobel business, and he had then only recently escaped from the Russian revolution, having lost all his property in that turbulent country. He was in anything but a peace-loving frame of mind.

The prize-giving ceremony lasts for five or six hours. Everyone who goes has to wear evening-dress, and as few of the prize-winners are good speakers the performance is tedious.

On my own initiative I visited the exhibition of Russian painting which was then being held in Stockholm. Here were pictures by great artists like Korovin and Repin. They were priced as low as fifty pounds. The dearest was marked at three hundred and fifty. Yet the gallery was empty. Not more than two or three pictures had been sold. The memory of mankind is short. In the welter of Bolshevism we have forgotten not only the sufferings of the Russian *émigrés*, but also the genius of the pre-war Russian artists.

On my last day in Stockholm I was taken by Carl Laurin to his house on the highest point of the South Island. It commands the finest view of the city, and the panorama stretches from Lake Mälar to the Baltic. In the dim watery sunset of a winter's afternoon the vista is almost intoxicatingly beautiful, and here I took my last farewell of Stockholm. It has been called by enthusiastic travellers "the Venice of the North". It may lack the warmth of Venice, but as a city built on water it has no equal.

Before leaving Sweden I had to lecture in Västerås and Göteborg. I had been reluctant to go to Västerås, which is a small manufacturing city and the headquarters of the Asea, the great Swedish electrical concern. It is the simple truth that I enjoyed myself there more than anywhere else during my tour. The hospitality was overwhelming, and I saw a working-class population so clean and so happy-looking that I felt sad because my own country fell so short of this standard. The Swedes believe in making of their factories places where work is not only hygienic, but also attractive. They take a pride in the architecture of their buildings. The walls are gaily painted. You could eat off the floor of any department, and I soon discovered that the Asea directors, who have also a factory in England, were shocked by the untidiness of the average English factory. In the various departments there were no "bosses" or foremen. The workers—the women pink-cheeked, well-dressed, and passingly beautiful, the men strong and vigorous—were on piecework. In winter they have an hour and a half for luncheon in the middle of the day in order that they may spend at least some of the daylight in the open air, and at eleven-thirty I saw them all trooping off home on bicycles.

The Swedes are justly proud of their industrial prowess. They admit that they acquired much of their knowledge in the United States. Now they say modestly that they have little more to learn from the Americans. It is not, I think, an over-statement. Certainly, when I was in the United States, I saw no factory with a higher standard of efficiency or with anything like such a happy relationship between capital and labour.

Even more impressive was Göteborg, a beautiful city with a cultural life of its own and a theatre and a concert hall of which London might be proud. Göteborg is the home town of the S.K.F., the huge concern which supplies ball bearings to every country in the world. Owing to the post-war barriers against free trade, the S.K.F. have now their own factories in most of the leading countries. The company keeps very careful records of the respective efficiency of the workmen in the different nations. As production is standardised, the records afford a very fair standard of comparison. I was shown them. For the tiny ball bearings, which demand agile fingers, the French women came first. In the other categories the Swedes just beat the Americans. Very little behind came the Germans.

"And where do we come?" I asked.

The finger went down to the bottom. "Easily last," said the manager. "I'm afraid the British won't work or have forgotten how to."

Modern Sweden impresses me. She has made immense strides since 1918, and has to-day reached a higher standard of civilisation than any other country in the world. She has a finer conception of life than either Britain or France or, at least, she has been more successful in realising it. She is industrially as efficient as the United States, and a hundred years ahead of that country in social legislation. Her youth is, I think, without any exception the healthiest and, in the most comprehensive sense of the word, the best-educated in the world. For the harassed peoples of Europe, for all pessimists and defeatists, Scandinavia is the finest tonic that I know. If there were fifty million Norwegians and Swedes, there would be peace in Europe. Unfortunately, the combined total of the two populations is only nine millions, and their prosperity and their progress must be ascribed mainly to the fact that for more than a century they have been spared the horrors of war. It is a blessing which small nations are not prepared to exchange for the risks of collective security.

After Norway and Sweden, Denmark was something of an anti-climax. Perhaps it was the weather which was to blame. In Norway and Sweden I had enjoyed dry cold with delicious sunshine on a background of crisp snow. In the thaw Copenhagen was like London on a raw and slushy winter's day.

Certainly I had no reason to complain about my welcome. The Danes were as friendly and as hospitable as their Scandinavian cousins. They were, too, just as efficient and even more intellectual. Their factories were the last word in modern progress. Like nearly every British subject who comes to Copenhagen I was taken to the vast brewery concerns of Carlsberg and Tuborg. I would not say a word in favour of one beer against the other, but the Carlsberg brewery interested me more if only because Carl Jacobsen, the son of the founder, was a passionate lover of art, and left the business to a foundation which now devotes all the profits to the furtherance of painting, literature, music and science. I visited the charming old Jacobsen house situated in a secluded park adjoining the main brewery. It is now given to a famous writer or scientist so that he may live as a great man ought to live. I could not help wishing that every British brewery were run on similar lines.

The Danes know and understand Britain even better than the Norwegians and the Swedes, and there are many Danes who speak English without a trace of accent. The Anglo-Danish Society has the largest membership of any foreign British society, and with little help from Britain does a great work in promoting British culture in Denmark.

This interest in Britain is not wholly idealistic. It has a strong material side. Britain is by a long way Denmark's best customer. In spite of frequent denunciations of the British-Danish Trade Pact in certain sections of the British Press, the trade is not entirely one-sided. In order to keep her export market Denmark has inaugurated a "Buy British" campaign, and its results are already to be seen in the English clothes, ties, socks, shirts and collars of almost the entire male population of Copenhagen.

Of the hospitality of the Danish people I cannot say enough. During my five days in Copenhagen I did not have a meal by myself. I was entertained by the students of the English faculty at the University. They were having an end-of-term celebration, and I heard several amazingly good English speeches by students who had never been in England. I talked politics to politicians and economics to business men. The Crown Prince and the Crown Princess came to my lecture, slipping quietly into their places without fuss or ceremony. The Crown Princess, who was Princess Ingrid of Sweden, flattered my vanity by saying that she had been the first of her family to read my books. She is deservedly popular in a country where the monarchy is an even more democratic institution than our own, and where the King walks daily in the streets unaccompanied and unguarded.

Denmark is essentially a country where opportunity is open to everyone with talent and a capacity for hard work. The most striking instance of this aspect of democracy was afforded by my talk with M. Ingolt. He reminded me that in 1918 he was the clerk at the Danish Consulate in Moscow who accompanied me and the members of my mission to the Finnish frontier after our release from prison. He is now president of one of the largest banks in Denmark. Until quite recently his father was an hotel-porter.

As the Danes live by night, I had a night out in Copenhagen. My pilots were journalists, one the son of an admiral, the other a Dane educated in England. Both were charming and highly intelligent. We began at the Ambassadors, a luxury establishment with a cabaret. It was crowded with rich Danes and foreign diplomatists, more intent on dancing than on the entertainment. We finished up at a low night-club with dancing dames for hire. They were well-dressed, and with their blue eyes and flaxen hair good to look upon. But their smile, fixed with a hard line of lip-stick, was cold. The general effect was depressing. Copenhagen is the Paris of the North, and of all forms of night-life the Paris variety is the most boring and the most commercial.

The Danes have a strong streak of the Latin in their temperament. They are the greatest readers in the world, but they read even more French than English. Copenhagen is a city which caters first and foremost for women. Oslo, and especially Stockholm, are male cities. For that reason I cannot help feeling that the Danes lack some of the more solid virtues of the Norwegians and the Swedes.

In spite of these Latin tendencies, the Danish political conception of life is strongly Anglo-Saxon. With a Nazi problem of their own in Schleswig-Holstein, the Danes have little affection for Germany. As flying time from the German frontier to Copenhagen is to be calculated in minutes and not in hours, their dislike is circumscribed by a natural anxiety, and even more than the Swedes and Norwegians their hopes of peace are centred on Britain.

Like the Dutch, the Danes feel that British diplomacy neglects them. I realise that at a time like the present, when our Foreign Office has to deal almost daily with a fresh crisis in other parts of Europe, there is an inevitable tendency to regard the Scandinavian countries as a quiet backwater which, thank God, causes no commotions. After making allowance for these difficulties, I should like to see British diplomacy in the Netherlands and in Scandinavia much more active than it has been in the past. It is a ground which, if intensively cultivated, will yield excellent results.

On my way home via Esbjerg I took in Odense, the birthplace of Hans Andersen. It is extolled as a town of churches and of a famous tower. But to-day there are more factory-chimneys than spires. The manufacture of spirits flourishes, and the first glass of "schnapps" that I drank in Denmark came from an Odense factory. Surrounding the factories are rows of drab streets with small gabled houses, and on the outskirts of the town I saw hundreds of the little garden allotments which Danish industrial concerns make a habit of giving to their employees.

The country was dead flat, and my first impressions were rather dismal. But at Odense there was snow. The streets were garlanded with fir leaves. In every house there was a Christmas tree, and soon, without any effort, I could feel something of the atmosphere which inspired *The Little Match Girl*. Hans Andersen is one of my special favourites, and it always amuses me to recall that he and Stalin share a curious parentage: a cobbler father and a washerwoman mother.

Andersen is still a universal favourite. Every year 30,000 worshippers visit the house in which it is claimed, rather doubtfully, that he was born. I am glad to say that a goodly proportion of these 30,000 is made up by English admirers. The British race, which has been brought up on Hans Andersen, will always have a special affection for the country which gave birth to the most human and humane of all the world's great writers.

BOOK II

THE PEACE PENINSULA

D

"YOUTH IS A period of formation and acquirement. It must be judged by its fruits."

CHAPTER ONE

IT WOULD BE gross hypocrisy on my part if I were to say that
I did not enjoy my tours in Central Europe and Scandinavia.
I did, but my enjoyment was qualified by one limitation. In
my capacity as an agent of the British Council I had been in
a semi-official position. Officialdom imposes obvious restrictions on personal liberty. My two tours had whetted my appetite for Europe, but they had not satisfied it. Very soon after
my return to England, I made up my mind to go back to
Central Europe and the Balkans at my own time and in my
own manner.

There were strong reasons for my decision. The ten years
that I had spent in that part of Europe from 1919 to 1929 had
been the period of the Versailles Treaty. In itself the Treaty
was not so bad as many of its critics had made it out to be.
But it contained certain fundamental defects which should
have been remedied, and the failure to do so was partly, but
not wholly, responsible for the tension which now prevails.
I had analysed this period very fully in my book, *Retreat
From Glory*, which ended in 1929 with the death of Stresemann and with my forecast of the Nazi rise to power. The
advent of Hitler had wrought vast changes. Until 1932 the
smaller countries of Central Europe had assumed that
France and Britain would never allow Germany to re-arm.
Germany presented no danger and no menace, and they felt
themselves secure to consolidate their gains with little regard
for the interests of the minorities entrusted to their care. It
was not so much that they maltreated these minorities as
that they failed to make concessions which would have been
acceptable at the time but which to-day are noisily spurned.
Now the Treaty of Versailles was little more than a scrap of
paper, and there was the impact of an all-powerful and ambitious Germany on the whole Central European and Balkan
complex.

I wanted to study these changes. There was also the personal desire to revisit old friends in whose company I had spent or misspent the most important years of my life. And this was perhaps the strongest urge of all. I set out in January of 1938 with a free programme and an indefinite time limit.

As I stepped into the Simplon Express on which I had once travelled so often, I felt like a schoolboy who ought to be reading Seton Merriman. I slept, too, like a schoolboy, not waking until I reached Lausanne. A misty drizzle was falling, and in the semi-dark I had some difficulty in distinguishing the waters of Lake Geneva, mournful in the morning rain. At Stresa Lake Maggiore was half-hidden in a low grey mist, and the Isola Bella, where the ill-fated Stresa Conference was held, looked dark and gloomy. Only to the North, in the line of the Berlin-Rome axis, was there any gleam of light. High above the mist the sun was shining on the topmost mountain peaks. Everywhere else the winter of discontent lay heavy on the land. The scene seemed unpleasantly symbolic of the rift in Anglo-Italian friendship.

I know much of the inside story of the Stresa Conference. It cannot yet be published in full, but, when the facts are more widely known, they will or should blast the reputations of more than one British Cabinet Minister. Stresa was the last opportunity of settling the Abyssinian question either on the terms of the subsequent but belated Hoare-Laval pact or by a strong diplomatic hint to Signor Mussolini that high-handed action on his part would incur our active opposition.

At the Stresa Conference Abyssinia was not even mentioned, although the opportunities were both numerous and propitious. By the time Mr. Eden went to Rome, the Duce had already 50,000 troops on their way to Abyssinia, and nothing short of war could have made him call them back. Very rightly we did not start a world-war, but by our subsequent action we pushed Italy into Germany's arms.

This was the first time that I had ever seen Stresa in such

sad guise. Northern Italy was then undergoing a spell of very severe weather. There was snow not only on the mountains but on the plain. There was snow at Milan, which looked drab and dirty. There was snow at Verona, scarcely visible in the greyness except for the tall chimneys of its countless new factories and the huge magazine of the Italian Red Cross. In a backyard I saw turkeys sitting on fences in order to keep their tails and legs out of the snow and hens warming themselves on the straw of a smoking dung-heap. Under the black sky the town looked more like a North of England factory town than the scene of Shakespeare's *Two Gentlemen of Verona*. It is true that there was no snow at Venice, but in a pale and watery sunset the city looked cold and almost forbidding.

At Trieste where we stopped for ten minutes I got out and bought an Italian newspaper. The top of the front page was black with huge headlines: "The German Reich Celebrates the Fifth Anniversary Of Its National Unity." And then immediately below, in print of similar size as though the Italian editor intended to stress the dual importance of the two dictators, a home-news headline: "To-morrow the Duce Will Review The Armed Guards Of The Fascist Revolution." The much-flaunted axis was working on paper at least. Was the old Anglo-Italian friendship dead? I felt a momentary sadness, for I like Italians. Did they now dislike us?

Any apprehensions that I may have felt proved groundless. As far as their outward behaviour was concerned, the Italian officials were unaggressively polite and even friendly. I had no trouble with the Customs authorities, who did not even open my rather suspicious-looking travelling book-case. I suffered no inconvenience at the hands of the currency control officials who here, as in all Continental countries, have made travel even more irksome than it was in 1919. The trains ran punctually and, miracle of miracles, I could go to the restaurant-car leaving my luggage in my compartment without fear of theft.

It was long past midnight when I reached Zagreb which was to be my first stopping-place. Here, at any rate, the weather was friendly. The air was warm and the sky star-lit. There on the platform was Conrad Sejk, my old Croatian fishing friend, to meet me. We went straight to a café, for Zagreb sits late by night, and for an hour we talked fishing and politics alternately.

On going to my hotel, I could not sleep. In my room I found a large bottle of "slivovica", the plum brandy of Yugoslavia, beautifully encased in wicker-work and decorated with red, white and blue ribbons, the national colours of Croatia. This was a present from my good friend, Stanko Šverljuga, the former Finance Minister of Yugoslavia. There was also a huge bouquet of red carnations, the national flower of Slovenia. These were from Madame Šverljuga, a Slovene and the former Lady-in-Waiting to Queen Marie.

The "slivovica" was not the cause of my wakefulness. I was excited. The years in Fleet Street seemed to have rolled away, and I was back where I had left off nine years ago. Certainly I felt nine years younger. I unpacked my things and set out my Greek Testament, my Odyssey and my language books. It was five in the morning before I could sleep, but I was up at nine and dressed and ready for Dr. Jakić, the young university graduate, who was to give me my daily lesson in Croatian.

As we went out into the street, the sun was shining from a blue sky. The air was warm in our faces and heavy with the scent of the Southern spring. I had a busy day before me: a round of official visits to make, a score of old friends to re-visit. But I turned my steps to the market-place.

If there is a more beautiful market-place than Zagreb's, I do not know it. True, on the buildings of the Jelačić Place there were many new signs. They were mostly foreign: Philips Radio, Telefoni Ericsson, Tungsram Lamps, Singer Sewing Machines, and even the modest and therefore re-assuring advertisement of a British Insurance Company.

There was, too, a new hotel, American in design with a high tower and a turret suite of apartments like the Waldorf-Astoria in New York. But the market-place was Croatian and unchanged, and very lovely it looked in the sunlight with the grey towers of the Cathedral in the background. On the market stands, shaded by huge red-and-white umbrellas, a riot of flowers and fruit was exposed: mimosa, willow blossom, violets, great bunches of red carnations, and rows of apples and oranges arranged in pyramid fashion. On the other stands were lace-work and gaily painted toys. And more attractive even than the goods were the Croatian peasant women, healthy, smiling and vigorous, in the white stockings, red ribbon garters, white skirt and gaily-coloured apron and kerchief head-dress of their national costumes.

Resolutely I marched Jakić into the inside modern market-hall. I wanted to see the fish-market which has an unfailing charm for me. Nor was I disappointed. Here were hundreds of fish, many of them strange to English eyes and fresh from the Adriatic or from the river: scampi, oysters, lobsters, langoustes, sardines, big tunny, medium-sized tunny, baby tunny, brantsino, orada, pike-perch, rainbow trout, pike of all sizes, and huchen, the monster land-locked salmon of the Danube and its tributaries. On our way out we passed through the meat and vegetable market where a profusion of provisions of all kinds was marked at prices which would make a British housewife's mouth water. Jakić told me quite solemnly that German tourists faint when they visit the Zagreb market. They have never seen so much or so cheap food.

From the market-place we went up to the old town. It was once a fortress city and stands on a high hill commanding a superb view of the valley of the Save. Although it was January, the weather was more like a warm June day in England, and the river below was almost obscured by the heat haze. We turned into St. Mark's, the twelfth century St. Paul's of Zagreb, to see the new frescos of Kljaković and the Christ and the Madonna by Meštrović.

Like the Italian painters of the classical period Kljaković
has put his friends into the various Bible stories which the
frescos illustrate, and I very quickly spotted Meštrović as an
apostle, although I was not certain which. High above the
altar was Meštrović's Christ, a Christ totally unlike the
stereotyped Christs of most Catholic Churches, a Christ
emaciated and half-starved, a Christ symbolic of His own
suffering and of the sufferings of underfed, down-trodden
humanity throughout the ages. The Madonna is in stone but
is also modelled from the people. She is represented as a mother squatting like the scores of Croatian peasant mothers
whom Meštrović must have seen when as a poor boy he tended sheep on the mountain slopes of Dalmatia.

I liked both the Christ and the Madonna at once and expressed my admiration with enthusiasm. I should have been
more guarded. In Zagreb the Christ and the Madonna, the
work of the world's greatest living sculptor and the best-
known Yugoslav alive or dead, were the subject of violent
controversy. The city was divided into two camps: those
who admired the statues and those who wanted them thrown
into the Save. Naturally these artistic likes and dislikes were
strongly tinged with political colouring. Conservative Zagreb preferred orthodoxy to works of art, and to bourgeois
conceptions a Madonna who squatted like a roadside peasant
woman was the essence of unorthodoxy. To admire the
emaciated Christ was heresy, nay, worse than heresy. It was
incipient Bolshevism.

This quarrel is typical of the heat and fervour of local politics in Zagreb. The city is the capital of Croatia. It has a noble
history dating back to the days when the Kings of Croatia
were mighty monarchs ruling over more subjects and larger
territory than the Kings of England of that time. But to-day
its atmosphere is definitely bourgeois. At luncheon-time
and in the evening the citizens still walk five and six abreast
in the main streets, turning their busiest thoroughfares
into a Corso. Time moves here on a leisurely stage, and

every hour is a fresh opportunity for conversation. As most Croats are highly intellectual and very well-educated, there are very few subjects which they do not discuss. Discussion leads inevitably to controversy, and, not content with quarrelling with the Serbs, they quarrel among themselves.

The domestic quarrels are probably the more serious, for after twenty years of constant bickering the Serbo-Croatian dispute has become almost a legend, powerful, deep-rooted, and dangerous, but not so bitter as the personal grievance against one's immediate next-door neighbour, who has animadverted on the quality of one's wine or cast dubious reflections upon one's domestic bliss. A foreigner who lives in Zagreb must possess great strength of character in order to avoid being drawn into local camps and local feuds, and the state of domestic discord is well illustrated by the fact that in a city, where one society would be ample, there are no less than three separate societies for the promotion of cultural relations with Great Britain. This sturdy exhibition of democratic independence would not be tolerated in a totalitarian state. I feel that it is perhaps a little out of place in Zagreb. But the Croats are not wholly responsible. The English who live in their midst have been infected by the same virus.

I should not like to create the impression that the Croats are an embittered race, because they ventilate their grievances with a ready volubility. They are, in fact, an attractive, friendly people with some of the light-hearted inconsistency of the Viennese. In particular, the Zagreb bourgeois are cultural disciples of Vienna. But they are not mere borrowers. They have a fine culture of their own, are passionately devoted to music and to the theatre, and have as wide a knowledge of European literature as I have found in any other Continental city. I have been many times in Zagreb for Štrossmayer's Day. Štrossmayer, one of Croatia's national heroes, was an Archbishop, who during the long reign of the

Emperor Franz Josef, was the foremost champion of Croatian independence and of the Croatian language. He was the founder of the Yugoslav Academy and the first man to persuade the Austrian Government to sanction the use of the word Yugoslav.

During my last visit to Zagreb I was taken as a guest to the commemoration session of the Academy. Here, surrounded by poets, painters, publicists, priests and professors, dressed in morning-coats and looking like a Parliament of crows, I listened in solemn silence to a long philosophical discourse which was several thousand feet higher than bombing distance over my head. I was, however, vastly impressed by the ascetic appearance of the Academicians. They looked like scholars. They had the refined features that I feel a scholar should have. Many had moustaches and neatly trimmed white beards. I felt like a Rugby football player or a prize-fighter in a gathering of Wickham Steeds.

The Croats, too, are superbly honest in their literary and artistic judgments. When you say to a Croat professor "how high does Monsieur X. stand in Croatian literature?" and he replies quite solemnly: "I hate the man with every fibre in my body, but I am bound to admit that he can write poetry", you know, at least, that Monsieur X. is a poet and that the criticism is more honest than most English criticism. To-day, the Croats are suffering from the fact that, having been denied for centuries the right to rule themselves, they are being compelled to learn again this difficult art from the beginning. I like them immensely, and many of them are my friends.

Chief among these are the Šverljugas to whom I owe nearly all the many happy months and days that I have spent in Croatia and from whom I have absorbed some of their love of their beautiful country. In my banking years Stanko Šverljuga was the managing director of the Croatian bank in which my own bank had a financial interest. Owing to this connection I saw much of him and learnt to admire his many sterling qualities. His advice to me was always sound. I never

knew him make a promise which was not immediately fulfilled. His kindness and patience were limitless. A man of
great knowledge and culture, he has been, since those early
days, Finance Minister of his country. The experience has
widened his horizon, and he is one of the very few Yugoslavs who possess the English sense of compromise and who
can sum up a situation on its merits without party or national
bias. He is a tremendous worker, still the first to arrive at his
bank, of which he is now president, and still the last to leave.
The hour of leaving varies; being first to arrive means eight
o'clock in the morning.

Incidentally, English banking experience in Yugoslavia
seems to be a useful stepping-stone to a political career. Apart
from Stanko Šverljuga, two other members of our Zagreb
bank have been Ministers since my time. Moreover, M.
Stojadinović, the present Prime Minister and the strong man
of Yugoslavia, began his career as Serbian sub-manager of
the Belgrade branch of the British Trade Corporation. Our
British bankers, perhaps rightly, prefer to work off their
superfluous energy at golf.

Stanko Šverljuga has only one defect. He speaks no English. The defect is made good by his wife, who not only
speaks and writes our language with consummate ease but
also is very widely read in English literature. She is pro-
British and, as the former Lady-in-Waiting to Queen Marie
of Yugoslavia, had probably some influence on King Alexander's decision to send his two sons to England to be educated. From their earliest days the two boys have been
brought up in an Anglo-Scandinavian atmosphere. Their
tutor, Mr. Parrott, is an Englishman and a former master at
Edinburgh Academy where he taught my "rugger" international nephew. Their governess was a Norwegian. This
Anglo-Scandinavian combination produced an Anglo-
Scandinavian romance. Mr. Parrott married the Norwegian.

The tragedy of King Alexander's death put a premature
end to the school career in England of Prince Peter who, on

becoming a boy King, had to be brought back to Yugoslavia. The decision was inevitable, but is regretted by many Yugoslavs who feel that both the young King and the country would have benefitted if he had been allowed to spend a few more years in England before being projected into the guarded seclusion of the Yugoslav Court. Both boys are fond of open-air life and are keen anglers. King Peter is good-looking with delicately chiselled features and a rather serious expression which would seem to indicate that he already feels the burden of Kingship on his young shoulders. Prince Tomislav is the livelier of the two, chafes at all forms of restraint, and takes a special delight in giving the slip to the detective who guards him.

If the Šverljugas are the kindest and most hospitable people that I have ever known, another old Croatian friend of whom I am very fond is Želimir Mažuranić, a former Minister and now the President of the Yugoslav Senate. He is the grandson of Croatia's greatest poet, and he himself has much of the romantic in his nature. He is a great linguist who more than once has represented his country at Geneva. He speaks seven languages with great fluency, and can make an excellent speech in Latin. To these talents he adds a comprehensive knowledge of music and a passion for Russian gipsies. He plays the piano, sings with gusto, and knows by heart every Russian gipsy song that was ever written. He is a protector and benefactor of the large Russian *émigré* population in Yugoslavia, but has never been in Russia. He says that he has no need to go there. In Zagreb Russia comes to him. In his joy of life, his many-sided talents, and his generous and expansive nature, he is the Croatian Maurice Baring. With him I have spent many pleasant Croatian days and nights, drinking the new wine from his vineyards and listening to the endless repertory of his songs.

Želko, as he is known to a host of friends in half-Europe, has all the qualities of the Russian temperament save one. When needs must he can be serious and very dignified, but he is never depressed.

CHAPTER TWO

AMONG MY OTHER Croatian friends I hope that I may include Ivan Meštrović, who is a great patriot as well as the world's greatest sculptor. He is one of those rare men whom you have only to look at in order to realise that they are not fashioned in the ordinary mould. He is short, rather thick-set, and slightly bald with high, protruding forehead and a small, dark, straggling beard. But what rivets your attention at once are his eyes, keen and full of lights that sometimes flash and always penetrate. He hates social functions, but will talk for hours to his friends, and in his own house he is a hospitable and attractive host. He is a good listener, answers questions patiently, and, when he talks himself, has always something original and instructive to say.

Meštrović is a peasant genius. He began his life tending sheep on the mountain-slopes near Split, the beautiful Dalmatian seaport where the Emperor Diocletian ended his days. The rocky Dalmatian coast is rich in stone, and soon the young shepherd longed to fashion things in the material which surrounded him. While still in his 'teens, he was apprenticed to a stone-mason in Split, and there he learnt the rudiments of the art which was to make him world-famous. But as a sculptor he has had only one master. This is Michel Angelo, on whom he has written a remarkable book. Later, he went to Vienna and to Paris, where his work attracted the notice of Rodin.

Meštrović has prospered. He has made statues for nearly every city in the United States, and he has a charming villa at Split commanding a superb view over the Adriatic and a fine house in Zagreb, where he also owns considerable property. He is quite unspoilt by success, and has not altered his mode of living. He likes the wine of his native Dalmatia and, on occasions, will sit up late, especially if he is talking politics. But he is, first and foremost, a worker, and when he

53

is engaged on a new statue, shuts himself off from everyone. At the present moment he has the largest temporary studio in the world. It has been specially built for the huge equestrian statue which he is now making for the Rumanian Government.

For many of his statues he takes himself as his model. British tourists who visit Split and fail to see Meštrović in the flesh have only to ask for the Marko Marulić statue on the piazza just off the harbour front. Marulić was a great Croatian poet of the fifteenth century. In stone he is the perfect image of Meštrović. Incidentally, the statue is one of Meštrović's best.

I have already indicated that Croats have a passion for politics. In this respect Meštrović is a hundred per cent. Croat. He was one of the most active champions of Yugoslav unity, and during the war, when he was still nominally an Austro-Hungarian subject, he had to live in exile. He still stands, I think, for the Yugoslav idea, but he has been embittered by much that has happened since the new kingdom came into being, and feels the wrongs which Croatia has suffered with all the vigour of his ardent temperament. He is moderately Radical in his political outlook and, like most Croats, supports the Croatian Peasant Party. He is, however, no strong Party man, and differs from the official leaders on several points. The official leaders were and still are bitter critics of the late King Alexander. Meštrović believed in the King, and believes to-day that Alexander was more the victim of his Serbian environment than the conscious executor of a policy of repression.

Meštrović, who was on terms of friendship with the late King, told me that just before King Alexander went on his fatal journey to Marseilles, he sent for the sculptor, told him that he saw now that his policy towards the Croats had been mistaken, and that he was going to settle the Croatian question on his return from France. He never returned, and the Croatian question is still unsettled. I should add that most Croats are convinced that it would not have been settled even if the King had lived, and I quote Meštrović's statement to show that he is capable of taking his own view and his own line in political matters.

During the war Meštrović, who was a member of the Yugoslav Committee, spent some time in England. He is an Anglophil and brings up his sons on English lines. But, like many foreigners, he is genuinely afraid that we have grown soft with luxury. I remember with delight a lively luncheon in his house in Zagreb. The only other guest besides myself was Kljaković, the Croatian painter, and for two hours I drank various sorts of Dalmatian wine, including the famous "prošeko", and discussed the international situation. During the meal Meštrović's son, aged eight, came into the room. He was dressed in an English sailor-suit, and I asked him what he was going to be when he grew up. Like a flash came the answer in perfect English: "I *was* going to be an English admiral. Then came the Abyssinian affair, and you didn't close the Suez Canal. So now I don't know."

I expect the boy takes his politics from his father. At any rate Meštrović was delighted with the reply, and at once told me another story of his son's precocity. Not long before, the boy had been having a geography lesson from his English governess, who was taking him round the map of the British Empire.

"Canada", said the governess, "is a Dominion."

"What's a Dominion?" said the boy.

"Oh, it's like a kingdom or a part of a kingdom."

"But how can Canada be a kingdom? It's in America, and America is a republic. In any case, who is King of Canada?"

"The King of England."

"H'm," said the boy, unconvinced.

"Australia is a Commonwealth, also part of a kingdom," continued the governess.

"And who is its King?"

"The King of England."

"H'm."

Next came India, and the governess explained that India was an Empire and that the King of England was its Emperor. This was too much for the young Meštrović, who shook his head.

"Miss Taylor," he said gravely, "you'll be telling me next that Heaven is an Empire and that the King of England is the good God."

The arrival of the boy switched the conversation to a discussion on education. Kljaković was an ultra-modernist who did not believe in sheltering boys from the dangers of life, holding that repression was more harmful than complete liberty. Meštrović was prepared to give a good trial to English discipline. But he showed no irritating obstinacy in his views, and I admired the balanced judgment with which he summed up the merits and demerits of both systems. Indeed, whether he is talking art or politics or even trivialities, he weighs his sentences and fixes you with his eye as though he were measuring the perspective for a statue. He is saved, too, from the ardour of his Slavic temperament by his sense of humour. Although a fearless critic of the Serbs, he can see the faults and weaknesses of his own countrymen and make fun of them. He is an impressive figure whom you must either like or dislike with equal intensity. I count myself among the hero-worshippers.

I cannot include the Croatian political leaders in the category of friends, partly, because it is difficult to be on intimate terms with a politician unless one is one's self a politician, and, partly, because I dislike party politics, holding that both national and class hatreds are fostered by the professional politicians for party ends. But inevitably I talked politics in Zagreb because more politics are talked there than in any other city in Europe. Inevitably, too, I talked with Dr. Maček, who in 1925 succeeded Stjepan Radić as leader of the Croat Peasant Party.

I was in Yugoslavia when Radić was shot down in the Skupshtina, the Yugoslav Parliament, in Belgrade, and, as soon as the news was received, every town and village in Croatia went into mourning. By his death Radić became a martyr.

In Croat eyes Dr. Maček is also a martyr, for he has spent many months in prison. But in many respects he is the complete antithesis to Radić. Not even his warmest admirers can say to-day that Radić was a practical man. He was a brilliant but volatile talker, who lost himself easily in constantly changing formulae. In private conversation Maček, who like most Croats can deliver a demagogic speech, is a man of few words. Short and thick-set, with small moustache and plump hands, he prides himself on the constancy of his political views. He is a lawyer by profession and a man of considerable erudition. In his own party he occupies an almost dictatorial position, but, like most modern dictators, he practises the simple habits of a democrat.

Some years ago Colonel Cooper, the American engineer who built the famous Dnieper barrage for the Soviet Government, gave me a graphic account of his various meetings with Stalin. On one occasion he spent a day alone with the Soviet dictator at Gorki. At luncheon the two men were waited on by a Russian girl, who dumped the dishes down on the table and then withdrew, leaving Stalin to serve the food and hand the plates to his guest.

Stalin did not miss his opportunity to sow the seed of propaganda.

"You saw that girl?" he said to his guest. "You noticed that she refused to wait on us?"

"Sure," said the Colonel.

"Well," said Stalin, "she's been like that for three years. Foreigners say that I am the dictator of 180,000,000 people. But I can't do a thing with that girl. She's working for her university degree, and she says it's beneath the dignity of an educated woman to wait on any man."

I should be loth to accuse Dr. Maček of pose. He has no vices. In order not to smoke too much, he makes his own cigarettes, carrying his tobacco in a little silver box. Even the

E

Serbian politicians, who suspect few of their opponents of
honesty, admit that he is honest. Yet he has one foible which
always strikes me as a deliberate attempt to impress his peasant
followers. On each occasion that I have seen him, he has always worn the short black coat of the ordinary professional
man, but his neck has always been collarless and his shirt-
front open and tie-less.

Dr. Maček received me in his little Zagreb office in Prilaz
No. 9. It is a badly furnished, untidy room. Night and day a
policeman stands on duty on the opposite side of the street.
Other police agents, not in uniform, dog the Croatian
leader's every step. Also present at our meeting was Dr.
Kosutić, a political exile amnestied by Prince Paul and now
Dr. Maček's chief lieutenant.

Our talk followed the same restricted course as previous
talks that I had had with him. Radić was readily indiscreet;
Dr. Maček is a man of caution. He limits his political creed
to three short sentences: "I accept the frontiers of the Yugoslav state. I recognise the dynasty. I demand a new constitution." He may accept the frontiers, but what he really wants
is a wide measure of autonomy for Croatia. He may recognise the dynasty, but he is a severe critic of the late King
Alexander, whose death, he told me rather bitterly, was no
loss to the Croats.

I asked him what progress he had made since our last talk
a year ago towards an understanding with the Serbs. He
quoted the "sporazum", the written agreement which he
concluded with the United Serbian Opposition in 1937. As
a political document it is not impressive. It provides for free
elections and the consideration of a new constitution if and
when the Opposition comes into power. In the unlikely
event of the Opposition achieving power the whole question of the constitution would have to be thrashed out again,
and a squabble would be inevitable. Moreover, the old
political parties in Serbia have lost much of their former
power. The three leaders of the United Serbian Opposition

are old men. Their combined ages exceeds two hundred and thirty, a fact to which M. Stojadinović, the present Prime Minister, refers with considerable effect in almost every speech. When one bears in mind that, although there are no class divisions in Serbia, there is little of the democratic spirit in the Serbian politicians, and that the only substantial difference between the so-called democratic politicians and the so-called dictatorships is that the politicians want the spoils of office to go round quickly, it will be realised that the "sporazum" is not a very promising document. Dr. Maček knows all the difficulties of the situation, and he probably regards his adherence to the "sporazum" more as a sound tactical move than as a constructive piece of work. The "sporazum", however, has one practical asset. It represents to the rank and file of both peoples the first attempt at Serbo-Croatian political co-operation. For the first time a Croatian leader has put his signature to a document which tells his followers in black and white that he is prepared to work with Serbs.

It is the tragedy of Yugoslavia that, whereas other European states are burdened with immense and almost insoluble problems regarding racial minorities, the great Yugoslav dispute is one between two peoples who belong to the same race and who, to all intent and purposes, speak the same language. The quarrel dates from the first days of the creation of the new state. With the passage of time it has increased in intensity, and feeling is now much more bitter than it was when I was resident in Yugoslavia twelve years ago. It has eaten into the heart of the Croatian youth, which is now much more radical than it used to be. In pre-war days ninety per cent. of the students of Zagreb University were ardent champions of a Yugoslav state. Now, the same percentage is anti-Serbian and even anti-Yugoslav.

During my recent stay in Zagreb I saw some of the cleverest of the young generation. It would be unfair to them to give their names. But I can summarise their attitude. They see no solution of the Serbo-Croatian quarrel. The

river Drina, they say, has been for over a thousand years the
boundary between Western civilisation and Eastern civilisation. Croatia belongs to the West. Serbia is still the Orient.
The gulf cannot be bridged. In a future European war the
Croats will side with anyone who is against the Serbs.

This attitude is exaggerated and must not be taken too
seriously. It illustrates a capacity for wild talk which in post-
war Europe is not confined to the Croats. On the other hand,
the Croats have genuine grievances. Both in numbers and in
importance they form the second partnership in the new
kingdom. Yet they find themselves shut out from all the
high posts in the army, in the diplomatic service, and even
in the navy for which their special qualities would seem to
predestine them. The Serbs are not a seafaring people. For
five centuries the Croats have given to Venice and, later, to
Austria not only splendid sailors, but also famous sea-
captains. Moreover, since 1918 the Croats have seen money
lavished on Belgrade, which has now overtaken Zagreb both
in size and in economic importance. And their indignation
at the extravagance and corruption of the Belgrade administration is not without some justification.

An impartial observer might reasonably conclude that this
neglect of Croatia is the direct result of the Croat refusal to
co-operate with Belgrade. The Slovenes, who are the third
partners in the Yugoslav kingdom, have not suffered in the
same manner as the Croats. On the contrary, they have received many favours. Those Croats, who believe obstinately
that the first preoccupation of every Belgrade government
is to keep Croatia down, regard these favours to the Slovenes
as a clumsy attempt on Belgrade's part to play off the smaller
minority against the larger.

But there is another aspect of this particular problem.
There have been moments when various Belgrade admini-
strations have been prepared for their own political advantage to give minor concessions to the Croats. Had these concessions been accepted, the Croats were strong enough to

have consolidated them. They might have advanced, trench by trench, to their objective. The Croat leaders, however, lack political experience. Maček, in particular, has always refused to budge from his "all or nothing" attitude. On the other hand, Dr. Korošec, the Slovene leader, is a shrewd and experienced politician. Both as a Catholic priest and as a former deputy of the old Austrian Parliament, he understands the necessity of political compromise. It is a curious and illuminating fact that Dr. Maček is almost more bitter against Dr. Korošec than against any individual Serbian minister.

The attitude of the Serbs is almost as uncompromising. They are irritated by Croat claims to a superior culture. They feel that in the war, which led to the creation of the new state, they made the greater sacrifice. Whatever concessions may eventually be given to Croatia, the Serbs are determined that they themselves shall be the dominant element in the new state, and that Belgrade must be the capital and the administrative centre. Few outside observers will deny that in a small country of fifteen million inhabitants three capitals are two too many.

Certainly the Serbs have made many mistakes. They are an attractive, proud and rather cocksure race. They have a firm faith in their own destiny, and are not given to studying the psychology of other peoples. They believe in their own methods, and perhaps their greatest fault has been their persistence in trying to make a final bargain with Dr. Maček, instead of carrying out a definite policy of conciliation irrespective of the attitude of the Croatian political leaders.

No Serb is likely, either now or in the future, to grant the full demands of Dr. Maček. But such concessions as will one day have to be made might well be granted now. Even if unacceptable to-day to the majority of Croats, they would not be without effect. It is true that Dr. Maček has behind him the vast bulk of the Croat people and that when elections take place Croatia presents a united national front. But it is also true that many Croats, especially among the bourgeoisie, are not satisfied with Dr. Maček's policy of inactivity and passive resistance. They see the benefits which have accrued to Slovenia and draw the inevitable comparison. Unfortunately, the Serbian attitude towards Croatia is also one of passive resistance. If Belgrade adopted a more liberal Croatian policy, many influential Croats would be satisfied with the realisation of forty per cent. of Dr. Maček's demands. Admittedly, the Croatian bourgeoisie is numerically insignificant. But it possesses the best brains.

Both among the Croats and among the Serbs I have met several men of intellect and administrative ability who are prepared to meet each other half-way in order to work for a united Yugoslavia. I am bound to admit that such Serbs receive little concrete encouragement in Belgrade. As for the Croats, anyone who tries to co-operate with Belgrade is at once labelled by Dr. Maček's henchmen as a traitor or a self-seeker, and such is the power of Maček's influence that the label sticks.

There is another potential rift in the Croat national front. Dr. Maček and his lieutenants, if anti-Bolshevik in their economic views, are Popular Front in sympathy and accept the Franco-Soviet Pact. For this reason they dislike the present Belgrade "politique de bon voisinage", which really amounts to nothing more than cultivating friendly relations with Yugoslavia's two best customers, Germany and Italy. To many of the Croatian bourgeoisie, who accept the "politique de bon voisinage" as an economic necessity, Soviet Russia is anathema and the Popular Front definitely unpopular. By a more generous policy towards Croatia, the Serbs could strengthen the Yugoslav idea without sacrificing the unity of the state. Instead, they have adopted a hole-in-the-corner and rather Oriental policy which consists in an effort to win over some of Dr. Maček's lieutenants by methods which are akin to bribery. The policy has proved and will continue to prove futile, and its only result has been to convince many Croats of all classes that the Serbs want, not a Yugoslavia, but a Greater Serbia.

It is difficult to be optimistic about the outcome of this unfortunate quarrel. Like the old Scottish clans, the Slav races have a peculiar capacity for quarrelling among themselves, and the nearer they are to each other the more readily they squabble. Croats and Serbs are so closely allied in speech, in physical attributes, and even in character, that a foreign resident of long standing finds it hard to tell one race from the other. Yet there are fundamental differences: the difference of culture which comes from centuries of different domination by alien rulers, and, above all, the difference of religions. The Serbs are Orthodox; the Slovenes and most of the Croats are Catholics, and in Bosnia and Herzegovina there is a strong minority of Mohammedan Slavs who are more conservative in their Islam orthodoxy than most other followers of the Prophet. These religious differences have created another cause of irritation. Although there is less difference between Serbian and Croatian than there is between the dialects of Yorkshire and Lancashire, the Serbs use the Cyrillic script and the Croats the Roman. And the Serbs insist overmuch on the use of the Cyrillic script in places where it is unnecessary.

For these reasons the quarrel is likely to be of long duration. The Croats themselves foresee no immediate settlement of their grievances. And in one respect their position is without hope. They cannot expect to establish a new independent state. Secession to a neighbouring state—and since March, 1938, the choice is confined to Germany, Italy and Hungary —would be both unpopular and unfeasible. And in despair they fall back on a solution which is as ingenuous as it is unrealisable. Many of them told me that their only hope lay in a Franco-British ultimatum to Belgrade. In this connection they have been disappointed by successive British Ministers to Yugoslavia, who have rightly refused to entangle themselves in an internal dispute. And, as a result of this disappointment, the Croats now lean more towards the French, who have lost influence and prestige in Belgrade owing to their intrigues with the Opposition.

The tragedy of the situation is that both races seem to think that time is on their side. The Serbs, who are political realists, are not impressed by Croat volubility. They regard Dr Maček, for all his obstinacy and unwillingness to compromise, as a man without initiative, as a man slow to take action in the form either of an understanding with Belgrade or of a revolt by his own people. They are not afraid of him. Undoubtedly, they prefer him to some unknown but almost certainly more active successor. To the foreign visitor they refuse to admit the existence of a crisis.

It may be granted that the crisis is latent and therefore not serious in peace-time. The Serbs, who are never afraid to act, are masters of the necessary force. But if Yugoslavia were involved in another war the situation might alter. The Croats might extend their tactics of passive resistance. In 1937, when the Yugoslav manœuvres were held in Croatia, the Belgrade administration had to appeal to Dr. Maček to prevent the Croatian peasantry from refusing transport facilities and provisions to the troops. The Yugoslav army, if excellent in fighting spirit, is weak in equipment and in transport, and, had the boycott continued, the manœuvres might have been brought to a standstill. In wartime a boycott of the mobilisation would have far more unpleasant consequences.

This long-standing dispute is the more deplorable because, of all the new states in Europe, Yugoslavia is at heart the soundest and the most virile. Both in 1937 and in 1938 I was forcibly impressed by the immense material progress which had been made in every part of the country since 1928 and, especially, since 1921 when I paid my first visit. I have the warmest affection for all the Slav races of Yugoslavia and for the country itself, and I feel poignantly that it would be a European catastrophe if the new state were to be undermined by fratricidal dissensions which to the foreign observer seem unnecessarily puerile. Yet it is a quarrel in which no foreigner can help by taking sides, and I regret that so many English visitors become so violently partisan on the briefest acquaintance with the country. Anglican clergymen, anti-Catholic by tradition and obsessed by the prospect of a fusion between the Anglican and Orthodox Churches, champion the Serbs. Liberal and Labour politicians, who spend a week-end in Zagreb, lend a ready ear to the grievances of the Croats. The lesson of Ireland should make us particularly chary of taking sides in a foreign country. We should remember that, however futile they may seem to us, the Serbo-Croatian differences are deep-rooted and that faults and mistakes have been made by both peoples.

A gradual amelioration of the situation must depend on Belgrade. The present state of Europe should make the Croats realise that a spirit of compromise must be shown by both sides. For, if Britain desires a strong and prosperous Yugoslavia, there are other countries who have very different ambitions. Neither Croats nor Serbs should forget that Yugoslavia's neighbours, more particularly, Germany, Italy and Hungary, have a special interest in prolonging the quarrel and in keeping the wounds open as long as possible.

CHAPTER THREE

A BRITISH VISITOR, strolling through the streets of Zagreb, might come to the conclusion that he was in a small and rather shoddy provincial town. The conclusion would be wrong. The shops, it is true, are unimpressive, and the drabbest of British provincial towns boasts a better cinema. But, apart from its ancient history, Zagreb is still a living city, possessing more of the atmosphere, if less of the appearance, of a capital than Edinburgh. Politically and culturally it may well be compared with the Dublin of pre-war days. Its Consular Corps is more concerned with politics than with commerce. Half-a-dozen daily newspapers represent the different currents of local political thought. If the Zagreb cinemas provide no creature comforts, the city possesses an opera, a ballet and a theatre which won the highest praise from so great a critic as M. Stanislavsky, the co-founder of the Moscow Art Theatre.

The culture is European. The bookshops are full of German, Russian, French, and even Italian literature. British culture is neglected, partly, I think, because Britain has neglected Zagreb. While I was in Yugoslavia in 1938, the French were holding a large and representative book exhibition in Zagreb; the Germans had organised a similar exhibition all over the country, and the Italians had just concluded arrangements to send to Belgrade the same magnificent collection of Italian paintings which they exhibited in London a few years ago. British efforts at cultural propaganda are still in their infancy. So far they have been concentrated mainly on music. Both Miss Myra Hess and the Fleet Street Choir, who toured Yugoslavia under the auspices of the British Council, achieved a remarkable success in Zagreb. But I cannot help feeling that, as propaganda, music is of small value. People go to hear music because it is good, not because it is British. The Germans and the Italians spend their money on a very dif-

ferent form of propaganda, offering every kind of inducement
to foreigners to send their sons and daughters to German or
Italian schools and universities.

Few Croats visit Britain, although I was glad to learn that
Viktor Ružić, the Ban or Governor of Croatia, had sent his
daughter to England to be educated. With encouragement
more Croats could be easily persuaded to follow his example. Incidentally, M. Ružić's future is worth watching.
His acceptance of the post of Ban implies his willingness to
co-operate with Belgrade. He is young, able, hard-working,
and essentially practical. He is a man of few words and is one
of the few Croats who practise abstinence as a form of self-
discipline.

Zagreb society splits itself readily into small groups. It is
rich, for the city possesses a large industry. But the richest
citizens are Hebrew, and, indeed, it is no exaggeration to
state that the commercial prosperity of Zagreb has been
created by the Jews. Hitherto, there has been no Jewish question in Yugoslavia. But since the advent of Hitler the first
signs are already faintly evident. Jewish refugees have come to
Croatia from Germany. Like most Jews they are hard-working, intelligent and thrifty. They soon succeed in business.
So far there is no active anti-Semitism, but from more than
one quarter I heard murmurs of discontent.

During my visit I was entertained by one of Zagreb's
richest Jews. The hospitality was lavish and the conversation
intellectual. But I could see that not only my host but other
prominent Zagreb Jews were perturbed by the spreading
wave of anti-Semitism in Central Europe and that, like
many British Jews, they regarded the influx of German
Jewish refugees with some anxiety. In view of the barbarous
treatment which has been meted out to Jews in Germany,
it is difficult to discuss the Jewish question dispassionately.
I have lived with it for twenty years: in Russia, in Germany
and in the Danubian states, and I have come reluctantly to
the conclusion that, in Central and Eastern Europe at any

rate, it is largely a problem of proportion. As soon as a country acquires more Jews than it can absorb, a Jewish question at once arises. Philosophers, scientists and economists can give a hundred excellent reasons why this should not be so, but, unfortunately, human nature has not yet learnt to act reasonably.

In Zagreb I did not spend all of my time with the rich and privileged. I also saw much of my poor friends. With young Jakić, my Croat mentor, I made a first-hand study of university life in Zagreb. The poverty of the students was pitiful. Many lived in the barest of hostels. Others shared a garret with one or two fellow-students. The majority, I think, had rarely more than one meal a day, and the meal usually consisted of bread and a dish of soup with meat or vegetable stock. Some of the students looked and, undoubtedly, were under-nourished. But what struck me most was the cheapness of the education. A student can and does "do" Zagreb University on a total budget of forty-five pounds a year. Of this sum thirty-eight pounds are required for board, lodging and clothes. The remaining seven pounds cover all university fees including the cost of graduation.

Even if one admits that forty-five pounds go twice as far in Yugoslavia as in Britain, the contrast with Oxford and Cambridge is startling. In Yugoslavia, as in Japan, poverty is a badge of honour. It is also an incentive to work. At the end of his university course the Zagreb student will lack the physical attributes and the self-assurance of the Oxford and Cambridge undergraduate. He will not know one end of a horse from the other. He will have played no games, and for the improvement of his physique he will have to depend on his period of compulsory military service. But the range of his knowledge will be wider and more comprehensive than that of the average Oxford or Cambridge student, and the number of hours that he has devoted to work will be twice as great. In Zagreb the preoccupation of the educational authorities is to prevent the five thousand students from over-working and under-eating. The average Oxford or Cambridge undergraduate is under-worked and over-fed.

The conditions of university life which prevail in Zagreb are duplicated in the other university towns of Yugoslavia and, indeed, of Bulgaria, Rumania and Czechoslovakia. They set a difficult problem both to British and to Yugoslav educational authorities.

As far as Oxford and Cambridge are concerned, we have to ask ourselves two questions. In the present state of the world how long can we continue to afford an education which costs five times as much as the average university course in Europe? How far are the results achieved commensurate with the extra expense? The questions must arouse grave doubts in many minds. It is true that in Britain we have other universities where first-class educational facilities are provided at a low cost, and that the wide extension of our scholarship system has opened the doors of even the most expensive colleges to poor students. But, rightly or wrongly, I cannot help feeling that the attitude of the average student in the new countries towards his university career is very different from that of the upper and middle class British student. In particular, the average foreign student knows that he can expect little or nothing from his parents, and in this respect the self-reliance that he acquires is a distinct advantage.

In Yugoslavia and in the other new states of Central and South-Eastern Europe the educational problem is a different one. Faith in their new destiny has stirred all these peoples to a great effort. The urge for education is universal. Sons of peasants desert the land to go to the university. They work like ants, because when you are bone poor study is both work and pastime. And the vast majority does well. Then comes the task of job-finding. It is not easy. A university degree in Yugoslavia qualifies you for a post as a government official, as a doctor, as a lawyer, or as an engineer. But already Yugoslavia has a superfluity of bureaucrats, engineers, doctors and lawyers, and the supply of jobs is no longer equal to the demand. The over-production of intellectuals has now reached a point where it is hard to secure a post even as a bank-clerk or a book-keeper without a university degree. The inevitable result has been the creation of a disgruntled intellectual proletariat. And the intellectual youth of Yugoslavia is definitely radical in thought and outlook.

In Zagreb I was entertained by some of my poorer Croatian friends, and I enjoyed that evening more than any other. They were young, and the excellent, cheap wine loosed their tongues. They were much less internationally-minded than our British intellectual proletarians, and their radicalism was strongly tinged with nationalist sentiment, admittedly in the Croatian rather than in the Yugoslav sense. Their talk was witty. They disliked the semi-dictatorship of M. Stojadinović and gave point to their dislike with a typically Croatian story of the Yugoslav Prime Minister's visit to Berlin. After a busy day M. Stojadinović sups alone with Herr Hitler. "May I ask you one question?" says the Yugoslav to the Fuehrer. "As one dictator to another, tell me how many of your people are against you?"

The Fuehrer thinks for a minute and then replies: "Confidentially and in all honesty I should say not more than fifteen millions."

"Just the same with me," says Stojadinović delightedly.

The total population of Yugoslavia is approximately fifteen millions.

Still less did my young friends like the dictatorships in Germany and Italy. To-day, the most popular form of story in Yugoslavia is the letter puzzle. Out came a pencil, and one of the young men handed me a card with the cryptic message "Februar, 1940." Could I decipher it? A similar card was supposed to be received by Herr Hitler at Christmas and, as it bore no signature, the Fuehrer's mystic curiosity was aroused. He sent for General Goering. He summoned his cipher experts from the Wilhelmstrasse. He offered a reward to the soothsayers. No one could solve the message. At last an old Rabbi came to the Fuehrer's palace and, after demanding and being granted full immunity from persecution, volunteered to decipher the puzzle. Each letter represented a word, and the message, which had to be read forwards and then backwards, ran as follows: "Frankreich, England, Belgien, Russland, und Amerika rechnen auf Untergang des Reiches bis Ende Februar, 1940."[1]

After our dinner my friends took me to a wine-cellar much frequented by the students and by the poor. The long narrow room, rudely furnished and foul with cheap cigarette smoke, was full. A small orchestra of a piano, a guitar, a concertina and two violins was playing a Viennese song. The musicians were all young. They were, my friends told me, university students who worked here by night in order to pay for their education. A waiter in a dirty white coat found a table for us, and presently the leader of the orchestra, a swarthy, young Adonis with a soft tenor voice, began to croon a Croatian song. The tune was not so plaintive as a Russian gipsy song, but the affinity was unmistakable. It was extraordinarily pleasant, and I was glad that Zagreb or at least the poor of Zagreb had not yet succumbed to the deadening monotony of "jazz". I was fascinated by the public. They were of all ages and ranged, I imagined, from plutocratic hotel porters and waiters to young clerks and students. At the tables couples predominated, and as most of the women were young I guessed that there were more mistresses than wives. They were cheaply but neatly dressed. Most of them were artificial blondes with dark eyes and lips liberally smeared with carmine. Some would have walked straight into a beauty chorus in London or New York. Yet, although morals are easy in Zagreb, there was no looseness of behaviour. These people took their pleasures with unaffected but respectable gaiety. Even the men who had

[1]France, England, Belgium, Russia and America reckon on the downfall of the Third Reich before the end of February, 1940.

drunk too much were quietly somnolent. Soft music and wine produce a more romantic and less rowdy effect than "jazz" and hard liquor. To me it was a pleasant and harmless experience. It was certainly not harmful to the pocket. For here one could sit until the early hours of the morning for the price of a few pence, and a whole carafe of local wine costs less than a packet of ten Players.

Under the influence of the Croatian music the nationalism of my friends reasserted itself. Out came the pencils again, and I was given a new letter puzzle. "Why is Yugoslavia surrounded by 'brigama' (difficulties)?" "Because 'brigama' stands for: Bulgaria, Rumania, Italy, Greece, Madjarska (Hungary) and Austria." So much for neighbourly love and the popular nationalism of Croatian youth!

As befits a sub-capital with a fairly prosperous bourgeoisie, Zagreb has also a more expensive night-life. It is more provincial and less sophisticated than the night-life of Vienna; a little less primitive than the night-life of Belgrade. It takes place in "bars", a name borrowed from America but possessing here a Viennese significance. In Central Europe a "bar" consists of a dancing-floor, which also serves as the stage for the cabaret turns, a dais for the orchestra, rows of tables, and behind the tables a semi-circle of low boxes. In an anteroom there may be a real bar, but it is not much in evidence.

Zagreb has its full complement of "bars". Some advertise themselves as "open all night". The two most expensive and, in that sense, the most exclusive, are the Pik "Bar" and the Ritz "Bar". I revisited both and marvelled a little at my powers of endurance. The programme was long. The artists included a lightning calculator, a trio of lady contortionists, a young man, obviously Austrian, who sang an English song and performed a Lancashire step-dance, a German-speaking American negress, and a real Indian nautsch-girl. At side-tables at the back sat half-a-dozen blond Viennese Animierdamen who chain-smoked as the cheapest antidote to boredom. The presence of the Viennese ladies and of the Indian

nautsch-girl indicated Zagreb's exact geographical situation
on the map of night-life. It is the half-way house between the
West and the East.

Even here the entertainment was not expensive. Unless
one drinks French champagne, life, both human and material, is very cheap in Zagreb. Nor was there much gaiety or
even the attraction of lewd behaviour. Till the end of the
cabaret programme the audience, which contained a fair
sprinkling of married couples, was solidly respectable. When
the married couples left, the Animier-damen roused themselves from their lethargy. Their animation, however, was
half-hearted. Correctly but joylessly they danced with good-
looking young men with polished nails and sleek hair, while
the orchestra played American music without the American
sense of rhythm. I was surprised to see how quickly luxury
creates decadence even in a country where there is little inherited wealth. Night-life in Belgrade may bring many surprises: noisiness, drunkenness, even a brawl. But, at least,
there is something virile in the conduct of the revellers. Here
in Zagreb the young men had obviously plenty of money.
But they looked bored and satiated. Doubtless, the satiation
was the cause of the boredom. There is, indeed, only one
exciting feature of Zagreb night-life, and this is provided,
not by Croats, not by Viennese, but by the Russians.

With Želko Mažuranić I went to a Russian *Nachtlokal*
where a Russian orchestra, complete with gipsy singers,
played and sang until the last guest chose to leave. The hour
was late and the room, lit with the dimmest of lights, was
thick with cigarette smoke. Through the cloudy atmosphere
I could just see that the windows had stained-glass designs.
Was I in a converted church? I felt a little uncomfortable. A
closer inspection revealed that the figures in the windows
were not saints but semi-nudes who looked like hermaphro-
dites. At tables, separated by flimsy, low partitions. sat the
public: men of all ages and classes; some alone .others with
painted doll companions who obviously came from the

F

streets. One or two were rather drunk, and several were in that state of boredom which leaves one tired but unable to go to bed. Among the guests there was considerable coming and going. Some dropped in to have a drink and hear a gipsy song and then left. At some moments the room was nearly full, at others almost empty.

I had come prepared for disillusionment, expecting at the best to meet some old friend like Jurie Morfessi whom I had heard sing in Russia in the pre-war days and again, after the war, in Prague, in Belgrade, and in Paris. I was loth to revive memories which were better kept unsullied. But Morfessi was not there. In his place were new faces; above all, young faces. The orchestra, fourteen strong, was composed of young men. Most of them looked intelligent. One or two were good-looking youths with clear-cut features and well-knit frames. One of the lady singers was middle-aged. The other was a young girl with the face of a madonna. Their demeanour was quiet and dignified. Compared with the public, they looked like thoroughbreds at a fair of cart-horses.

As the guitars struck their first minor chord, I thought vaguely of the money I had squandered on Russian gipsy music. Through my mind flashed Pushkin's lines:

"Mechtam i godam nyet vozvrata,
Nye obnovlyu dushi moyei . . ."

For me, too, there would be no return of the dreams and years, no renovation of the soul. Never again should I yield with the same abandon to the follies and enthusiasms of youth.

But in spite of myself my interest was roused. These Russians represented a type that was new to me. Since I had lived in Yugoslavia, a new generation of Russians had grown up that had been born abroad or were too young to remember the Russia from which their parents had been driven. They were the children of the remnants of Denikin's and Wrangel's White army, and their fate in a foreign country had been hard. Sons and daughters of monarchists, they had been brought up on monarchist lines, for of all countries Yugoslavia has shown the greatest sympathy to the Whites. The boys had been educated at the Kadetski Corpus, a kind of Russian Sandhurst sanctioned and aided by the Yugoslav government, the girls at the Russian Institute, a replica of the aristocratic Smolny Institute in St. Petersburg which subsequently acquired a new fame as the first headquarters of the Bolshevik Party. Here they had spent a few happy years in sheltered seclusion, the boys being trained as the former Tsarist officers were trained, the girls learning to curtsey and to dance the mazurka and the polonaise. Then, at the age of seventeen, they had been thrown penniless into the whirlpool of Balkan life. Some of the young men found employment. A girl was lucky if she found a Serbian husband. But for the majority there were no jobs. And so they had banded themselves into orchestras to work all night in order to pay for advanced education by day.

Although they bore no resemblance to the professional gipsies of Tsarist days, they had mastered this form of entertainment thoroughly. The guitars and violins struck the necessary note of melancholy into one's soul. A burly bass sang with the necessary abandon the drinking-songs which invite the guest to empty his glass. There was a young man with a superb tenor voice which in the old days would have made his fortune.

The most curious feature of the evening was the singing of new Soviet songs, for the performers were anti-Bolshevik to a man. Russia cannot have changed very much. The songs, doubtless transcribed from the Soviet radio, were indistinguishable from the Tsarist songs. The themes were the same: unrequited love, champagne and vodka. One song about street lamps, with a stirring chorus beginning "Fonariki, Fonariki moji", was a special favourite of Mažuranić, to whom the very name of Bolshevism is anathema. This typical example of Slav inconsistency broke down my defences. If my sentimental emotions were not disturbed, I was amused and abandoned my reserve. The choir, which received a miserable salary from the proprietor, depended for its living on the contributions of the guests. Every half-hour or so, at the end of a song, one of the girls took a plate and solemnly walked round the tables to make a collection. I looked at the stained-glass windows. I thought of my Presbyterian upbringing in Scotland. And I contributed more generously than I could afford.

I went back several times to this place. I got to know the young men and the girls rather well. I went with them to other Russian establishments, for both Zagreb and Belgrade have several restaurants and cellars where Russian choirs and Russian singers provide the entertainment. I took them out into the country to dine at little restaurants by the banks of the Save or at the top of the Sljeme mountain. And gradually I learnt the story of their lives.

It was a story of tragedy relieved by courage of the highest quality. Most of the young men had managed somehow to go through a university. They told me stories of their student days and of life on one hundred and fifty dinars a month. One hundred and fifty dinars represent thirteen English shillings. Life on so small a sum means sharing not only a room with three companions but also sharing a suit. They went in rotation to their studies, the three suitless students remaining in bed till the fourth returned. They told me their story without complaint. They even laughed as they explained to me how it was necessary to beg or borrow a suit for the tallest. He could hardly go to the university with sleeves to his elbows and half his shins showing below the trousers. With half-a-dozen safety-pins and some amateur tailoring they could fit out the shortest student more or less respectably.

Most of them were still learning some useful subject. One was qualifying as a surveyor. Another had taught himself English, including a tolerably good pronunciation, from a book. While I was in Zagreb, the young tenor took two days off in order to sit for his final examination as an engineer. He was married, had a baby daughter, and, like most of the others, had joined the choir to pay for his education. He passed brilliantly, but he was pessimistic about his prospects of obtaining a job.

After the war the Yugoslavs were very kind to the White Russians. They accepted their professors, their staff officers, their engineers and their military doctors, and both Russians and Yugoslavs benefited from this arrangement. But twenty years have passed since the war, and Yugoslavia has made great progress. Her universities have now turned out hundreds of trained Yugoslavs. There are nearly twenty thousand Russians in Yugoslavia. Their position is like that of Jews in other countries. They are too numerous to absorb. Competition to-day is too severe. And, if the Yugoslavs are not unkind, they nevertheless are forced to consider their own people first.

But it was the story of the girl with the madonna face which amazed me. She told it with a simplicity and lack of emotion which convinced me of its truth. Her name was Tatiana. Her father, a colonel in the White Army, was killed in the civil war. In the scurried evacuation of the Whites after Wrangel's collapse in 1920 Tania, then aged four, was separated from her mother. A British ship took the mother to Egypt. Another bore Tania and her young sister to Constantinople. From that city she was brought to Bulgaria, where there was a scheme in force for the adoption of Russian refugee children by Bulgarian families. For several days Tania was exposed with other children in a kind of booth while the Bulgarian housewives, impoverished by the war and seeking cheap servants, came to inspect this human cargo. Tania was not selected. She was too young to be useful in the house.

From Bulgaria she was brought by other Russian refugees to Yugoslavia. She was educated in the old-world, sheltered atmosphere of the Institute. After eight years she was re-united to her mother who had since re-married, and, on leaving the Institute at the age of eighteen, she went to live with her family. She was beautiful, and there was trouble with the step-father. She ran away and joined the choir. Times were hard for her, for the rewards of night-life are small in a poor country like Yugoslavia. After King Alexander's tragic death, when official mourning involved the closing of all places of entertainment for several weeks, she lay penniless with pleurisy in a damp cellar. Now at the age of twenty-four she helps to keep her mother, her step-father and her brother. She has kept something more: a fine, un-spoilt character and her self-respect.

I have something more than a sentimental admiration for these exiled Russians of the new generation. Unlike the Russian *émigrés* of fiction, they do not call themselves counts or princesses. They are, however, the sons and daughters of educated parents: professors, doctors, army officers. They are a fine type of youth, stronger and more self-reliant than the previous generation. Strangely enough, they have also far less fear of poverty, war, revolution, and all the other terrors of life in Europe to-day than the men and women of fifty. Although they have known hardly a moment of what we should call happiness, they have remained normal. Some admittedly fall by the way, but in a situation which seems almost hopeless the vast majority has not lost the hope of youth.

If I were young, I should choose a wife from the new generation of Russian *émigrés*. They know life as the previous generations never knew it. And their courage is superb.

I could wish that Mr. Somerset Maugham would write a corrosively corrective story on the theme of Russian *émigrés* and national pity. To-day, Britain is moved by an immense sentimental pity for the persecuted Jews of Germany and the Spaniards. It is a proper and highly creditable sentiment. But cynics might point out with some truth that our pity is often prompted more by political indignation than by any other emotion. As far as the Spaniards are concerned, most of us, I think, reserve our sympathy and our cash for one side or the other and only rarely is our charity extended to the suffering masses of both sides.

In any case these movements of national pity are remarkably transient and evanescent. Many people will remember the huge wave of sympathy which swept Britain during the Great War when the first refugees arrived from Belgium. Within two years it had considerably subsided. Although Russia, with France, was largely instrumental in helping us to prepare for a war for which we were not ready, the Russians have been forgotten. Perhaps the first *émigrés* were in some respects responsible for their own failure. But the new generation are not to blame for the shortcomings of their forbears. They have endured an exile as barren, if not as harsh, as that of the Jews. They are the victims of a civil war as cruel and as savage as that of Spain.

CHAPTER FOUR

NO ONE WHO lives in Central Europe to-day can help feeling grave anxiety about the future. There is a nervous tension in the atmosphere which communicates itself all too readily to the foreign traveller. For myself I was obsessed by the premonition that, even if this were not my last journey, there were many things that I should never see again in their present form. After ten days in Zagreb I felt an irresistible longing to return to the Dalmatian Coast.

My Croat friends did their best to dissuade me. The beginning of February was not the season for Dalmatia. Without the sun the coast would be very bleak. Had I forgotten my *Twelfth Night*? With better knowledge of maritime conditions than he is given credit for, Shakespeare had wrecked Viola on the Dalmatian Coast. I should, of course, escape that fate, for the Yugoslav boats were good. But I might have a rough and unpleasant passage.

I ignored these warnings. I had seen the Coast in all seasons, and my luck had never failed me. I was determined to put it to another test.

At first the weather-god did his best to punish me for my obstinacy. I left Zagreb in a dense, damp fog which refused to lift. As we began to climb the rough slopes of the Gorksi Kotar, the mist lay so low and white around us that it was scarcely distinguishable from the snow, and only the stunted birches, leafless and ghost-like, satisfied me that the train was, indeed, on earth and not enshrouded in the clouds. At the highest point of the line, more than two thousand five hundred feet above sea-level, we entered the Sljeme tunnel. When we came out, not even Jack, on reaching the top of his beanstalk, could have had a greater surprise. The sky was the clearest of blues. We had left the snow behind us. Below me was the Adriatic, like a huge aquamarine in a platinum setting, with Sušak, Fiume and Abbazzia nestling at the head of the bay in a bath of sunshine.

At Sušak I was met by a nephew of Dr. Šverljuga, and went at once on board the *Yugoslavia* to be entertained to a sumptuous luncheon with fresh "orada" and "plavać", the rich Chianti-like red wine of Dalmatia. I was the only passenger. Indeed, but for the mail contract, the Adriatic shipping lines could not run during the winter. I was, too, the captain's guest. Stanko Šverljuga, whose grandfather had founded the line, and Božo Banać, the Dalmatian shipping magnate, had sent instructions that I was to be looked after, and I was treated like a king.

As we slid gently out of the harbour, I could spot with the naked eye the guns on two Italian destroyers lying off Fiume. To-day, this port, still more Croat than Italian, is separated only by a bridge from the neighbouring Yugoslav port of Sušak. I could not help recalling the escapade of D'Annunzio by which, in defiance of the peace-makers, the Italians had made Fiume their own. It was true that under the Treaty of London the Italians had been promised a part of the Dalmatian coast. Because that treaty had not been implemented, Italians now maintained that they belonged to the "have-not" nations. But Italy had acquired one immense benefit from the war: the break-up of the Austro-Hungarian monarchy, which for years had prevented Italy's natural expansion in the Balkans. With a saner policy Italy could have made herself the natural protector of the Balkan States. She could have found not only useful allies, but also a valuable outlet for her industrial products. But she had chosen the path of violence, and, by so doing, had sown the seeds of mistrust in what would have been a profitable field. The seizure of Fiume had been a cardinal blunder. One day Germany's drive to the south-east might make a saner Italy regret her mistake.

I did not let my thoughts dwell long on politics. Here Nature was at peace, and I wanted to enjoy it while it lasted.

After a star-lit night I arrived at Split soon after dawn and spent some hours on shore. Since my last visit the town had doubled in size. There were new villas on the outskirts and a new hotel. Some old friends like M. Bulić, the famous archaeologist, had died. But the old landmarks had not altered. Here on the front were the rows of palms. In the harbour lay the long line of Dalmatian sailing ships with their gaily-coloured sails of green, russet-brown, blue, and orange, their neatly stacked cargoes of wine, fruit, oil, fish and olives, and their rudely painted names. On every hull figured the name of the Virgin Mary or of some local saint, for the Dalmatian sailors are Catholics and superstitious. The front was already thronged with people: clerks going to their offices, fisher-girls carrying fish to the market, house-wives, some in local costume with little caps not unlike the latest London fashion in hats, and sober Bosnians with fezes and trousers converted by dark puttees into knickerbockers. Both men and women were of splendid physique. Indeed, the Dalmatians share with the Bulgarians the distinction of being the longest-lived race in Europe. They live on fruit, fish, vegetables, wine and unrefined olive oil, and they attri-bute their longevity to the oil. To the British visitor it tastes evilly rancid. But apparently it has great virtues.

Unchanged, too, except for a huge new statue by Meštro-vić, was the old palace of Diocletian. And here I wandered for an hour, untrammelled by guides or tourists. It was to this pleasant retreat that Diocletian, himself a Dalmatian, re-tired after his abdication. It was from here that he wrote his famous message to his former co-emperor Maximian, who had invited him to reassume the Imperial purple: "If I could but show you the cabbages which I have planted here with my own hands, you would not urge me to relinquish the joys of happiness for the pursuit of power."

Gibbon does only the barest justice to Diocletian, although he praises the Emperor's choice of the site for his retreat. In these modern days, a world, more exhausted by the pursuit of power, would build the most sumptuous palace that money can buy for any one or, preferably, all of the dictators who might be induced to follow Diocletian's example.

All the way from Split to Dubrovnik, which I had decided to make my headquarters, the fine weather held, and the sun was warm enough to force me to sit on deck in my shirt-sleeves. From Split onwards I had a fellow-traveller, although not a traveller in the strict sense of the word, for he was an official inspector of the shipping line. He was an ex-sea captain, and, like the captain in *Twelfth Night*, could reply to any modern Viola's question: "Know'st thou this country?" with the same answer: "Ay, Madam, well, for I was bred and born not three hours' travel from this very place."

Powerfully built like most Dalmatians and widely travelled, he was a man of considerable shrewdness, reserving his judgments for matters which he understood. Like nearly everyone in Europe he wanted peace, and regarded Britain as the chief bulwark of peace in the terms in which every country except the dictator countries understands peace. During the last five years he had seen much of the British tourists who visited Dalmatia. He liked them, but was not impressed by the rather contemptuous manner in which they spoke of the Italians. As a sailor who had no love for Italian policy, he thought that we underrated the Italian effort both on land and sea.

Politics, however, were not his strong point, and he preferred local history, of which he had a great knowledge. I therefore welcomed his presence, more especially when we reached Hvar, the pleasantest island of the Adriatic with a winter climate which one day will make it a second Madeira. Here the steamers usually stop for only quarter-of-an-hour, but on this occasion the captain and the inspector arranged for a wait long enough to enable me to see the town more thoroughly than I had ever done before. Hvar is a miniature Venice set in a background of olive-trees, tamarisks and cypresses. It is dominated by its cathedral, but every little street is a nest of fifteenth-century buildings: ruined palazzi and villas with loggias. On the Cathedral Square beside the quay is an old building which once housed a Venetian arsenal and the first theatre in south-eastern Europe. Symbolic of the present insecurity of Europe, the theatre was over the arsenal, and the actors played on boards stretched above the barrels of powder.

Leaving the inspector to do his own business, I walked out to the Franciscan monastery. It stands alone in a grove of cypress trees on a small promontory. I went into the church to see Roselli's *The Last Supper*, which is the chief treasure of Hvar. The church was deserted, and I could not find the picture. Rather nervously I rang the monastery bell. A young Franciscan monk came to the door, and in my halting Croatian I explained to him my desire. He took me into a rather dark refectory, and there, surrounded by other pictures of less value, hung Roselli's huge masterpiece. The monk told me gleefully that a few years ago an English millionaire had come to Hvar in his yacht and had wanted to buy the picture. As the purchase price he had offered to cover the enormous canvas with golden sovereigns. I tried to make a lightning calculation, and arrived at the figure of £10,000, which in Yugoslav currency represents the impressive sum of 2,700,000 dinars. Actually, as the picture measures ten metres by two metres, the sum required, if the picture were to be wholly covered, would be nearer £40,000 than £10,000. But the Franciscan was not interested. "We never calculated the amount," he said proudly. "The monastery does not sell its religious treasures." It was, I suppose, the right attitude. But I was not convinced. The picture was badly hung and needed doing up.

I told the young monk that I hoped to spend a winter in Hvar. Could he help me to find a place where I could work in peace? "Certainly," he said, "we can put you up here. We should have to charge you four hundred dinars a month,

but you would have a room to yourself." Thirty shillings a
month for the most beautiful and most peaceful sojourn in
Europe! It seemed an inviting prospect. I thought of the
happy hours that I could spend with the local fisher-folk, of
the expeditions that I could make from this delectable spot.
Vis, the Lissa of British naval history, with its British cemetery as the standing memorial of Hoste's great victory over
the French, was only two hours' sail away, and Korčula,
another miniature Venice, was not much farther and more
accessible. Here in Hvar I could find the solitude which so
many of my generation sought to-day. Then I remembered
that in all probability the monastery had no bath and certainly no heating, and I went away sorrowfully, cursing the
softness of our modern civilisation.

As our steamer entered the narrow strait which separates
the island of Korčula from the peninsula of Pelješec, my inspector became quite excited. The strait, he told me, was the
favourite sailing ground of King Edward VIII when, during
his short reign, he came on his yachting cruise to Dalmatia.
The peninsula is the birthplace of most of the Croatian
sea-captains, and here they return to live when they
retire. They settle at Orebić and, although in summer it is
over-run by Czech tourists, it is as fair a township as any on
this enchanting coast. The little terra-cotta-coloured town
has one claim to fame. It possesses the only jackal hunt in
Europe. The jackals settled here in the sixteenth century, and
on a still night their howling can be heard even at sea.

Orebić was the favourite resort of the late Admiral Sir
William Fisher when he was Commander-in-Chief of the
Mediterranean Fleet. He did not come there to hunt jackals,
but to take exercise. Every day he landed and walked along
the coast for two or three hours. He had a companion, the
mayor of Orebić and an ex-captain who had sailed the seven
seas and who spoke English. The Admiral not only took his
exercise. He discussed with a rare desire for information
every aspect of local politics and every problem of the

Adriatic. The mayor, who had never walked so far in his life, was immensely impressed, and now Sir William Fisher's name is more respected than any other in Orebić. Because of the world-reputation which the British Navy enjoys, British admirals, who take an intelligent interest in human affairs, can do more for Britain than a whole train-load of peripatetic ministers.

The Dalmatian islands are well known to our Mediterranean Fleet, and, gun or rod in hand, our naval officers have wandered over most of them in search of game or fish. There are many jokes about naval horsemanship. They are now rather out of date when naval polo, stimulated by Admiral Sir Roger Keyes, has attained such a high standard of skill. There are also one or two shooting stories which can only be told far from the presence of sailors. On a certain occasion our Mediterranean flagship was anchored off an island, and early one morning the commander-in-chief went ashore in the barge to shoot. Several petty officers and ratings accompanied him in order to serve as beaters. The ship was due to sail at two p.m., and the Admiral, a stickler for punctuality, had made the necessary arrangements to be back at one-thirty. At the appointed hour there was no sign of the barge. At two o'clock the captain became anxious. At three he was agitated and was on the point of ordering a rescue party to go ashore when he saw the barge appear round the corner of a small promontory. It had a casualty on board. The coxswain had received a charge of shot in his pants. Who shot him remains a secret, for the Navy maintains its reputation as the silent service. In silence the Admiral came aboard. In silence the great flagship steamed her way furiously to her destination.

Sir Roger Keyes is another name to conjure with in Dalmatia, and at a time when Britain's prestige does not stand too high it is a pleasure to be able to say that among Yugoslavs the Mediterranean Fleet is not only popular, but also highly respected.

It is true that a Dalmatian lady told me that when the British naval ratings came ashore at Dubrovnik decent girls had to bar themselves in their houses. But she was a wizened old trout, who believed that the Turks were the only sailors who knew how to behave like gentlemen, and her evidence puts her in a minority of one.

Both the officers and ratings of the British Navy are natural diplomatists, and from every section of the Dalmatian population I heard tributes to their efficiency, courtesy, hospitality and excellent behaviour. The money which the Navy spends ashore is very welcome to the local inhabitants, and, when the bulk of the Mediterranean Fleet visited Dubrovnik some years ago, the Yugoslav Government did a smart deal. It opened a special branch of the National Bank which was given a monopoly for changing British money into dinars. What with purchases of stores and provisions and the expenditure of officers and ratings on shore, the Yugoslav Government netted about £80,000 of good British currency. In these circumstances Yugoslavia would welcome the visit of a British fleet once a month!

The sun was setting as we entered the Mljet Canal which forms the stupendous approach to Dubrovnik. The air was still warm. The sky had turned the deepest of blues. On the mainland to the east a few white clouds began to appear from behind the thin crest of snow on the mountains. On our right Mljet, the Melita where St. Paul stopped on his way to Rome, was already in the shadows. Soon it would look like some prehistoric monster asleep on the surface of the sea. It still shelters monsters of a minute shape. For many years it suffered from a plague of vipers, and then modern science with its urge to interfere in all things introduced the mongoose. And to-day the inhabitants are wringing their hands. The plague of vipers has been replaced by a plague of mongooses, and the islanders cannot keep a hen or an egg.

In ancient days Mljet was a kind of Devil's Island to which the Romans sent their political exiles, and here Oppianus wrote his poem on hunting and fishing. The Yugoslav Government sometimes uses the islands for the same purpose, and, after the dictatorship was established in 1931, Dr. Korošeć, the Slovene leader, was exiled to Hvar for two years. It is, at any rate, an almost idyllic place of banishment.

As the sun sinks lower in the sky, the sea changes from the wine-dark of Homer to a slate-velvet. The water is wondrously calm, and in the stillness the islands stand out in bold, black relief. To the left is Lopud, with its ruined fortresses and deserted monasteries. Farther ahead is Lokrum, with its memories of Richard Lionheart and the Archduke Maximilian, the ill-fated Emperor of Mexico, who was the last private owner of the island. To me Lokrum has personal memories of happy picnics beside banks of bougainvilia and of moonlit walks to a cliff grotto, where the sea splashes and burbles like a witches' cauldron. Only here the cauldron's contents are not slime and toads, but the clean, coloured waters where the rainbows end.

As the steamer slips almost silently through the channel, the clouds turn to a rich mauve. On the hillside of the mainland the last rays of the sun catch the windows of the highest cottages until they gleam as though lit by a thousand candles. Slowly the lights go out. The mauve of the clouds fades to the faintest of rose-pink. As the darkness falls, the new moon, which has been with us since the afternoon, sheds an opal radiancy on the water. With the rocky islet of St. Andrew on our right we turn the corner of Koločep, and there before me are the friendly lamps of Gruž. We are at the gates of Dubrovnik.

I went ashore in high expectation and with a new reverence in my heart. The summer evenings on the Coast are the greatest pageant that Europe can offer, but nowhere had I seen anything to equal the glory of that winter sunset. Here I felt I could forget the daily problems of my life and recapture for a while the lost years of my youth.

My optimism was a little foolish. For, like most experiences which one tries to repeat, Dubrovnik brought the inevitable disillusionment. It still retained its picture-postcard beauty. I was as enthralled as ever by the history of this little republic which had kept its independence from the tenth century to the time of Napoleon. I still yielded to the charm of the cypresses, although each tree seemed to shelter a gravestone. I found the same repose and peace in the orange-grove cloisters of the Franciscan monastery. But there was a difference, and the change was not only in myself.

When I came here just after the war, there were few tourists; above all, few rich tourists. Since then Europe had gradually invaded Dubrovnik. The Duke of Kent and General Goering had spent part of their honeymoons here. King Edward had walked its streets with his bride-to-be. Captain Cunningham Reid had brought his yacht. Other Western Europeans and Americans had followed in their train, and something of the sophistication of modern civilisation had transmitted itself to the local citizens. Even the romance had become westernised. Nearly every young Dalmatian is an Adonis. But he has been spoilt, and from more than one source I heard tales of easy foreign conquests beneath the palms and cypresses of this seductive coast.

It is true that the English have left little trace of their real culture. In the bookshops there were few English books, although in one window I saw a huge spread of Edgar Wallace's works. But a large red strip above them with the words "Wallace è irresistibile" soon revealed that the edition was an Italian one. It is in other directions that one must seek the signs of our superior civilisation: in the new shops with foreign scents and foreign face-powder, in the curio store run by the attractive and popular Hassan, in the rouged lips and painted faces of the young Dubrovnik girls, in the new hotels, and in the new café close to the Rector's Palace. For to-day Dubrovnik has a café-restaurant which its owner boasts has no equal in London. The boast is not exaggerated.

G

The food and wines of the Gradska Kafana are excellent, and the café employs the smartest negro page in Europe. According to the local legend he is the son of the favourite negro servant of the late King Nikita of Montenegro, and his rig-out, a bright scarlet Eton jacket, black trousers and white spats, is a sight for the gods. And by the force of the same progress Dubrovnik has also a "Bar". Only a few years old, it is already invested with a romantic story. It was started by an Irishman and made no headway. In the end the Irish-man went away, leaving the premises to his bar-attendant in lieu of wages. The bar-attendant carried on. One day the Duchess of Kent came there to dance, and from that hour the "Bar" became a going concern.

With these new developments Dubrovnik has lost, for me at all events, something of its old charm. I realise that my atti-tude is churlish and uncharitable. Like anglers, nature-lovers are selfish folk who always try to keep their favourite stretches of water or of scenery for themselves. I should be ungracious, if I failed to praise the hospitality, the friend-liness and the good looks of the Dubrovčane or Ragusans as I suppose most English people still call them. The advent of the tourists has brought wealth to Dubrovnik, and the local inhabitants are not ungrateful. They are especially friendly to the British, who are assured of a warm welcome, and the day is past when an Englishman need fear the fate of Sir Arthur Evans, the famous archaeologist, who as Mr. Evans of the *Manchester Guardian* was imprisoned here in 1882 for seven weeks by the Austrians for interviewing the leaders of the Bosnian insurrection. He was released only after a British man-of-war had anchored off the harbour.

To those of my countrymen who wish to see something of the former glory of Dubrovnik I give the advice to come soon, for the place has become a favourite inspiration for novelists, and their enthusiasm will act as a stimulus to the tourist traffic. Young people who like to combine their scenery with excellent bathing and the noise of gramophones,

not to mention the seductive strains of Russian gipsy-music
—for in the season the Russians descend on Dubrovnik, will
have only one desire: that Dubrovnik should go ahead as
quickly as possible.

The real estate king of modern Dubrovnik is M. Božo
Banać, a Yugoslav shipping magnate, who is as well known
in London as he is in his own country. Shrewd and jovial, M.
Banać is a strong Anglophil who believes in progress. His
hospitality is unbounded, and many prominent English
visitors have had their first view of the beauties of the Dalmatian coast from the windows of his villa at Cavtat. He is
the last of a long line of successful Dalmatian business men.
Indeed, such few millionaires as Yugoslavia has given to the
world have been, I think without exception, Dalmatians. In
most cases their fortunes were made in foreign countries. One
Dalmatian millionaire was so foolish as to leave part of his
wealth to his native village. The results were unfortunate,
and on the theme of this form of charity some Yugoslav
Mark Twain might write another "The Man That Cor-
rupted Hadleyburg".

While I was in Dubrovnik, a Dalmatian millionaire died
in Buenos Aires. This was the well-known Miha Mihanović,
the founder of the first Argentine shipping line. When he
left his native village of Doli, Mihanović was little more than
a boy. He was then completely illiterate.

Although the Dalmatian has the forcefulness which makes
for success in business, the hot blood of the South runs in his
veins. It boils when politics are discussed. My first task in
Dubrovnik was to enlist the services of a Dalmatian teacher,
and with little difficulty I found a charming and cultured
young man with whom I revisited the whole countryside.
With his aid and without it I had numerous conversations
both with the citizens of Dubrovnik and with the peasants
in the neighbouring villages. I found them as radical as the
young men of Zagreb and staunch adherents of Maček, the
Croat leader.

Indeed, the Dalmatians have always played a virile and a vigorous part in Croatian politics, especially in the difficult days of the war when Croatia was struggling to be free. Frano Šupilo, who during the war did more than any man to convert the leading allied statesmen to the Yugoslav cause, was the son of a Dubrovnik mason. Ante Trumbić, who signed in 1917 with Pašić, the veteran Serbian statesman, the famous Declaration of Corfu which proclaimed to the world the unity of the three Yugoslav races, is a native of Split. He lives mostly in Zagreb, a gentle, erudite and disillusioned Croatian Seton Watson. Šupilo, a man of dynamic force, who made a great impression on the British Cabinet, died in London before he could see the triumph of his life's dream. His death was an irreparable loss to the Yugoslav cause. Had he lived, many of the differences which now divide Serbs and Croats would never have been allowed to arise.

Anti-Serb grievances of the Dalmatians are the removal of the old archives of Dubrovnik to Belgrade and the placing of this ancient capital under the administrative control of Cettinje. The archives were removed long ago by the Austrians. When they were returned after the war, the Serbs kept them in Belgrade. To the foreign visitor these may seem small pin-pricks, but, like most unnecessary pin-pricks, they irritate.

More creditable to the administration were the increased signs of material welfare which I saw everywhere. Nearly every day I made a long expedition down the coast or into the interior, revisiting all the villages and townships which I had known so well in my banking days. After the war the Montenegrins were wretchedly clad, making their clothes of old sacks, and in Cettinje or even in Kotor you could see men walking along the street with the letters "Portland Cement" stamped across the seat of their trousers. Both the Coast and Montenegro are still poor, but, at any rate, the inhabitants are respectably dressed. The famous Gulf of Kotor is also getting its share of the tourist traffic, and new developments at Budva, where Queen Marie has a summer residence, portend the creation of a series of holiday seaside resorts not only for the foreigner, but also for the city populations of Belgrade and Zagreb.

Perhaps the greatest transformation that I saw was in Trebinje, a small town in Herzegovina, with old fortifications, a garrison, a modern tobacco factory, and a population that still numbers a large percentage of Mohammedans. The town is surrounded by barren mountains and lies in a plain watered by the mysterious Trebišnjica river, which after a longish course disappears suddenly under the ground to rush forth again into the light some miles farther down the valley. The whole district looks wretchedly poor, but thanks to the sun the carefully-guarded soil yields more than one might expect.

Ten years had passed since my last visit to Trebinje. Then the Mohammedan women of all ages still wore trousers and were heavily veiled, and among the males there were many fine, old Mohammedan types, grave men who walked with dignity, and who between prayers spent the day in drinking coffee. In those days I had to use tact and diplomacy to gain admission to the mosque, and had, of course, to remove my shoes. Now all was changed. Only the old women still retained the Mohammedan trousers. I hardly saw a veil. The only sign of Islam about the men was the fez. The ready-made clothes-merchant had conquered the town.

As I passed the chief mosque, a service was going on. I asked a young Mussulman if I could go in. Without a moment's hesitation he led me to the main door and opened it. I stood for a moment at the threshold watching the prostrate figures. Then I turned away. The Mussulman seemed surprised.

"You can go in," he said with a smile. "All the tourists do. Most of them take their cameras."

As I came down the last step, there was a furious ringing of bells, and I stepped back quickly. Some young Mohammedans were having a bicycle race round the mosque, and they rode like devils. Others were lustily kicking a football in a neighbouring side-street. Here in the interior we were back in winter, and I went into a Mohammedan restaurant to drink a cup of hot coffee. I thought of Loti, who visited the place some fifty years ago. All that was left of the old Islam in Trebinje was the curious smell which floated through from the Mohammedan kitchen.

For a week I lived in a dream-world which only failed to realise my fullest expectations because I tried to extract too much from it. It was a spiritual dream-world in which material pleasures had no place. Resolutely I refused an invitation to spend an evening or a whole night in one of the low cafés in Gruž which tourists delight to visit, and where, indeed, they see life with more honest song and wine than they find in the expensive establishments of great cities. Perhaps because I had the premonition that I should never return to Dubrovnik, I was in high content and unwilling to depart. I was serenely happy in this environment of cypresses and cemeteries and of standing stone which told the story of five civilisations.

But on the seventh day the weather changed. The sirocco blew with an icy blast; the skies fell in; and a half-sleet rain came down in torrents. Without the sun this country of barren mountains, volcanic gulches and subterranean rivers is not merely gloomy; it is threatening and unfriendly. Hurriedly I packed and booked my steamer passage for the next morning. When I woke, I saw a white slush on the balcony of my room. For the first time in twenty years snow had fallen on the streets of Dubrovnik.

Even in the sheltered harbour the waves were dashing against the quay and, as I looked at our small steamer, I felt a momentary hesitation. I am a good sailor, but no one likes being knocked about. This was not the farewell to the Coast that I had visualised.

Fortunately, the good ship *Zagreb*, British built and with British engines, stood up splendidly to the heavy sea. And by the time we reached Hvar Nature performed yet another miracle. Although we were going north, we had run out of the storm and the snow back into the warmth and the sunshine. For the rest of the journey to Split the sea was as still as glass.

All day I had been engrossed in reading Ivan Cankar's story of *The Man Jernej*. Cankar, the greatest Slovene writer, has all the Slav sympathy with suffering humanity. The common man is fundamentally good; it is society which is wrong. *The Man Jernej* is the story of an old farm-hand. He has grown up with the farmer-proprietor, has tilled the fields, has even built with his own hands the house in which the family live. On the day of the farmer-proprietor's funeral Jernej is thrown out by the farmer's son because the farm-hand insists in his old age in talking of "our" farm and "our" fields. He believes in man's law and man's justice and sets out to seek it. He wanders through the country telling the story of his great wrong to anyone who will listen. He is mocked at by the children, robbed by a tramp companion, cursed by innkeepers, and told to be submissive and finally rebuked by a priest. Then in despair he goes to Vienna to see the Kaiser. Surely the head of the state will listen to him. But he is thrown into prison. In the end he comes back to the farm and sets fire to the house. He stands by, exulting in his own act of justice. The enraged farmers set on him and, after beating him to death, throw him into the fire.

Profoundly moved by this superbly-told story, I went on deck to enjoy the last hour of sunshine. The beauty of the scene held me completely. There was both peace and a great sympathy in my heart. In these surroundings it was easy to visualise a world in which men would act with charity towards their neighbours and not like savage beasts.

As we berthed at Split, the spell was broken. There on the quay was Rapp, our erudite and efficient Consul from Zagreb. He was on his way to Sušak. The Chinese crew of a British steamer had mutinied. They had discovered that the steamer was going to Japan in order to be sold there as scrap-iron. The iron would be used to supply Japan with material for her war against China, and the Chinese crew would not be a party to the transaction. Rapp, who had to settle the dispute, shouted to me to remain on board and to go on with him. But I shook my head.

I had two hours in Split before catching my train to Zagreb and to Belgrade. Before I returned home, I should have my fill of politics and disputes. I wanted to spend these last hours on the Coast in peace. On strolling on to the front, I saw little groups of people excitedly reading the local newspaper. I bought a copy. There had been a clash between the Croats and the police at Šibenik, a neighbouring port farther along the coast. A Serbian Fascist called Ljotić had come into this Maček stronghold and had tried to hold a Fascist meeting there. A hostile crowd had gathered and had refused to disperse. When the police tried to use force, the mob threw stones. Then the police had fired. Two Croats had been killed; several policemen had received head injuries.

It seemed an unnecessary provocation, and it was hard to see why a government, which controls most things, had not forbidden the meeting. On the other hand, the crowd had not behaved well. Obviously, the fundamental goodness of man was not sufficient to make two brother races love each other as themselves.

As I walked back to the station after a lonely dinner the moon was shining over Diocletian's Palace. Behind, stretching as far as the eye could see, the vast volcanic mountains, grey with the wisdom of countless aeons, looked down on the ruins of successive civilisations. I turned to the sea, which hides all the traces of man's folly, and there I took my last farewell of the Dalmatian coast.

CHAPTER FIVE

I DO NOT know what Belgrade suggests to the mind of the average Englishman. I do know that some members of the House of Commons are hazy of its whereabouts, although, doubtless, many of them remember the occasion in the Belgrade Skupshtina when a Serbian hot-head, irritated by the obstructionist tactics of the Croats, picked off the front row of the Opposition with a revolver. Probably to the average Englishman the city presents a picture of something that he understands as essentially Balkan, that is to say, of something savage and untutored. Of the new Belgrade he has almost certainly no conception.

Yet its wonderful site on a steep hill overlooking the confluence of the Danube and the Save has made Belgrade one of the great towns of history. It was a frontier outpost of the Roman Empire, and for many years was garrisoned by a Roman legion. Several Romans including Septimus Severus were proclaimed Emperor there or at the neighbouring Sirmium. Several Emperors, notably Aurelian, were natives of the district. The Emperor Claudius II died by the banks of the Save, and the museums of Belgrade are full of Roman monuments dug up from under the city's streets. Throughout the centuries the town has been the centre of interminable wars, and its rivers have run with the blood of Byzantines and Hungarians, Turks and Serbs, and Serbs and Austro-Germans.

When in 1717 Lady Mary Wortley Montagu visited Belgrade, she described how on her way she passed fields strewn with the skulls and carcases of unburied men and horses. They were the marks of that bloody day when Prince Eugene won his victory over the Turks. When I first went to Belgrade after the Great War, I saw indeed no skulls. But there were other signs, including shell holes and shattered houses, of the havoc wrought to a city which during those four-and-

97

a-half years changed hands four times. The name Belgrade means "The White City". Crimson would be more appropriate to its history. In the past only a people of deathless courage could expect to hold this key city, and courage is still the outstanding virtue of the Serb. No man, be he king, politician, or poet, can expect honour among Serbs unless he possesses the cardinal quality of guts.

Modern Belgrade is a new city with well-paved streets and spacious buildings. Since the war it has grown out of all recognition, and its population, only 5,000 strong in 1820, now exceeds 300,000. I should not like to live there permanently, for it is rather comfortless, but I confess that for a short visit I find it one of the most fascinating cities in Europe.

On this occasion the question of comfort did not worry me, for I was the guest of Sir Ronald Campbell, the British Minister. In Belgrade our Legation is British-built and British-furnished, and once inside its gates I was back in Belgrave Square. I had made no programme for my stay. Less than a year before, when I had lectured here for the British Council, I had had my fill of official entertainments. Now my programme was limited to a desire to see Prince Paul, M. Stojadinović, the Prime Minister, and Dr. Korošeć, the leader of the Slovenes. As such appointments always take some time to arrange, I had several days in which to follow my own inclinations.

According to my usual practice I engaged at once a Serbian tutor, a young man who was only seven years old when the war started. He had never left Belgrade. He had seen street fighting. He had seen his native city captured and recaptured. Most of these war years he had spent in a cellar. His experiences had not destroyed his sense of humour. In Zagreb and in Dubrovnik I had had Croat teachers. To them I had to say: "What is this in Croatian?" Here in Belgrade, although to the foreigner the two languages are identical, I had to say: "What is this in Serbian?" Every time that I forgot my cue, my young Serbian was vastly amused. Finally I solved the difficulty by drilling myself to ask: "How do you say this in Yugoslav?" And Yugoslav, I feel, is the right word. I am devoted both to the Serbs and to the Croats, but everyone who wants to see a happy Yugoslavia must foster the Yugoslav idea.

Out of a rather macabre curiosity I devoted my first incursion into the past to a visit to the former Austrian Legation where on the eve of the Great War the Russian Minister Hartwig collapsed and died of heart failure while he was discussing the ultimatum with the Austrian Minister. I was in Russia at the time and remember very vividly the excitement caused by the sensational announcement of Hartwig's death. Naturally, in the first heat of the war fury, the Russian newspapers asserted positively that Hartwig had been poisoned.

Although for several years I had lived for weeks at a stretch in Belgrade and knew where the old Austrian Legation was, I had some difficulty in finding my way, so greatly had the city grown. The Legation is now the Palace of the Catholic Archbishop of Belgrade, and when I rang the bell and explained the nature of my visit the doorkeeper seemed taken aback. A young priest secretary came to my rescue. He was friendly and helpful. I could not see the room in which Hartwig died, because the Archbishop was having his afternoon rest there. But, if I came the next morning at eleven, the Archbishop would be at mass and all would be well. I came back to the minute and was shown by a plump and gentle nun into a moderate-sized room with high ceiling and two long windows on the first floor. The windows looked on to a side garden. It was a very peaceful room. It gave me no feeling that here had been enacted one of the great dramas of history. Yet, so the nun told me, there had been only one alteration in the room. A picture of the Madonna now hung in the place of the portrait of the Emperor Franz Josef.

Almost every day I spent an hour or two on the Kalemegdan, which to me, and, I expect, to all Serbs is the glory of Belgrade. It is a kind of Kremlin on an Edinburgh Castle cliff. Its name means "battle ground" and a battle ground it has been throughout the ages. It contains all the records, both written and monumental, of Serbian history. Architecturally it is a somewhat incongruous mixture of the new and the old. But the splendour of the site and the huge expanse of view are unrivalled.

You enter the Kalemegdan by a park which is dominated by the massive Junoesque statue to France. The figure is semi-naked. On the pedestal is Meštrović's exhortation to his fellow-countrymen: "Let us love France as she loved us. 1914-1918." At the far end of the Kalemegdan, overlooking the steep descent to the two rivers, is Meštrović's superb statue of "The Conqueror". The hero, symbolic of the Yugoslav triumph, is represented by a titanic warrior in bronze with a sword in his right hand and a falcon poised on the open palm of the left hand. The figure is naked. The first intention of the city fathers was to place "The Conqueror" on the Terasie in the busiest centre of the city. But, although you may be surprised, there are prudes in the Balkans. The professors and schoolmasters protested. The statue, they said, would shock the young schoolgirls or perhaps turn their thoughts from their books. And so the statue was moved to the Kalemegdan. It was a happy move, for no statue could have a better site. But the prurient-minded have the last word. The statue, they say, was transferred to the Kalemegdan to enable "The Conqueror" to pay a nightly visit to the French Juno.

A hundred yards or so to the right of "The Conqueror" is a small terrace. It is a secluded spot where one is generally free from interruption. It has long been my favourite pilgrimage in Belgrade, and here I have come in all seasons. In the spring the air is fragrant with the scent of the acacias. On a sunny winter morning the still waters of the Danube gleam

with a silver sheen, in which are reflected the spires of Zemun.
In the heat of the late summer the sun goes down in a flame
of red over a plain of golden corn. Sunday is the best day for
a visit, for, during the week, steamers and barges ply busily
on the river and aeroplanes from the huge airport at Zemun
circle noisily over the plain. But on Sundays the steamers,
black with a white ring round their funnels, are tied up. The
aeroplanes are silent, and in the stillness the tiny islets of the
Danube add a pale olive-green softness to the tranquillity of
the scene.

It is a place for poets and for dictators, and more than one
dictator has stood here. From this point the Emperor Diocletian watched his soldiers hurling the early Christians into
the river below. But the spot has a more recent claim on history. On the terrace is a marble seat. Its back has been scarred
but the eye can still make out the proud eagle of Prussia. The
seat was placed there by the order of the German Kaiser to
commemorate his visit to Belgrade in January, 1916. He
came here when his troops were in possession of the city, and
fortune seemed to smile on the armed might of Germany.
He stood on the terrace and liked the view, for his imperious
sweep took in, not only as fair a scene as mortal eye can see,
but also the richest granary in Europe. Then he turned to his
generals and said: "All this is ours".

I wonder if the Kaiser, who knows his Byron, remembered the lines about the Persian king:

"A king sat on the rocky brow
Which looks o'er sea-born Salamis;
And ships by thousands, lay below,
And men in nations;—all were his!
He counted them at break of day—
And when the sun set, where were they?"

I expect not. We learn more from defeat than from victory,
and in those days of apparent triumph the Kaiser had a contemptuous opinion of the Serbs. Had he not once appended

to a despatch from his minister in Belgrade, warning the German Government that the Serbs wished to keep their dignity and their national sentiment, the famous marginal note: "They do not exist."

There are other incongruities in the Kalemegdan. Alongside the ruins of an ancient tower you will find a wooden pavilion with an exhibition of modern art. And in the dried-up moat of the old fortifications you will look down on a couple of tennis-courts. They belong, of course, to the Anglo-Yugoslav Club, and the tennis-courts of the Kalemegdan must rank with the golf-links under Cheops' Pyramid and the nine-holed course across the Chinese cemetery in Singapore as the most curious example of the British passion for games.

The most interesting building in the Kalemegdan is brand-new. It looks like a cheap seaside teashop. But the interior is heroic. It houses the Yugoslav War Museum which is unique in its macabre solemnity. Here, in pictures, in trophies, and in relics is the story of Serbia's gallantry in the Great War. There are grim paintings of that heroic retreat to Corfu when for the first time in history a nation that had seemed crushed out of existence reformed its forces and came back to fight again with unquenched determination.

There is no one who can visit this crudely simple temple without feeling an immense admiration for the Serbian people, without coming away with a renewed faith in the justice of the cause which makes men fight against a foreign aggressor. And in the museum are generous tributes from many nations. There is a Belgian room, a French room, a Rumanian room, an Italian room, an American room, a Czechoslovak room; in a word, a room for every nation which helped Serbia. I should have written *almost* every nation. For there is no British room. I do not know why. I was ashamed to ask.

The museum is also a memorial to the late King Alexander. Here in glass cases are set out all his personal belongings: his numerous uniforms, his swords, and even his shoot-

ing suits, his English cap and his Austrian hat with its cha-
mois-beard brush. My first impressions were mawkish. I
could not help remembering the glass case at Abbotsford
with the last suit of clothes worn by Sir Walter Scott. In a
certain golf-club in the United States I had seen a similar case
with the golfing-suit of the club's first president. There I had
nearly laughed. Here in Belgrade I felt uncomfortable.

It was on a Sunday that I paid my first visit to the museum,
and it was crowded with workmen and peasants. They were
solemn and reverent. If they felt any curiosity, they did not
manifest it. They were like pilgrims, and as I walked in the
slow procession something of their reverence communicated
itself to me. By the time we reached the last room the pace
was funereal. Here on a large catafalque, surrounded by four
huge candlesticks, the admiral's uniform in which the late
King met his death was laid out lengthwise in a glass coffin. It
looked almost like a mummy. The uniform had not been
cleaned. Tunic and trousers still bore the brown stains of
dried blood. In cases on the walls were the exhibits of the
Marseilles tragedy: the murderous pistols of the assassins, the
cartridge clips, and even the spent bullets. In the corners of
the room little tables with glass tops contained the King's
effects taken from his pockets after his death: his handker-
chief, his match-box and his white gloves. One glove had a
ragged hole at the top of the first finger. It may have been
caused by a bullet, but more likely, I think, he made the hole
himself by biting his glove through in his death agony.

Behind the catafalque, in a curtained annexe, stood the
French motor-car in which the King was shot down with
M. Barthou on his way from the Marseilles docks. Here the
crowd did show an inevitable curiosity. Men surged forward
to see the bloodstains on the drab seat-covers. Low murmurs
broke the silence. They were murmurs of indignation.

The motor-car, indeed, deserves all the scathing comments
which the foreign journalists made on it at the time of the
murder. It is a shambles of a car, more like an old taxi than a

car for a royal visitor, and its long running-board is almost an invitation to gangsters and assassins. There is only one new thing about it, and that is British. There is a new tyre on the spare wheel, and it bears the mark of Dunlop. It is the only British exhibit in the museum.

When the car was first placed in the museum, it made a shattering effect on the population of Belgrade. So bitter was their indignation against France that the French Government asked diplomatically to have the car withdrawn. The request was refused.

I went back to the museum several times and came away with the firm conviction that time will be on King Alexander's side and that he will become a national hero, not only to the Serbs, for he is that already, but also to the other Slav races of Yugoslavia. I have had the opportunity of discussing his character with Serbs and Croats who are closely associated with him, and with Sir Nevile Henderson who was probably the late King's closest friend. Their testimony agrees on two important points. Whatever mistakes King Alexander may have made—and there is no Croat who does not think that he was forced into making mistakes—he was a man of remarkable character and devotion to duty. He was a genuine Yugoslav. Above all, he was a man of fearless courage. When he came to Zagreb, where the problem of his personal security must have caused some anxiety to the local authorities, he insisted on walking about freely among the people. In the end his courage hastened his death. He received many warnings not to go to Marseilles. On the eve of his departure his servant begged him to wear the shirt of mail which had been specially made for him. The King refused. He was a soldier, and modern soldiers do not wear coats of mail.

His death on French soil has reacted unfavourably against France, who recently has lost much of her old privileged position in Belgrade. The loss of prestige is partly the result of the instability of the political situation in France, and I cannot believe that it will be more than temporary. Hundreds of prominent Yugoslavs have been educated in France, and the progressive part of the nation still looks to Paris as its cultural Mecca.

There is one thing that I envy the French in Belgrade, and that is their Legation. It is the most imposing foreign building in the city, but that is not the reason for my envy. For the design does not conform with local architecture. What I covet is its site opposite the entrance to the Kalemegdan and the long balcony terrace with its superb view. It was on this terrace that Leila de Dampierre, the wife of a former French Minister in Belgrade, wrote most of her Yugoslav poems. One which begins "Je vous écris le soir" expresses the spirit of Belgrade so completely that I take the liberty of quoting two verses:

"Le vent fait onduler au loin, en terre slave,
La moisson dont le pain fut si longtemps amer;
Il ne se pouvait pas qu'elle restât esclave
Cette plaine aussi vaste et libre que la mer.

Je pense à la douleur des milliers de mères,
Aux neiges que rougit le sang, tant de saisons;
J'entends encor les voix qui proclamaient: 'chimères!
Ils poursuivent un rêve!' Et le rêve eut raison."

If the Kalemegdan has been embellished, it remains an old friend, immediately recognisable and changed only in dress but not in heart. This cannot be said of the new city which has sprung up during the last seven years. The charm of Zagreb is in its old-world atmosphere. The new Belgrade is like an American city of the Middle West. Its pulse beats with the dynamic force of a feverish creation. Cement dust and the smell of stucco choke your nostrils. Gone are the old one-storeyed Turkish houses, and only one or two have been retained as historical mementoes of an Oriental domination that is gone, let us hope, for ever. In my time Yugoslav Ministers were housed where they could find accommodation, and the

H

Ministry of Finance had its headquarters in the villa of an American business-man. To-day, there is a whole quarter of new Ministries, each as spacious as our own War Office. There is a new Senate and a new Skupshtina. My old friend Mažuranić was in Belgrade during my visit. I went to see him several times at the Senate. His presidential suite would make our Lord Chancellor envious. There is a magnificent new Patriarch's Palace, and new buildings like the House of the Combattants of the War would make the heart of a Kansas City burgher rejoice.

As for the new Skupshtina, it has at last been finished. Begun years before, it had long stood as an empty shell. Lack of funds was the excuse given for its non-completion, but the superstitious Serbs had their own views. The site was ill-omened. The Turks had slain Saint Sava there. During the Turkish domination a mosque had defiled the spot. Everyone connected with the new Parliament had experienced bad luck. King Alexander, the people said, had been influenced by these omens, and now the King had perished at the hands of Croat assassins.

In one sense the superstitions have not been stilled. The new Parliament is grandiose. Its vast corridors impress the delegations of peasants who come almost daily to see the Yugoslav ministers. The ministers themselves have splendid rooms. But the Parliament is only a semi-Parliament subordinate in most things to the semi-dictatorship.

As for the old Skupshtina, it has now been turned into a theatre. When I think of my visits to it twelve years ago and of the hours I spent in listening to interminable wrangles and fruitless discussions, I feel that even then it was more of a theatre than a Parliament.

Modern Belgrade is a stupendous achievement, but its newness is a little overwhelming. And the dust and the noise, more than the principles of modern hygiene, have driven the richer elements of the population out of the city. For Belgrade has moved south to the leafy slopes of Topčider, Košutnjak, Dedinje and even lofty Avala. Here new garden cities are in process of rapid formation. There is a special "colony" for state officials. Where in my time there was only one house, there is now a whole quarter of Ministerial villas. One day I drove out with a friend to lunch at one of these villas. I could hardly recognise a district which I had once known well.

"Whose are all these new villas?" I asked.

"Ministers'," replied my friend.

"You must have had a lot of Ministers since I was here last."

"We have, but you need be a Minister only three months in order to get a villa."

I do not quote this rather candid comment in order to sneer at Balkan morals. Belgrade society is now passing through the transition stage from peasantry to bourgeoisie, and the process is always a difficult one. Ministers are poorly paid. The prestige of their country demands that they should represent it adequately. In order to meet their expenses, they find ways and means which in older countries would be considered unorthodox. These methods are the growing pains of a new country, and we should do well not to make them the theme of a pharisaical homily. Since the war we seem to have made a habit of indulging our passion for moral indignation at the foreigners' expense. This lecturing angers our enemies and irritates our friends. After all, while we rightly pride ourselves on the rigid honesty of our civil service, we have our own black spots. No one who has investigated the history of ribbon-development in the South of England since the war would hand a white lily to the representatives of our local government bodies.

The Belgrade Court has also moved South, and the old Palace buildings which, with their gardens, occupy a dominating site in the centre of the city are no longer inhabited by the Royal family, although Court balls and official receptions are still held there. They now house the famous art collection of Prince Paul who, I imagine, is happier with his books and pictures than with despatch-boxes. The gallery has a special interest for the English visitor, for it contains a representative collection of modern English painting including pictures by John, Sickert, Tonks, Paul Nash, and Duncan Grant.

In the same room is a striking picture of Prince Paul by Sorin, the famous Russian who has been for several years the leading portrait-painter of New York. It is a half-length portrait, and the Prince is shown in profile in the white uniform of a Serbian officer. The pallor of the delicate face and the whiteness of the tunic contrast strangely with the dark eyes and the black hair. It is the portrait of an ascetic aesthete rather than of a soldier. In the big hall at the head of the stairs is a group of statues by Meštrović, and from the tall windows one can look down on the garden plot where stood the old Palace in which in 1903 King Alexander and Queen Draga were assassinated.

The new Royal Palace is several miles outside the city and stands in a splendid park on the hill of Dedinje seven hundred feet above sea-level. Like Herr Hitler, the late King Alexander was keenly interested in architecture, and the new Palace is an imposing edifice, approached by marble steps and built in the old Serbian style. Close by is the new Palace of Prince Paul, snow-white and pleasantly attractive in the classical simplicity of its design.

The new Palaces afford a reposeful contrast to the florid stucco of Belgrade itself, but the most imposing edifice of all Yugoslavia and perhaps of all Europe is still farther outside the town. This is the Yugoslav temple to the "Unknown Warrior" on Mount Avala. The mountain, twenty-five miles distant from Belgrade, stands sixteen hundred feet above the sea. It was on a sunny February afternoon that I paid my first visit to the temple. It had only recently been finished, and the place was deserted. Slowly I made my way up the long, steep marble steps, and, as I climbed, the impression of solitary grandeur made me afraid of the sound of my own footsteps. The temple itself, severely simple in design, is open at the sides and shelters the classical figures of nine maidens representing the nine banovine or provinces into which Yugoslavia is divided. And beneath this majestic mausoleum rest the remains of the "Unknown Yugoslav Warrior". The temple is impressive, but it was the view which exalted me. For a radius of forty miles I could look unimpeded in every direction of the compass over a land of noble mountains, fertile valleys, broad-winding rivers and rich plains.

The temple is the work of Meštrović, but the idea was King Alexander's. It is true that, just as Culloden has been desecrated by tea-shops and petrol-stations, so, too, the solitary grandeur of Avala has been profaned by the erection of a modern hotel a little farther down the mountain. This notwithstanding, the conception of the cenotaph is magnificent, and it has given to Yugoslavia the national shrine most appropriate to a race that has fought its battles in the mountains and that loves, and lives by, the soil.

On my way back to Belgrade I passed two battalions of Yugoslav soldiers marching out to the manœuvre ground. Their uniforms were rough and badly cut, but the men themselves looked splendidly fit and virile. Many writers have descanted upon the fighting qualities of the Yugoslavs. Doubtless, their long struggle for independence has bred in them a military tradition. But if they are a race of warriors, it is a mistake to call them warlike. To-day, they remember the war—and Avala itself is a reminder—but they have not forgotten its horrors. They are, at heart, a kindly, hospitable people who want only to live at peace, and to be left in peace by their neighbours. They will defend their country to the last man. But their own ambition is to develop their rich resources and to make good the long years of lost progress when they were under the heel of Austrian and Turkish domination. Like Britain, Yugoslavia has all the territory she wants and has much less to hope than to fear from the hazards of war.

CHAPTER SIX

IF THE EXTERNAL appearance of Belgrade has changed, so has the life of its inhabitants. When I first came here a year or two after the war, society was organised on a primitive basis. Certainly, there was the Court and the diplomatic circle. But Royal family and diplomatists lived a life apart, and the average Serb knew them not. The standard of living was low and the shops were small and full of shoddy. A modern apartment was an almost unknown luxury and most of the hotels were bug-ridden. The city looked like an overgrown village. The sartorial effect of the streets was more in keeping with a provincial township than with a capital. Even Ministers paid little attention to their personal appearance, and at official functions grotesque anomalies of dress were not uncommon. Except at the Royal Palace unpunctuality was the rule rather than the exception.

Above all, Belgrade was a man's town. The more prosperous Belgrade man breakfasted off "slivovica", combined business with politics, lunched and dined at his favourite hotel-restaurant, drank his coffee in one of the small cafés, and in the evening went to the Jockey Club to play poker or to one of the three low *Nachtlokal*. On Sundays he set off with his male friends on a full day's shooting expedition. The Serbian woman's place was in the home.

The Belgrade of those days had touched, but only just touched, the fringes of the West. There was a cultural and literary life, but it was confined to the university professors and to a small group of intellectuals. It was poor both in cash and in quality, and it hardly obtruded itself on the everyday life of the average citizen.

The last fifteen years have transformed Belgrade. The broad, well-paved streets are now lined with shops which, if not yet equal to those of Bond Street or Fifth Avenue, make quite a brave showing and cater adequately for most of

the needs of a great city. There is even a Belgrade equivalent
to Woolworth's.

The best shops are now the women's shops, for the Belgrade woman has come into her own. She dresses well, keeps
pace with the latest fashions, and is both vivacious and attractive. She is a high-brow, and can discuss art and literature
with more knowledge and assurance than the average London or New York society woman. She goes to the opera and
to the ballet and to excellent concerts. She dines out, plays
bridge, and dances in hotels. Dancing, in fact, has conquered
all Belgrade from the twenty-stone Prime Minister down-
wards, and public balls, organised for charity, have become
almost a public nuisance. One of the old *Nachtlokals* has been
replaced by a first-class modern cinema hall, and, if the low
haunts have not disappeared, there is a new form of night
entertainment, with, of course, the inevitable Russian gipsy
choir, to which the Belgrade bourgeois can take his wife.

The progressive emancipation of the Belgrade woman has
had the effect of smartening the men, and solecisms in male
attire are no longer tolerated. At a recent reception to a distinguished foreign diplomatist a newly-appointed Yugoslav
Minister, who did not know his Belgrade, appeared in full
evening dress supplemented by a pair of white spats. Doubtless, he had heard some American refer to the diplomatic
corps as the "white-spat brigade" and had adopted his attire
to suit the occasion. He was told diplomatically by an emis-
sary from the Prime Minister to remove either himself or the
offending articles.

Side by side with this sartorial and social progress there is a
flourishing cultural movement, and Yugoslav literature, and
especially Yugoslav art and music, are rapidly making a name
for themselves. Bookshops abound, but their foreign wares
are mainly French, Russian and German. British books are,
unfortunately, rarely seen.

For signs of British culture in Belgrade one must look to
other spheres and, first and foremost, to the new golf course,

opened by Prince Paul with a slice to point and now frequented not only by the foreign diplomatists, but also by the bourgeois *élite*. Great Britain may also claim with legitimate pride some credit for Yugoslavia's remarkable advance in other fields of sport. Even twelve years ago sport in Belgrade was in its infancy. Football, indeed, had been played for some years. But the standard was low, and as late as 1926 I remember watching the youth of Belgrade being initiated into the mysteries of hockey by those two stalwart British diplomatists, Sir Howard Kennard and Mr. George Ogilvie Forbes. For his splendid services in Madrid during the civil war George Ogilvie Forbes has since been knighted by his Government. I feel that the Yugoslav Government should have given to Sir Howard Kennard the Grand Cross of the Order of the Red Tiger.

To-day, Yugoslavia's ardour on the field of play is a joy to watch. Has she not within the last year whacked the British Davis Cup team at tennis and defeated an English First League side at football? She has. But does she realise that these victories really date from those early days when the British Minister, then in his forty-fifth year, used to charge down the field, with stick, arms and legs forming a human Catherine wheel, exhorting his Serbian followers to one last desperate effort, and instilling in them the spirit which never owns defeat until the last whistle blows, and even after it has stopped? Sir Howard was a great figure in the Belgrade of those days, working his secretaries as hard as he worked himself, and making the whole Legation staff learn Serbian.

I also found a great change in the attitude and behaviour of the Serbian officers. During the immediate post-war years the country was poor and the army badly equipped. All the officers, except the very youngest, had fought in the war and, like officers in other countries, they wanted to enjoy the fruits of victory. It was a period of celebration and of some truculence. They had been brought up in a hard school.

Nowadays, if you have won their confidence, senior officers will tell you quietly stories of their early training: queer tales of after-dinner pranks in the mess when the lights were put out and, in order to practise courage, the officers drew their revolvers and fired at each other in the dark. As cadets both Prince Paul and the late King Alexander are said to have been put through this form of "courage-blooding". Certainly in the victory years some of the gayer spirits were inclined to indulge in these practices in the early hours of the morning in some *Nachtlokal*.

These days have gone for ever. The army has been re-formed and remodelled, and the Serbian officer of 1938 is so poorly paid and so hard-worked that he has little time or opportunity for the wilder forms of amusement. He looks very smart in his flowing, well-cut overcoat. He is dignified, reserved, and, above all, serious, and even the most rabid Croats will tell you that his behaviour is exemplary. Admittedly, some of the generals play a part in politics, but the average officer talks little except his own shop. He is, first and foremost, a soldier and, if he has his political preferences, he keeps them to himself. As his first preoccupation is the strength and efficiency of the Yugoslav army, he probably understands the necessity of placating the Croats better than most of his countrymen. As a soldier he has a certain respect for the military qualities of the Germans, a respect which the Nazis strive their utmost to cement into a friendship.

Not long ago a Serbian Colonel of the General Staff had to go to Berlin on official business. He was received by General Goering. In the room was a large portrait of Germany's Air Chief. The only order on his huge uniformed breast was the Serbian Order of the White Eagle!

The Serbian officer, and I write Serbian purposely because he is the controlling force of the Yugoslav Army, is pleased by such compliments, but he is not taken in by flattery. He is a fine type of man, strong, courageous but unaggressive, and imbued with a high sense of duty towards his brother officers, his men and his fellow-citizens. He is, too, a good family man, and on Sundays I was surprised to see the number of Serbian officers walking soberly with their wives and children on the Kalemegdan. Incidentally, the sons of an officer introduced me to a new Belgrade fashion. They wore knickerbockers which reached to the ankles. In the cold winter it is a sensible fashion. Long trousers catch the snow or the slush. Long knickerbockers keep the lower part of the leg warm.

On the whole, although he is a good trencherman and likes strong drink, the average Serb is sober-minded and self-reliant. He has no inferiority-complex and thinks, probably rightly, that no foreigner understands the Balkans. His self-confidence makes him tolerant, and during the last fifteen years I have heard only one Serb speak in real anger against the Croats, and the Serbs have not lacked provocation. The speaker was a woman, and she did not spare hard words.

If Belgrade has become mundane, it has also undergone a political transformation. When I first came to Belgrade after the war, the biggest man was Nikola Pašić, a shrewd and fearless peasant patriot and the ablest statesman that the Balkans have produced. There has always been a sturdy democratic spirit among the Serbs, although it has never manifested itself politically in the sense that we should call democratic. With the formation of the new Yugoslav kingdom there came to the Belgrade Parliament a host of new deputies, many of them peasants with no political experience and no sense of compromise. From the beginning the parliamentary machine was in travail. Unbridled oratory provoked unbridled hate: hate between the three Slav races, hate of the Habsburgs, hate of the Italians who had so wantonly seized Fiume, and who boasted so openly of their intention to make Dalmatia their own.

While Pašić lived, his cunning hand controlled the growing turbulence. After his death at the end of 1926, the flood gates were broken down. There was an unseemly wrangle for the political succession. Government succeeded Government with stultifying rapidity. The political divisions became more marked. The spate of oratory swelled into a torrent, and the scenes in the Skupshtina became so violent that in 1928 pistols took the place of words. A new country, which had little experience of ruling itself, had tried an experiment in Western democracy, and the experiment had failed. In 1929 King Alexander suspended the Constitution and appointed a dictator. Two years later he proclaimed a new Constitution which divided the country into nine provinces. In an attempt to cut across racial divisions the old title of Kingdom of the Serbs, Croats and Slovenes was abolished, and the name of Yugoslavia was given officially to the country.

The dictatorship had many enemies, and in 1934 King Alexander was assassinated. As his son and heir, King Peter, was a minor, a Regency was appointed with Prince Paul as the chief Regent.

Prince Paul relaxed some of the rigours of the dictatorship, and in 1936 Dr. Milan Stojadinović, the new strong man of Yugoslavia, became Prime Minister. A member of the old Serbian Radical Party, he has been doing his best to form a new Yugoslav Radical Party called for short the "Yerezé". His régime, which depends for its support on a coalition of his own followers, the Slovenes, and the Bosnian Mohammedans, is nominally parliamentarian, but Parliament is boycotted by the Croat deputies. The régime may be fairly called a very limited form of parliamentary government occupying a halfway position between Fascism and democracy.

In foreign politics M. Stojadinović has made an important *volte-face*. Not wishing to see his country involved in a clash between two rival groups of Great Powers, he has ceased to rely entirely on the old friendships with France, Britain and the Little Entente, and has instituted the so-called "politique de bon voisinage". He has made the pilgrimage to Berlin and to Rome. He has made his peace with Germany and

Italy. This does not imply that he intends to alienate France
or Britain or even the Little Entente. It merely means that he
desires to make the best of both worlds. He is an old poker
player. He is now playing poker politics with sufficient success to be courted by many Powers and to be envied and
imitated by his Balkan neighbours.

It would be foolish to assert that the new régime is popular
in Belgrade, let alone Croatia. It has many opponents. There
is the so-called democratic Opposition. Above all, the students of Belgrade are radically opposed to the dictator countries, and are therefore pro-French and pro-Czech in sympathy. When Dr. Beneš and M. Delbos visited Belgrade in
1937, both received tumultuous ovations in the streets. I have
met, too, Serbian generals, who, if they did not condemn the
policy of good neighbourliness, were very suspicious of the
goodness of some of their neighbours. After all, Yugoslavia
fears only two countries, and they are, of course, Italy and
Germany.

Nor is the new Yugoslav Radical Party, the Yerezé, very
popular, although I should not say that it has failed completely. But, according to Balkan practice, considerable pressure is put on civil servants to join it, and there are therefore
many stories against it.

In Belgrade I heard this one: The three leaders of the
régime, Stojadinović, Korošeć and Spaho, were on their way
to Skoplje in order to hold a propaganda meeting for the
Yerezé. Suddenly their special train stops in the middle of a
lonely country district. Stojadinović sends for the engine-
driver and asks what is wrong. The engine-driver tells him
that there is a cow on the line and that it refuses to budge.

Stojadinović heaves himself from his seat. "I'll deal with
this," he says to his colleagues. He walks up to the cow.

"Old girl, I'm the biggest man in this country. Hop it or it
will be the worse for you."

The cow sits tight, and Stojadinović then asks Korošeć to
intervene.

"I am the leader of the Catholics," says the Slovene leader humbly. "In the name of the Almighty I request you to remove yourself to safety."

The cow pays no attention, and in despair the two big politicians turn to Spaho, the leader of the little party.

"You try," they say in unison. Spaho shrugs his shoulders, creeps up to the cow on tiptoe, bends down and whispers something in its ear.

The cow throws up its tail and bolts from the line like a startled rabbit.

The politicians go back to their saloon car. For several minutes Stojadinović sits in puzzled silence. Then he addresses Spaho.

"Tell me," he says, "what did you say to the cow to make it shift?"

"Oh, that was easy," replies the Mohammedan leader. "I just whispered: 'If you don't get out of here at once, Stojadinović will make you join the Yerezé.'"

In spite of these adverse criticisms the régime works, and is, I think, not nearly so unpopular as the professional politicians assert. Many Serbs are flattered by the increased importance which their country has acquired through the new foreign policy. They regard it as a policy dictated by commonsense and by the necessities of the country's geographical situation. Trade has benefited greatly from the new agreements with Italy and Germany, and in 1937 these two countries were Yugoslavia's best customers. Money talks, and in a new country, which has made remarkable material progress, the get-rich-quick spirit is strong. The Serbs are realists both in politics and business. Many of them feel that the country has had an overdose of politics, and there is, I think, little doubt that the old political parties have lost much of their prestige.

In a lesser degree some of these feelings are shared by prominent Croat business men, although, of course, not by the politicians, who represent the vast majority of the Croat people. Personally I feel that what Yugoslavia needs most is a few years of efficient and honest administration and some relaxation from the incessant political wrangling. More hours of work have been lost in Yugoslavia through political gossiping in government offices, business-houses, cafés, universities, fields and factories than in all the strikes in the world in a quarter of a century.

The man most likely to provide the requisite period of peace is M. Stojadinović. Neither by tradition nor inclination is he a Fascist, nor is he likely to be driven into the totalitarian camp.

Of all the Yugoslav politicians he has by far the best understanding of the complicated problems of modern finance and industry. In this connection the highest compliment that I heard paid to him was a remark made to me by a Croat politician, who had been fulminating against the Serbs. At last I interrupted him.

"After all," I said, "you have to work with them. If you became Prime Minister, would you discard men like Stojadinović?"

He scratched his head.

"No," he admitted grudgingly, "I'd keep him as Minister of Finance."

The new orientation in foreign policy has in varying degrees affected the Serbian attitude towards France and Britain. France, once the dominant external influence in Belgrade, has undoubtedly lost much of her former prestige, mainly because of the spectacle of internal weakness which her frequent changes of government have presented to the outside world. Most Serbs have a horror of Bolshevism. They dislike the Franco-Soviet Pact, and they attribute most of France's internal troubles to Communist agitation.

The attitude towards Britain is slightly different, and may be described as one of perplexity. At the end of the war the average Serb had a profound faith in the might of Britain. Recent developments in Europe have shaken this faith. He finds it hard to make anything of British public opinion which in relation to foreign affairs seems to speak with a thousand different voices. He hears these different voices even in the Anglican Church. He reads in his newspaper the opinion of an Anglican Dean that General Franco is a gentle knight-errant fighting the battle of Christianity. On the same page he finds another Anglican Dean extolling the Spanish Government as the administration which Christ would have approved. As he is severely realist in his judgments, he concludes that Britain is a country divided against itself. He is inclined to think that, like the Romans of the Empire period, we have enjoyed too long, and therefore abused, the advantages of luxury and wealth. He may be a little envious of the wealth, but he is not impressed by the display of luxury.

He compares the rich young English tourist, whom he sees sprawling on the beaches of Dalmatia, with visitors from other countries and draws his own conclusions. The first question that he puts to a British friend concerns our virility as a race and the quality of our man-power in the event of war.

After all, virility is his own strong suit. He has not been a bourgeois very long. Belgrade—and grass was growing in its streets as recently as 1889—may have become a modern city, but even to-day you have only to turn aside from the main thoroughfares in order to meet the famous pigs that caused the Great War and kids who are descendants of the goat that guided the Crusaders on their way to Jerusalem. The spectacle is a reminder that the Serbs are a peasant race and draw their manhood from the soil.

The Serb has another grievance where Britain is concerned. He resents the fact that his country rarely, if ever, figures in the British newspapers, except in connection with some scandal or unsavoury sensation. He complains that, while the scandals are nearly always exaggerated, no mention is ever made of the amazingly rapid progress that has been achieved in almost every walk of life. Even the genial Pepič, the Serbian secretary of our Belgrade Legation, is a little put out when he reads in an English book that Serbian peasants amuse their children by filling a sack with live frogs and then tying it to the wheel of their cart. Nor has he forgotten his first day in London when his landlady asked him if matches were now in general use in Yugoslavia. I should add here that, according to a Serbian superstition, if you kill a frog your mother dies.

Although he rarely shows his resentment, the Serb dislikes the British habit of lecturing and of finding fault with every institution and every form of government that does not conform with British standards. This dislike has been strengthened rather than diminished by the few British politicians who have visited his country. Himself a Slav, knowing Russian and the Russian mentality, he may listen politely while a British duchess tells him that he has no need to fear either Russia or Communism. She has studied the question and she knows. But when she leaves the lecture-room, he will either curse or laugh incontinently.

Although our prestige has not fallen so low as that of the French, I am afraid that we have lost ground in Belgrade. The loss, I think, comes mainly from the new interest which the British public now feels qualified to take in foreign affairs. The interest itself is a natural legacy of the Great War. It received a powerful stimulus from the ideal of the League of Nations, which, alone among the nations, Britain accepted with the fervour of a religious movement. It has been fomented and spread by the radio and by the Press until to-day it has become a national epidemic.

In his admirable essay on *The English Genius* Professor Macneile Dixon defines the chief virtues of the English as a willingness to act in accordance with the inexorable conditions of life, to respect, like the Greeks, its limitations, and to bear in mind, in legislation, as in everything else, what is possible for human nature. By way of contrast, he quotes the aphorism of the Greek sage: "It is a disease of the soul to be in love with impossible things."

To judge by the public voice or voices of England, this moderation seems to be no longer a characteristic virtue of the English people. In relation to foreign affairs we have allowed our desires to outrun the ability of our performance. In our striving after the impossible, we have been violently partisan, taking sides in European quarrels of which we have only the vaguest understanding. We sought to establish the millenium through the League of Nations. It was an honourable endeavour, even if our conception of the League was an English conception. We forgot that a schoolmaster cannot put all the boys of his school into one form and expect a uniform standard of excellence. We set an example in disarmament, hoping that the rest of the world, including the defeated and despoiled nations, would follow our example. Then, being disarmed and almost helpless, we took refuge in formulae like "collective security". There were moments when our enthusiasm for collective security bordered on collective hysteria.

Another formula was the platitude that "better knowledge of peoples makes for better understanding". I do not deny its truth, which I hope will one day be universal. But the knowledge is obviously slow in coming. You have only to go round the map of Europe in order to realise that the greatest enmities are those between next-door neighbours who, presumably, know each other better than, say, the Papuans know the Hottentots. In our passionate idealism we were like a man walking in a wood with his eyes on the trees and breaking his ankle on the roots.

Admittedly, democracies are hampered in their conduct of foreign affairs by the contradictions and inconsistencies of party politics, and in recent years British foreign policy has suffered from these defects. I shall give only two instances. In the summer of 1938 British ships, doing a profitable and risky trade with Republican Spain, were being bombed by

I

aeroplanes operating on behalf of General Franco. And in Parliament we saw at once the curious spectacle of Labour politicians jumping up and with jingo fervour taunting Mr. Chamberlain with his cowardly failure to protect the lives of British seamen. Is there any honest member of Parliament who will deny that, if the picture had been reversed and a Spanish Government, holding supremacy in the air, had bombed British ships bringing supplies to General Franco, we should have heard indignant Tories clamouring for the punishment of the bombers and Labour taking the same line as Mr. Chamberlain?

The second example was afforded to me on my return to London in April, 1938. I arrived on the day when the result of the West Fulham by-election was declared. In her speech the victorious Labour lady candidate ascribed her success as a triumph for the League of Nations and for collective security. At that very moment the three Prime Ministers of Norway, Sweden and Denmark were putting their signatures to a resolution pledging their governments not to commit themselves in any circumstances to one or other of the groups of Great Powers in Europe, and on no account to allow themselves to take sides in a possible European conflict.

In course of time our new interest in foreign affairs will produce, I hope, profitable results. But for the moment I cannot help feeling that it has been accompanied by a lack of expert knowledge of which the majority of the country seems to be supremely unconscious. In the post-war Britain it is a fact that the average man will hesitate to express his opinion on scientific or technical problems. He will say with modesty that he does not understand these matters. He does not observe the same reticence about foreign affairs, and will lay down the law about half-a-dozen countries of whose special problems and even of whose whereabouts he has perhaps only the haziest idea.

In its callow stage this new national interest in foreign affairs presents obvious dangers. Indeed, there is much truth in

Mr. St. John Ervine's statement that the world is not a pleasant place just now, "because a lot of high-minded and sincere people have been let loose on it lately, with the result that it is in an appalling mess." Idealism is a splendid thing, a goal that we must keep always before our eyes. It is, however, abstract, and in foreign affairs it represents the long view. But the handling of the day-to-day problems on which the immediate peace of the world depends demands a long training and first-hand experience. It is a technical job like any other, and, although I hold no special brief for diplomatists, I believe that they are better qualified to perform the job that they have spent a lifetime in learning than others whose knowledge is derived from books and from the daily newspapers.

Since the war the British diplomatic service has been subjected to severe criticism by our new self-styled experts on foreign affairs, and even in British periodicals of high standing I have read statements to the effect that our foreign correspondents represent the people of Britain much more adequately than our diplomatists, and that the United States is much better informed than Britain about European affairs because its Press is represented in Europe by a brilliant band of specialists.

These statements represent a curious confusion of thought. There are three forces which operate in the field of foreign affairs: the diplomatists who, controlled, of course, by the Secretary of State, are charged with the conduct and secrets of policy; the historians and academic experts who make special studies of certain countries and certain aspects of foreign policy, and the journalists who report the daily events abroad. All three help to mould public opinion, but in a democratic country the influence of the journalist is probably the greatest because his reportage is the source from which the man in the street moulds his opinion.

The academic expert performs a useful service so long as he confines his activity to academic studies. When he des-

cends into the arena of day-to-day events he is more dangerous. He has no responsibility except to himself. His own
special field is generally a limited one. He is inclined to consider it all-important, to be dogmatic, and to show irritation
when his recommendations are not immediately put into
force.

As between the journalist and the diplomatist the scales of
knowledge are heavily weighted on the diplomatic side. No
journalist, least of all the modern special correspondent who
rushes from capital to capital, as the crisis of the moment calls
him, can expect to acquire the expert knowledge of the best
diplomatists. Foreign governments very often do not wish
him to know too much. At the best they desire him to state
their case. The journalist plays a lone hand. The diplomatist
has a powerful organisation to help him. It is a mistake to believe that diplomatists lead a secluded and sheltered life far
removed from realities. They may move in a narrow circle.
But their sources of information go deep.

There is another difference, and it is an important one. The
diplomatist's task is to observe, collect information, weigh
evidence, and report. He is taught, and rightly so, to shun
enthusiasms and to put the fine comb of discretion through
his public utterances. No good diplomatist ever makes public
more than ten per cent. of his knowledge. The good
journalist has to supplement a ten per cent. foundation of
knowledge with intelligent deduction. This is what is called
"flair". It is the most important of all journalistic qualities,
and the great American news agencies and special correspondents possess it in a very high degree. But the general
public should learn to distinguish between "flair" and
expert knowledge. "Flair" makes occasional or many mistakes
according to the ability of the journalist, and it is fortunate
for him that his mistakes are so soon buried in the columns of
forgotten yesterday.

The diplomatist has the added advantage of a superior
linguistic ability, although too proficient a knowledge of

languages is sometimes a pitfall. The greatest diplomatic poly-
glot that I have ever met is Mr. John D. Prince, the former
American Minister in Belgrade. He could talk to nearly
every one of his foreign colleagues in the colleague's own
language. Albanian, however, defeated him, but, not to be
outdone, he once tackled the Albanian Minister in Turkish
at a large reception. The effect was not quite what he intended. After the conversation the Albanian came to the
British Minister and said in halting English: "What a strange,
what a silly, are these Americans. They have a Turk for their
Minister to Yugoslavia."

On the other hand the diplomatist labours under one
severe handicap: the growing tendency of cabinet ministers
to run their own diplomacy and to eliminate the man on
the spot. For the professional diplomatist it is an unpleasant
tendency, for, when things go wrong, he is certain to be
blamed. In diplomacy, as in marriage, the absent are always
wrong. He has, therefore, to move warily. But when he
really knows his job, there is no one who can replace him in
his own particular field.

Fortunately, in recent years British diplomacy has been
strongly represented in Belgrade. Sir Nevile Henderson, now
ambassador in Berlin, was the late King Alexander's most intimate friend, and in that capacity enjoyed a privileged position. Sir Ronald Campbell, the present Minister, is the rising
star of British diplomacy and, given health and an average
run of luck, is obviously destined to go to the top of his profession. Shrewd, intelligent, tactful, yet firm, he has all the
qualities of the best professional diplomatist, and is the outstanding personality of the Belgrade diplomatic corps. He
possesses the confidence of Prince Paul. He has won the respect of so astute a judge of men as M. Stojadinović, and his
influence has done much to correct any Serbian tendencies
to regard Britain as a spent force.

In 1914 we were poorly represented in the Balkans. In
1938 our representation was the best of any country. The

average Serb knows this and is sufficiently vain to feel flattered by the fact that we have sent one of our best men to Belgrade. His attitude towards Britain may be best described as one of "wait and see". If his confidence in Britain's strength has been slightly shaken by the vanities and volubilities of certain sections of British public opinion, he does recognise that the British are the most incalculable people in the world. Nor does he forget that more than one country, which has made the mistake of underestimating Britain's latent force, has paid dearly for the error. He is realist enough to avoid falling into the same fault. He remembers 1914. The same realism makes him suspicious of all political ideologies, more especially as the elements of ideological warfare are present in his own country. He dislikes being patronised and resents being told either by Fascists or democrats that he must do this and that or perish. He has a very good conceit of himself.

On the other hand, he admires the British conception of life and would like to imitate it, although he thinks—probably rightly—that his own road towards this goal must be a long one. With ambitious neighbours on his frontiers, he understands better than most people the truth of the old Greek saying: "Right, as the world goes, is only in question between equals in power, while the strong do what they can and the weak suffer what they must." He has made himself as strong as he can. He wants Britain to be strong.

Mr. Winston Churchill's plan for the salvation of Europe is a combination of ten states pledged to resist aggression. As far as Yugoslavia is concerned, there is only one way to realise this combination. Create a Britain strong enough to make her word respected by the most powerful aggressor, and you will have Yugoslavia among the ten states.

CHAPTER SEVEN

I WAS THOROUGHLY happy in Belgrade. I enjoyed and, I hope, benefitted from my talks with Sir Ronald Campbell who takes all things including golf with impressive seriousness. He was brought up in the old school of diplomacy, for his father was an Under-Secretary in the Foreign Office.

Soon after Sir Ronald entered the service, he went into his father's room. During the course of their conversation, the young diplomatist referred to Sir Edward Grey as Edward Grey.

He was at once pulled up by his father. "Do you know the Foreign Secretary on these terms?"

"No."

"Then in future please give him his proper title."

Sir Ronald has not forgotten. There is nothing flippant about him, and his attitude affords a striking and, I think, a pleasant contrast with that of the new school.

When Mr. Eden was Foreign Secretary, even the newly-joined fledglings never referred to him in any other terms except Anthony. It was, too, a very young Foreign Office clerk, I think, who coined the cruel and quite untrue aphorism on the gentle Lord Halifax: "Rien comprendre, c'est tout pardonner."

My own life in Belgrade afforded a contrast of another nature. In the Legation l was serious and spiritual. Outside its gates, I reverted mildly to my old Balkan ways, going with Mažuranić to hear the Russian gipsies and crawling back on tiptoe to my room like a Harrow schoolboy returning from a stolen trip to London. I had, of course, a latchkey, but such is my innate regard for British respectability that I do not think that I was ever out later than two a.m.

This same regard for the proprieties combined with a slight awe of Sir Ronald led me into an error of judgment.

It is difficult for any British subject to roam about the Balkans with no apparent reason for his roaming. I was no exception, and my presence in Belgrade titillated the curiosity of the journalists. As I was staying at the Legation, I did not want to give an interview. Still less did I wish to give one under Sir Ronald's roof. But being easy-going by nature, I was inveigled into accepting an invitation to see over a Belgrade newspaper office.

I was received with great kindness. Much against my will I was persuaded to drink a morning glass of "slivovica". It was, I knew, an old Serbian custom and honoured by all who crossed the threshold of a house or office for the first time. I emptied my glass in the Russian fashion. I thought I heard a suspicious click and looked round quickly, but saw nothing.

Graciously, and with a proper sense of my own importance as a guest of the British Minister, I explained the reasons which made it impossible for me to give an interview. I left the office on good terms with everybody and not least with myself. I was convinced that I had handled a delicate matter with consummate tact. Above all, I was elated by the remark of the newspaper-men that there was no one so difficult to interview as a brother journalist.

A year's absence from Fleet Street had blunted my own sharpness, and the smart journalists of Belgrade had the last word. On the Sunday the *Vreme*, which has nothing to learn from the most advanced Anglo-American journalism, published a whole page containing the most lurid details of my Russian and Central European career. The facts, taken admittedly from my own books, were embellished with fanciful exaggerations. There were two large photographs. One showed a thick-set and rather plump Scot, unmistakably myself, emptying a glass of "slivovica" and obviously looking as if he wanted more. The article was friendly. It compared my career with Sir Ronald Campbell's, and stated that, great diplomatist as he was, he probably envied the "rich excitements" of my life. It suggested that I was in Yugoslavia on an important secret mission. The sting was in the large headline, flattering but quite untrue: "The Northern Lawrence in Belgrade."

From that moment, everywhere I went I noticed a little group of three men whose identity was betrayed by their obvious boredom.

There was plenty of minor excitement in the domestic politics of the country. M. Stojadinović had just emerged from his long struggle with the Orthodox Church and the Opposition over his Concordat with the Vatican. It had been what one Minister described to me as a real dog-fight. Religious in origin, the dispute had become purely political, and the Opposition had used the unfortunate Concordat as a handy stick for beating the Government. At the height of the crisis the Orthodox Patriarch Varnava had died. The Opposition spread the rumour that he had been poisoned. M. Stojadinović had emerged, bruised but not defeated, from the battle and was now preoccupied with the issue of the election of the new Patriarch.

The dispute, tense but not cardinally important, is an illuminating example of the political passions of new countries. It also afforded yet another instance of the British passion for interfering in the internal affairs of other countries. The Anglican Church, or a section of it, anti-Catholic by tradition and pro-Orthodox by the hope of eventual union, sympathised with the Opposition, and at least one English Bishop came out more or less openly on the side of the Serbian Church. Shortly after the Patriarch's death another English bishop came to Belgrade. Naturally he was deeply interested in the question of the moment, and eager to know the truth he asked a local Englishman if it were true that Patriarch Varnava had been poisoned.

"Not by the Government," said the Englishman, "for that would have been the stupidest thing they could do. Possibly by the Opposition or by his mistress."

"Did I hear you say 'mistress'?" said the bishop in an awed whisper.

"Yes," said the Englishman. "Why not?"

The bishop was shocked. He need not have been. Yugoslavia is a strong, energetic and progressive country with a great future before her. But Balkan methods and manners are still different from ours, and advocates of a universal brotherhood of nations do not take into account the gulf of centuries which separates the stages of development of the different peoples even of Europe, let alone the whole world.

In this stimulating atmosphere the days passed pleasantly, and the time of my stay was nearly up before I remembered that my requests for appointments with Prince Paul, M. Stojadinović and M. Korošeć had remained unanswered. It was time to take action. I went to see my old friend, Dobrivoje Stošović, a former Cambridge undergraduate and now Minister of Public Works. I told him that I was leaving for Sofia.

"But you've seen nobody yet," he said.

"I know, but all the same I'm leaving the day after to-morrow."

He shook his head. "Too bad," he murmured sympathetically. Then he handed me a box of cigarettes and took up his telephone. It takes a long time to get to the fountain-head in Belgrade, but, when you do, Yugoslavs can hustle. When I returned to the Legation for luncheon, there was a message for me to say that all three appointments had been arranged for the next day. By the grace of Providence and perhaps by Stošović's good organisation the times did not clash.

Punctually the next morning I arrived at the Yugoslav Foreign Office where I was to have my talk with M. Stojadinović. He is said to be carefully guarded and to drive always in a bullet-proof motor-car, presented to him by a German firm! But on my way upstairs I saw no signs of special precautions. I was shown into an ante-room. Remembering the unpunctuality of the Belgrade of the early post-war years, I wondered how long I should have to wait.

I picked up a newspaper—the *Samouprava*, which is M. Stojadinović's special organ. Herr Schuschnigg, the Austrian Chancellor, had just come back from his visit to Herr Hitler, and the morning newspapers were full of the Berchtesgaden Agreement which meant the virtual end of Austria's independence. The very title of the *Samouprava* leader, "blood is not water," gave the clue to M. Stojadinović's attitude. He was obviously prepared to accept the Anschluss as a natural union.

Before I had read halfway through, the clock struck the hour for my appointment. A door opened, and two Orthodox priests in black robes and flower-pot hats walked out. They left the room, and a second later in came "Stoja", as the English in Belgrade call him. Eighteen years ago he had worked in the Belgrade branch of the British Trade Corporation which my old bank subsequently took over. His appointment had been a curious one. The English directors of the bank wanted a Serb who could bring them local business. Several candidates, including "Stoja", were suggested to them. They picked "Stoja" who was then in receipt of a salary of 4,000 dinars a month as a Secretary of the Ministry of Finance. The Englishmen offered him 14,000 dinars or approximately £50 a month, and "Stoja" jumped at the chance.

I had known him well in those days, but had not seen him for several years. As he came in, he seemed to fill the whole room, so huge and massive had he grown. He was dressed in a morning-coat, and it must have been the biggest morning-coat ever made. With his enormous chest, his powerful sloping shoulders, and his bushy, coal-black eyebrows, he would look like a fierce bear but for the good-humoured smile and twinkling eyes which light up his face very pleasantly.

"Stoja" has grown mentally as well as physically. To-day, he is in every sense of the word the strongest man in Yugo-slavia: big in courage and ideas; huge in bulk; tireless in energy. During his Berlin and Rome visits he exhausted everyone including Herr Hitler and the Duce. When I first knew him, he used to shoot, dance, smoke, drink, and sit up all night playing cards. Now he works day and night. He has discarded all the foibles of youth; all, that is, except dancing. For he still dances, although he has to hold his partner to one side.

He has the self-confidence of most successful men, but no conceit. And he is never ruffled. When he was shot at in the Skupshtina two years ago, he showed no sign of fear or emotion, but walked out of Parliament at a snail's pace with arms folded and a contemptuous smile on his face. It is true that his assailants were well covered by his own supporters. But his nonchalance impressed the deputies. Perhaps his chief fault is that he is too contemptuous of his opponents.

The Serbs say of him: "You cannot deceive 'Stoja'; he can only deceive himself."

By under-estimating the strength of the Opposition he deceived himself over the Concordat.

There are also stories that he is run by Madame Stojadino-vić. They are ridiculous. If ever there was a he-man in the Balkans, it is "Stoja", and to-day he is the outstanding per-sonality in Central and South-Eastern Europe, as important in his part of the world as were Dr. Beneš and Count Bethlen in the first post-war decade.

I received a specially huge smile by way of greeting, as he took me by the arm and lead me into his room. "You've been keeping my intelligence people busy," he said. "What are you here for?"

I tell him, and he laughs. He knows quite well. He has a thousand things to do, because he is leaving in two days for a Balkan League meeting in Angora. But he gives you the impression that he has the whole day for you.

"Well, never mind," he goes on, "I know you are a friend of my country and I hope you are a friend of mine. I'll talk to you frankly."

And he does; first, about himself and the internal situation. "I suppose you have been told that I am a Fascist. I'm not. I'll explain my system. By going to Berlin and Rome and making agreements with Germany and Italy I forestalled the Fascists in this country. First I went to the Right as far as I dared in order to win over the potential followers of the would-be Fascists. Now I go as far to the Left as I dare. And so you see I try to keep a balance. It is a middle course if you like, but it is my interpretation of democracy for this country."

He leans forward in his chair and makes a little gesture with the huge open palm of his right hand as if balancing were the easiest thing in the world.

In his turn he asks a few questions about Britain: how is rearmament progressing? What are we doing in the air? Are we satisfied with our man-power? I draw an optimistic picture, and he pays Britain a few compliments, expressing his gratitude for our financial aid during sanctions and his satisfaction at the increasing trade between his country and mine.

The satisfaction is genuine. "Stoja" is a *Realpolitiker*. He knows how dangerous it is for a small country to be under the economic yoke of one Great Power. Germany is an important factor in Yugoslavia's economic existence, almost too important, for with Austria she now does nearly forty per cent. of Yugoslavia's total trade. Good relations with Germany are therefore necessary and inevitable. But safety and independence lie in multiplicity of customers, and it may be taken for granted that "Stoja" will seek to redress the disadvantages of German economic preponderance by further extensions of the trading arrangements with Italy, Britain, France and, indeed, with any country which offers a reasonable opportunity for the exchange of goods.

I ask him a direct question about Austria and refer to the "blood is not water" leader in his own newspaper. The great shoulders bunch themselves into a shrug.

"At any rate," he says quietly, "the new situation has one advantage. It puts an end to eighteen years of make-believe. The cards are on the table, and we know where we are."

I see that already he regards Austria as part of Germany. He raises his voice ever so slightly. "Do you think we like what has happened? We don't. But do you expect us to put our head into the dragon's mouth when you aren't even going to swing his tail? In life you have to deal with realities and not with dreams. A few years ago we were on bad terms with nearly all our neighbours. I have altered this. We have gone all out for peace: appeasement in our own country, good relations with our neighbours. I think that we have set a good example to the rest of Europe."

He heaves himself out of his chair, and, as I say goodbye, I feel that, if I were a Yugoslav, I should support Stoja-dinović, not perhaps as the perfect Prime Minister, but as the best available choice. Only that morning I had seen some of the advance propaganda literature for the tourist season of 1938. Yugoslavia and the Balkans were "boosted" as Europe's "Peace Peninsula". There was some truth in the boost. Political life in the Balkans was subject to many un-certainties, but "Stoja's" foreign policy was dictated by commonsense. It was the right policy for his country. Its reversal or his own eclipse at the present moment would almost certainly be followed by chaotic conditions.

From the Ministry of Foreign Affairs I strolled down the Miloša Velikog to the vast new Ministry of the Interior to keep my appointment with Father Korošeć, a priest and a former member of the old Austrian Parliament in which he was the foremost champion of Slovene independence. He has suffered for his political convictions, and his long experience of the rough side of politics has made him the shrewdest politician in Yugoslavia. He is essentially a man of peace and bears no resentment against his persecutors. He is not liked by the Serbian Orthodox Church or by the Croats. But he understands the art and the wisdom of political compromise, and by his co-operation with Belgrade he has been able to obtain great benefits for the Slovenes. He is now over sixty, and is clean-shaven, broad-shouldered and rather plump. He suffers from diabetes.

Like M. Stojadinović, Father Korošeć received me to the minute. There was no sign of the cleric about him. He was dressed in a well-cut lounge suit of Scottish tweed. After a few minutes' conversation about Slovenia, which because of the simple friendliness of its people and of its splendid trout streams has a special place in my heart, we plunged into the vortex of the Hitler-Schuschnigg agreement. I found the Slovene priest much more perturbed by what had happened than the Serbian ex-banker, and the reason was obvious. Three hundred miles separate Belgrade from Austria; the Germans are on the Slovene frontier. And for that reason, although he is a man of peace, the Slovene leader wants a strong Yugoslavia and would like to see the Serbo-Croat question settled. It goes without saying that he also wants a strong Britain.

As far as internal politics are concerned, Father Korošeć is an admirer of M. Stojadinović and thinks that the present Prime Minister stands alone among post-war Serbian politicians. Perhaps too much alone, for "Stoja's" Cabinet is very much a one-horse vehicle and he has few able Serb lieutenants.

I went back to the Legation to prepare some questions for my audience with Prince Paul. At six in the evening he sent his car for me, and I drove out to the White Palace on the hill of Dedinje. The route was lined with gendarmes. They were even behind the trees of the long avenue which leads to the Palace door. Prince Paul is heavily guarded. The Government has not forgotten Marseilles.

Indeed, the Obrenovici and the Karageorgevici, the two

royal dynasties which have provided Serbia with its princes and kings, have a tragic record. During the last hundred years Serbia has had nine different rulers not counting the present boy King of Yugoslavia. Only two kept their throne from the moment they ascended it till their natural death. Of the other seven, two abdicated, two were driven into exile, and three were assassinated.

I was shown into a large drawing-room which might have come straight out of Eaton Square. Unlike the rooms of most royalties, whose tastes are generally petit-bourgeois, it was sparsely but exquisitely furnished. There was no horrible array of miniatures, snuff-boxes, cigarette-cases and family photographs. On a side table was a small green and yellow elephant of Ming pottery with a delicate cream effect. Over the mantelpiece hung a superb El Greco. It portrayed a white-faced Laocoon wrestling with the serpents before a background of clouds gathering menacingly over a city not unlike a Balkan capital. While I waited, the picture claimed all my attention. Was it the wildest flight of fancy to imagine that the struggles of the Trojan priest were symbolic of the difficulties of Prince Paul, an aesthete and an artist who has been forced by tragic circumstances to become the Regent to a boy King?

An adjutant came in and took me to Prince Paul's study, again an English room lined with shelves of books. A rather frail figure in khaki undress uniform came forward to meet me. In the history books, Kara-George, the founder of the Karageorgevic dynasty, who led the first Serbian revolt against the Turks, is portrayed as a massive figure of a man with bristling moustache, broad shoulders and pistols in his belt. It was hard to see in the delicately chiselled features of Prince Paul any trace of his descent from the tough Serbian warrior. Kara-George had a fist like a ham. Prince Paul's hands were the hands of a painter or a pianist. His dark, well-set eyes contrasted strangely with the pallor of his face. A racking cough interrupted his gentle smile. He looked ill.

And indeed he was. He had just got out of bed after a heavy "flu" cold. He conquered me in the first minute.

"I ought to be in bed now," he said, "but I wanted to see you. I feel that we are old friends."

I had met him in London fifteen years ago, but it was not to this meeting that he referred. He told me that he had come to Yugoslavia after his cousin's death to find a dictator-ship without a dictator. He was worried and unhappy. He could not sleep. He could not even read. Then one day his step-father gave him one of my books. He picked it up, and his insomnia was cured.

It was perhaps a doubtful compliment, but, being human and therefore vain, I took it at its more flattering value.

From books we passed to Scotland. Prince Paul is a Scot-tish enthusiast. He loves the country and would like to settle there when his job as Regent is ended. His best friend, he told me, is a Scot, the present Duke of Buccleuch. The two men were at Oxford together.

Then he talked to me very simply of his own task in Yugoslavia and of the difficulty of establishing anything like the British system of democracy within a few years. If by few he meant fifty, he was probably right. Of the internal situation he spoke with a confidential frankness which I must respect. His only complaint, and it was a very mild one, was with reference to the attitude of certain sections of the British Press. He gave me no details, but told me that he was not referring to the so-called popular newspapers. I imagine that he had in mind certain statements to the effect that he was pro-German and, therefore, presumably anti-British.

I remember reading in a high-brow British periodical a cruel comment on Prince Paul. It described him as "a neuro-tic with shattered nerves." I believe firmly in a proper ven-tilation of public affairs as a necessary safeguard for a pro-perly conducted democracy. But there are certain things, especially when they are inaccurate, which are better left un-written and unsaid. In pre-war days there was a tacit under-

K

standing that heads of foreign states should not be subjected to personal abuse. It was a good rule. It would be an excellent rule to-day. We are not so all-powerful in the world that we can afford to make enemies gratuitously.

I believe that, like his admiration for Britain, Prince Paul's good-will and good intentions towards his own country are beyond suspicion. No man looks less like a ruthless dictator. He spoke with sympathy and understanding of Dr. Maček. He would undoubtedly like to settle the Croat question. But he is hampered, I think, by the feeling that he is only one of three Regents and that he must do nothing to compromise the future of young King Peter.

It is hard to believe that after meeting him anyone could dislike him. Yet in Yugoslavia he has his enemies and detractors. There are malicious tongues which say that he is ambitious, that he wishes to prolong the Regency indefinitely, and that for this reason there is friction between him and Queen Marie, the boy King's mother. Although, doubtless, there are ambitious politicians who try to play off one Court against the other for their own ends, these stories are ridiculous. But they do not make Prince Paul's life easier. The position of every Regent is always difficult. Prince Paul's is peculiarly so. His mother was a Russian, and there is perhaps a streak of Russian mysticism in his character. Probably it stimulates his strong sense of duty, but it certainly does not make him covet a post which separates him from all that he likes best in life. He is an interesting and attractive personality, for he has a fine intellect and a remarkable understanding of all human problems and weaknesses. He is, too, a superb linguist, speaking half-a-dozen languages with an enviable facility. This gift is not a manifestation of genius. But it certainly adds to Prince Paul's charm, and never have I heard a foreigner speak English with so pure a diction and so attractive an accent.

Before I left, he asked me what impression I had formed of Yugoslavia after so long an absence. I told him truthfully that the strongest impression of my visits both in 1937 and in 1938 was one of material progress and appeasement, and that this impression was not confined to Yugoslavia but included all the Balkan states. I expressed my firm belief that, if only the Great Powers would leave them alone, the small states would soon solve not only their own difficulties but also the problem of their good relations with their neighbours.

His face lit up. "That's it," he said. "That is the whole problem."

As I drove back to the Legation, the lights of Belgrade shone brightly in the clear night air, and from the height of Dedinje I could see, as never by day, the whole expanse of the new city. It represented something of the same virile progress as had marked the growth of the United States half a century ago. In fifty years, I reflected, Yugoslavia would probably have a population as large as that of Britain. It was time for us to revise our estimate of this part of the world. It was still possible to come to the Balkans with a mud-rake and gather scandal and front-page news-stories of Yugoslavs who bit dogs or who married for the thirteenth time at the age of a hundred and twenty. Mud-raking was not a very difficult or noble achievement. After all, there were mud-heaps in our own country which needed a bigger rake.

The Balkans had changed. I thought of the difference between 1914 and 1938. In 1914 the Great Powers were afraid of an explosion in the Balkans. To-day, everyone in the Balkans is afraid of a clash between the Great Powers.

The next night I left Belgrade for Sofia. After saying good-bye to Sir Ronald and Lady Campbell, who had been so kind and helpful to me, I went down to the Bristol to spend an hour with Želko Mažuranić before my train left. The restaurant was empty, but for Želko the Russian orchestra outdid itself. Amid a host of old tunes there was one new song, written by an *émigré*, which appealed to me, partly on its own merits and partly, I expect, because I had heard Tania, the young Russian girl in Zagreb, sing it so often:

> "Sleep, my poor heart, sleep;
> Vain is all your yearning.
> Days that are gone have no morrow,
> Lonely the vigil you keep.
> Sleep, my poor heart, sleep;
> Past love knows no returning.
> Why lie awake with your sorrow;
> Sleep, poor heart, sleep."

The words were sugary and banal, but there was a minor note in the haunting melody which was well attuned to my own melancholy. I suppose that I shall be restless and homeless till I die, but I have never been able to conquer the emotions of farewell. Now that my pleasant sojourn was ended, I did not want to leave. I liked these friendly Yugoslavs, so hospitable, so warm-blooded, so responsive to appreciation. Their virtues far outweighed their faults, and in a scrap I would rather have them beside me than the men of any other race except my own.

Želko drove me to the station and on the steps outside kissed me warmly on both cheeks. It is a form of Slav greeting to which by now I should have grown accustomed, but, although I felt flattered to be embraced in this manner by the President of a Senate, I was at first taken aback. Then I began to count my friends and to wonder how many were as generous and loyal as the warm-hearted and impulsive Želko. As I entered my sleeper, I registered a solemn vow to return to this country whose valleys still breathed the spirit of the Roman legionaries, whose mountains and running streams reminded me so much of my own Scotland, and the beauty of whose coast and islands was first praised by the ancient Greeks.

CHAPTER EIGHT

BETWEEN BELGRADE AND Sofia I saw with my own eyes the beneficent effects of the policy of good neighbourliness. Only a year ago I had made the same journey and had been held up for tedious hours at the frontier. Then there were still barbed-wire entanglements between the two countries, and my journey had been like a war-time Odyssey. Now I passed through without delay. The barbed wire had gone. Even the "Komitadji", who, between the intervals of staging assassinations and murdering one another, had for years been appealing to Europe to come over into Macedonia and help them, seemed to have stayed their hand. The contrast, created by twelve short months, was both pleasant and hopeful.

I advise the first-time visitor to Bulgaria to make the journey from Belgrade by night, because then he awakes at the Bulgarian frontier and, if the morning is fine, as it nearly always is, he can enjoy the superb approach to Sofia, which nestles in a high plain surrounded by a complete oval of snow-capped mountains. It is a country with more shepherds than ploughmen. In most Februaries the snow lies thick on the ground. But in this wonder year of 1938 Nature had advanced her time, and the only sign of winter were the oaks still russet-brown in the withered bloom of their summer glory. The villages are few and far between, and the local church towers high above the lowly cottages. The villages look poor, but the stations are well-built and clean, and the railway officials with their long overcoats and Boris moustache are smart and scrupulously polite. If hirsute imitation is the sincerest form of flattery, every Bulgarian station-master admires his King.

I still take a boyish pleasure in listing countries in my memory by their bird-life. I associate the high moorlands and valleys of my own country with peewits and oystercatchers, whose mournful piping laments the barrenness of the soil. Bulgaria to me means magpies. All the way from Dragoman to Sofia you can play the game of counting them: "one for sorrow, two for joy, three a marriage, four a boy." If you are superstitious, it is generally a dangerous game, but here you may play it with complete impunity. You see so many magpies together that the rhyme does not go far enough to include all your blessings, unless, indeed, it increases the number of your progeny, in which case your blessings will lead to financial disaster.

On arriving in Sofia I was met on the steps of the Legation by Sir Maurice Peterson with the longest greeting that I have ever heard from him. "Well," he said with his hands in his pockets and without a note of emotion in his voice, "Eden and Cranborne have resigned." Even in placid, out-of-the-way Sofia I was not to be free from the repercussions of power politics.

By virtue of our opposite natures Maurice and I are old friends. His father was Rector of University College, Dundee, at a time when my father had a preparatory school nearby. Later, he became Principal of McGill University. He was a great scholar and a great classic.

Maurice has inherited his father's brains and his father's scholarship. At Rugby he was a distinguished ornament of a brilliant Upper Bench and beat Philip Guedalla for the King's Medal. His career at Oxford, where he won a history scholarship, was equally distinguished. Yet he failed by one place in the Foreign Office examination, and his only hope of an appointment lay in the unlikely resignation of some official during the next six months. He had lost many marks for bad handwriting; otherwise he would have passed in easily.

His father sent him to see Lord Morley who, when Maurice arrived, had already looked into the case.

"Mr. Peterson, I see that you lost marks for bad handwriting."

"Yes," said Maurice, "I had to race to finish some of my papers and in my hurry I had to do a good deal of scratching out."

"H'm," said Lord Morley severely, "you know what Palmerston said about people who erase words when they are writing. It shows grave defects of character."

Then the old gentleman sat down and wrote a tactful letter to Sir Edward Grey. The letter coincided with the resignation of a senior Foreign Office official, and Maurice got in. In the Foreign Office to-day handwriting is probably at a discount, but in Sir Robert Vansittart's ante-room a minute by Palmerston calling attention to the virtues of good penmanship still hangs in a glass frame by the side of the fireplace.

Maurice's case is yet another instance of the unreliability of examination tests. But for a chance resignation Britain would have lost one of her ablest diplomatists. Taciturn in speech, forcible on paper, and decisive in action, Maurice has had a remarkably successful career. His merits have been recognised. At the early age of forty-seven he was promoted ambassador over the heads of some twenty of his seniors. I had arrived in Sofia just in time. He was leaving for his new post at Bagdad three weeks later.

Sofia itself has the finest situation of any capital in Europe, and Bulgarians have it, with what authenticity I know not, that Constantine the Great, who was born at Nish in Yugoslavia, had serious intentions of making it the capital of his new Roman Empire. It is a city of Legations and Ministries, of spacious squares and wide, tree-lined boulevards. Its buildings are attractive and colourful. The Opera House is a rich raspberry fool; the King's Palace, once a Turkish Pasha's house, is a pale apricot; the National Museum has a rose-pink façade. Our own Legation is English-built and is, I imagine, the most comfortable house in Sofia. From my bedroom window I looked out on Vitosha, the magnificent snow-clad mountain which overshadows the city. The word Balkans means mountains, and Vitosha, like a giant pyramid, is the noblest, if not the highest, peak in the Balkan range.

The city itself seems to be a stone monument of Bulgaria's gratitude to Tsarist Russia and to the Russian troops who died in the war of 1877-1878 for Bulgaria's independence. Dominating all Sofia by its site on the highest point of the city is the huge cathedral of Alexander Nevski. It is a landmark for miles around, but it is too ornate and bizarre to please Western eyes, and to the cynical it looks like a huge tin mould for a blancmange shape. On the same square is the Narodno Sobranie, the Bulgarian Parliament. Above the main portals are the words "Union is Strength", a motto which, in the not distant past at least, was scarcely in keeping with the fierce party divisions of Bulgarian politics. Opposite the Sobranie is the vast bronze statue to the Emperor Alexander II, the finest monument in Sofia and one of the few great equestrian statues in the world. Round the pedestal are groups of Russian and Bulgarian soldiers led by the heroes of the war of Independence, Gourko, Skobeleff, the Grand-Duke Nicholas, and on the base is the inscription: "To the Tsar-Deliverer from a grateful Bulgaria." When I first saw this statue, it was surrounded by scaffolding. The frost had made a large crack in the Tsar's horse. At the time I could not help seeing in this rent in Tsarist glory a symbol of the cataclysmic changes in Russia.

The crack has long since been repaired. But during my 1938 visit I saw tangible evidence of the influences of the new Russia. To-day, Solonjevitch, a former Bolshevik Commissar and now leader of a new anti-Bolshevik, semi-Fascist movement, lives in Sofia. Two days before my arrival a parcel was delivered at his house. Fortunately for him, Solonjevitch was out, and in his absence the parcel was opened by his wife. In a few seconds both she and a young student, who was in the room at the time, were blown to bits. The parcel contained bombs. The senders were never traced, but few

Bulgarians and no Russian *émigrés* have any doubt whose hand ordered the sending.

Every day on my walks into the town I passed the Bolshevik Legation. The Minister was my old acquaintance Raskolnikoff, whom I had not seen since 1918. After the October Revolution he was the first Russian naval officer to throw in his lot with Lenin. My insatiable curiosity where things Russian are concerned tempted me to seek a meeting with him. But Stalin was then purging his own diplomatic corps as well as Fascist *émigrés*, and Raskolnikoff was wisely lying low.

I did meet the Bolshevik military attaché at our own Legation. He was a quiet, reserved man, like the new type of silent Russian airmen that I have met in various parts of Europe. Although he was willing enough to talk about the Russian army, telling me how hard it worked and how every officer had to learn thoroughly at least one foreign language before gaining promotion, he avoided politics. He did not even ask where I had learnt Russian. Only once did he put a personal question, and this was in the form of a volunteered statement rather than an interrogation.

"Before I came here," he said slowly, "I was in Afghanistan, in Kabul. The British military attaché was called Lockhart."

"My brother," I said.

He smiled. "He was a nice man," he added solemnly.

Then he relapsed into silence. Doubtless, he had received the confirmation that he sought.

I saw everywhere the same signs of building fever which are so manifest in Belgrade. Even since my visit in 1937 new houses had sprung up on all sides. The Bulgarians are a stolid, sober people, full of purpose and of national pride. They are determined that their capital shall not fall behind in the race with Belgrade and Bucharest. And they have held their own in spite of their poverty. For the Bulgarians are poor beyond the margin of subsistence. The Prime Minister's salary is only £400 a year, yet there is less administrative corruption in Bulgaria than in any other part of the Balkans.

Nowadays it is the fashion in Britain, as well as in the defeated countries, to blame the Peace Treaties for all the troubles and tribulations of Europe. The blame is somewhat exaggerated. The Treaties had many good points. They gave to many oppressed subject races, living on the verge of starvation, a new hope in life, and in almost every instance the races that have been freed, Czechoslovaks, Poles, Yugoslavs and Rumanians, have made good use of their hard-won liberty. It is precisely in the new states of Europe that the greatest progress has taken place since the war—perhaps because they had to build from the beginning. I must insist on this progress, because it concerns us. In all these countries there is a new generation which, in spite of many temptations, looks to Western Europe and not to Germany and Italy or Russia for its spiritual and material guidance. But I shall never deny that the treatment of Bulgaria, or rather of the Bulgarian people who were dragged into the war by their rulers, was savage and insensate.

Bulgaria's traditional friendship with Britain was broken by the war. But Britain is not forgotten. I never go to Sofia without some Bulgarian leading me insidiously to the old Hotel Bulgaria close to the King's Palace. He is not seeking a free drink. He wants to show me the room in which Bourchier, the famous *Times* correspondent, died. Even to-day Bourchier's name is known and honoured throughout the length and breadth of the country, and the *Times* has no one like him in the Balkans.

From the point of view of British cultural influence and of the informative education of our own people, I cannot help regretting the decline of the British foreign correspondent. His place and his influence have been usurped by the American, and, although, on the whole, the Americans have done their task admirably, I cannot regard our journalistic eclipse with equanimity. I should like to see the

Times represented by a first-class Englishman in every capital of central and south-eastern Europe, for never, I think, has our need of impartial, trained observers been greater.

Bulgaria has a small but highly educated intelligentsia, and in Sofia there is a whole army of painters and writers. I have always wondered how authors, writing in the language of a small country, earn their living. How the Bulgarian author exists is beyond my comprehension, for the total population is only six millions, and the average income of the inhabitants cannot be more than fifty pounds a year. Yet the country has a flourishing literature. It is sometimes bitter, reflecting the spirit of Bulgaria's post-war sufferings, like Jordan Jovkoff's story *Valkadin Talks with God.*

Valkadin is an old Bulgarian peasant whose three sons are at the front. During the war Valkadin works like a slave on the farm living for the day when his sons will return and he can divide the golden acres among them. The sons come back, but the old man's dream is soon shattered. The farm is split by the new frontier. The second son, shattered by the war, dies soon after his home-coming. The eldest son, who has acquired the bullying methods of a sergeant, is shot. Melin, the third son, who has been given the portion which is now in Rumania, is beaten up by the Rumanian police and dies of his wounds. The father, his mind affected by so much incomprehensible suffering, neglects the farm, and spends all his days under an elm tree on a hill, looking across the new frontier and asking God why goodwill has vanished from the earth and why the innocent must die and the poor be oppressed.

If the note of sadness is insistent, it is never depressing and never hopeless like much of the immediate pre-war Russian literature. The young writers are obsessed with the land. Their themes are the soil and its fruits and the virile love of strong men. Courage is the supreme virtue, and, as in Yugoslavia, only a fearless man can play any part in Bulgarian life. The courage springs from the glory period of Bulgarian

history, and there is throughout the country a vast sale of
cheap coloured prints illustrating the heroic episodes of the
wars of liberation against the Turks. Bulgarian heroes like
Vassil Levski are shown very large, fighting single-handed
against a horde of Turks. The drawings are grotesquely
crude, but they are to be found in every peasant's cottage.

For a small country the intellectual life of Bulgaria is
amazingly active and varied. The activity comes perhaps
from the popular belief that Bulgaria owes her freedom as
much to the pen as to the sword. And the pen is wielded not
only by poets, but also by caricaturists. In modern caricature
the national type is "Baj Ganju". Uncle Ganju is more of a
simpleton than John Bull. He is suspicious, but is always being taken in. He represents the disillusionment of the post-
war Bulgarian who believed in a new Europe of justice and
fair-play. One typical cartoon, which would appeal to
David Low, shows Baj Ganju, dressed as a peasant, sitting
before an empty plate at the rich buffet of the League of
Nations.

There is, too, in Sofia an excellent theatre in which the
repertory ranges from Shakespeare and Molière to Pirandello
and Maugham, and Bulgarian singers from the Sofia Opera
have won fame in other countries than their own. In my
Prague days the chief soprano at the National Theatre was
the colossal Morfova, a Bulgarian of Bulgarians. She must
have weighed twenty stone and, when dressed as the page in
Fidelio, was the most grotesque figure that has ever stood on
any stage. But her voice was superb.

It is, however, the reading urge of the Bulgarians which
stirs my admiration and to some extent my apprehension.
According to the statistics of the public reading rooms Bulgaria reads more than four million books a year, and, as
twenty per cent. of the population is still illiterate, the reading activity of the remaining eighty per cent. is extraordinarily high.

The English have so far never allowed education to be

more than their hand-maiden, and they have conquered the world. The Bulgarians have made education their goddess— a deity to be worshipped for herself. And she is a goddess of wrath, for she demands human sacrifices. Of the constant stream of intellectuals who finish the Sofia schools every year, only a small minority has any hope of profitable employment.

Sofia society is centred in the diplomatic corps. There are one or two rich manufacturers and bankers, but the most attractive Bulgarians are the travelled diplomatists like the Stancioffs, the father and brother of Lady Muir, who is Bulgaria's greatest champion in Britain.

M. Dimitri Stancioff, the head of this talented family, is the veteran Bulgarian diplomatist who, from the start of his active career to its end in 1924, was the foremost advocate of Bulgaria's adherence to the Entente. Heart-broken by King Ferdinand's decision to throw in Bulgaria's lot with the Central Powers, M. Stancioff came into his own again after the Peace Treaty when he was appointed Bulgarian Minister in London. His services to Anglo-Bulgarian friendship were recognised by King George V, with whom he was a special favourite.

Politically Bulgaria has suffered since the war from the existence of too many political parties and from the growing pains of democracy. Indeed, a too precocious childhood has nearly finished democratic government altogether, and for the last few years Parliament has been in abeyance, although recently there has been a return to a very modified and limited form of Parliamentary government.

In spite of the attempts to damp down the political fires, the professional politicians are not extinguished. They meet in the cafés of Sofia, where more than fifty years ago Pašić, then an exile from Serbia, discussed with the Bulgarian leaders the project of a Bulgar-Serb union under a common dynasty. The dream is not quite dead, but the Bulgar politicians of to-day rarely discuss it. They have more immediate dreams to realise. They have lost their jobs and want them back. They intrigue and plan new combinations. But it is hard to know how much support they command, and I have the impression that their influence, especially over the young generation, has declined.

At the end of the war the Bulgarian people were submerged by a wave of idealism. They expelled Tsar Ferdinand. They pinned their faith and their hopes on the Fourteen Points. They regarded Wilson as a saviour. To-day, they have been disillusioned by bitter experience, and the young generation, at any rate, has learnt to rely on itself. I remember Marshal Lyautey, the great French colonial administrator, telling a story shortly before his death. He had just come back to Paris from a visit to Strasbourg. He was in civilian clothes. As he was walking in the street, he saw a Moroccan soldier.

"Are you on leave?" asked the Marshal.

"Yes," said the Moroccan, rather surprised to be addressed so peremptorily by an unknown civilian.

"Where do you come from?"

"Rabat."

"Ah," said the Marshal. "Do they still remember Lyautey there?"

The Moroccan shook his head. Then he smiled, as memory returned. "I remember the name," he said. "One of the boats in our harbour is called Lyautey."

Wilson's fate has been the same as Lyautey's. To the young generation in Sofia Wilson is merely the name of a small and insignificant street not far from the British Legation.

Sofia has at least one other American-named thoroughfare. This is Carnegie Street. The University also boasts a grandiose Agricultural Faculty built with Rockefeller money. Moreover, in the rapidity of its growth Sofia, like Belgrade, invites comparison with the fastest American rate of expansion. According to the first census in 1880 Sofia's population was then barely 20,000. To-day, it numbers over 300,000.

Bulgaria, however, has only a tiny bourgeoisie. It is a land of soldiers and peasants. Eighty per cent. of the population lives by the soil, and it is a wonderful experience to drive out into the country and meet the long trail of peasants driving their carts for miles around into Sofia. The carts contain eggs, hens, vegetables, sheep, pigs and, of course, milk, for Sofia possesses more dairies to the square yard than any other capital in the world, and in each dairy you can buy the "jogurt" or sour milk which is supposed to be responsible for Bulgaria's longevity record. The produce of the carts fetches only a trifling price. The journey between town and distant village takes the whole day, and a passing car—fortunately, there are not many—raises a cloud of dust which envelops the long train of carts with a choking screen. But the peasant drivers neither curse nor shake their fists. Their patience is ineffable. On holidays when they put on their gala dress they make a brave showing. But they are poor, and in the villages I saw more than one man still wearing the military great-coat, or rather what remained of it, which he had brought back from the war.

Indeed, the Bulgarian has many of the qualities of the old-time Scottish crofter. The nature of his life has made him thrifty. Every lewa, less than a halfpenny in our money, has to be counted. He is musical. He plays among other instruments a kind of Bulgarian bagpipes. He is suspicious. On the Sofia plain every tiny flock of sheep, sometimes only twelve strong, has its own shepherd, who keeps watch all day against sheep-snatchers. Sometimes he plays a mournful melody on his reed-pipe, but generally you see him standing still, his sheepskin coat and hood huddled round him, a monk-like figure silhouetted against the landscape. He is unforgiving. Bulgaria has still its clan or family feuds. And he makes a splendid soldier.

A few years ago the soldiers were not much in evidence.

Now you see them everywhere, for Bulgaria, like the other defeated countries, is re-arming. You meet the soldiers on the plain, training and doing exercises. Morning and evening you pass them in Sofia as they swing down the streets. The passers-by stop, and you stop with them, not only because these Bulgarian peasants march superbly, but because they sing better than the Germans, better even than the Tsarist soldiers of Russia. During the long years of thraldom under the Turks, song was the Bulgarian peasants' only means of expression. The passion for song has bred a race of singers, and the gift has been handed down as a heritage to the succeeding generations.

I know little of its technical qualities, but for physique, courage and endurance I put the new Bulgarian army high. If ever the South Slavs can sink their differences and Slovenes, Croats, Serbs and Bulgars unite in one common South Slav federation, they will represent a military force which even the strongest Power will have to respect. I liked the Bulgarian officers whom I met. They took me to the Officers' Club, a building twice as large as the "Rag" or any of our London military clubs and more imposing architecturally. The Bulgars call it a casino, and here on a fine day you may see scores of officers of all ranks standing on the long balcony terrace and enjoying a before-luncheon cigarette. In their long overcoats they look like Russians. But they are more efficient and business-like, and they possess a stolidity of manner which is much more German than Slav.

As in Yugoslavia some of the generals try to play a part in politics. They receive little encouragement from King Boris, who, like M. Stojadinović, believes in an army attending to its own job. The belief is sound, for Balkan generals have the crudest political conceptions. Again, like Yugoslavia, but not to the same extent, Bulgaria has an unenviable record of political assassinations. Sofia looks the most peaceful city in the world, but occasionally its streets resound to the sharp crack of revolvers and to the rending roar of bursting bombs.

My favourite view-point in the Bulgarian capital is the corner of the Boulevard Marie Louise beside the old Turkish mosque of Bania-Bachi, from whose minaret the muezzin still calls the sons of the Prophet to prayer. For, although Bulgaria has happily no serious minority problems, there are still half-a-million Turks living in the country. They are well-treated, wear the fez, run their own schools, and are probably happier than any other minority in Europe.

From the mosque you look due south to Vitosha while the sun glistens on the domed roof and delicate arches of Sveta Nedelja. To me this church is the architectural jewel of Sofia. Externally it has none of the oriental ornateness of the Alexander Nevski Cathedral. The interior is severe and simple. Its name means in our language "Holy Sunday". Yet it has an unholy history. It was here that in 1925 King Boris came to attend a *Te Deum*. Communists had succeeded in placing a time bomb in the roof. During the service it exploded, and scores of people were killed. But the King was not in the church.

On the same morning he had gone to pay his last respects to a favourite gamekeeper, who after the war had saved the king from an attack by bandits, and who was being buried outside Sofia that day. From this funeral the King raced back by car in order to attend the *Te Deum* service. He stopped at the Palace on his way and was detained by his sister for a few minutes. There was a button off his uniform, and she sewed it on. When he arrived at the church, it was in ruins. The missing button and his sister's sharp eyes had saved him from a terrible death.

CHAPTER NINE

FOR ALL THAT I was able to see and do in Bulgaria I owe much to the kindness and hospitality of Sir Maurice and Lady Peterson. They gave me every opportunity to meet the leading Bulgarians including the members of the Government. Every day there were luncheons and dinners to which people likely to interest me were invited, and in the afternoons we made excursions into the country in order to enable me to see something of Bulgarian country life.

It was far too early in the year to make the long journey to Kazanlik or to see the Valley of Roses which provides Bulgaria with her world-famous attar of roses, still one of her chief exports. But I spent many happy hours inspecting villages, clambering up to mountain monasteries, sometimes far away from human habitation and often richly adorned with rare ikons and bejewelled ikonostasis, and admiring the costumes of the peasants. To inexpert eyes the costumes do not seem to differ much, except in detail, from other types of Slav costumes. But the women are clever with their fingers and make their own lace. In one village I saw women in their gala costumes with head-dresses not unlike those of Indian braves. They looked very attractive, and, indeed, the young Bulgarian girl must melt many hearts, although hard work in the fields soon gives her the legs of a professional footballer. Herr Hitler would admire the Bulgarian women. They have immense stamina, and with their broad hips child-birth comes easily to them.

Bulgaria has only one hundred and fifty inhabitants to the square mile, and within half-an-hour of leaving Sofia one is already in country as wild as the remotest parts of Scotland. The clearness of the atmosphere enhances the vast expanse of the vista, and the landscape inspires one with a sense of peace and infinity which I found uplifting.

The country roads, it is true, are bad. But they were once much worse. Bulgaria owes much to ex-Tsar Ferdinand. When he was ruling Bulgaria, he had a villa, or palace if you like, at Tcham-Korea, a mountain resort fifty miles distant from Sofia up the glorious valley of the Isker.

Tcham-Korea is a Turkish name. It means "Pine Forest", and the soothing effect of the pines has great health-giving qualities. But in Ferdinand's time the road was so bad that the Tcham-Korea doctors had to treat their visitors for kidney trouble instead of merely for nerves. Tsar Ferdinand had his own method of instilling "drive" into his Ministers. Every week he used to take his Minister of Public Works by car along that long, formidable road to his Tcham-Korea palace. The Tsar used to drive himself and put his Minister in the back seat. Every time the car gave a more savage bump than usual, Tsar Ferdinand would turn round to his Minister and growl: "Damned bad road this. Time it was mended." Then when he arrived at his palace the Tsar sent the Minister, luncheonless and hungry, back to Sofia with the chauffeur.

Maurice and I drove out to Tcham-Korea during my visit. The road was not like the Great West Road or the Berlin Avus. But we were not bumped!

Apart from the fact that he has inherited Tsar Ferdinand's brains, King Boris has few of his father's traits. By methods which are entirely different he has made himself as important a figure in Bulgaria and a more popular one. He is democratic in manner, both erudite and intelligent, and a born diplomatist who can mix with everyone with unaffected simplicity. Unlike the other Balkan kings he goes everywhere unguarded, likes camping out with his soldiers, and is at his happiest when talking to peasants. He does not see the diplomatists very often. In principle he is against favourites. If he saw one foreign Minister, he would have to see all. And that would be too many. He prefers his books and his butterflies to dinner-parties. On the other hand, he is always glad to receive English visitors to Sofia who are few and far between.

I have had two long audiences with him. The first was in the winter of 1937 and lasted for two hours. The King had a bad "flu" cold, and so had I. We commiserated with each other. At the end of the two hours I took my leave. Then suddenly the King stopped me.

"Your cold," he said. "I have the stuff for it."

Instead of ringing the bell, he rushed from the room. In two minutes he was back with a bottle of Roberts's Quinachina in his hand. "Take that," he said, "it will put you right in two days."

It did more. It restored my voice and carried me through my strenuous lecture-tour.

My second audience took place a year later almost to a day. As I entered the room, King Boris came striding towards the door and took me by the arm.

"Well, my friend," he said, "how are you and how's your health? You remember your cold. Did the Quinachina help you?"

His study is big and oblong-shaped. Like Mussolini, he has his desk at the end farthest from the door. Behind the desk is a fine portrait of Prince Alexander of Battenberg, the first Prince of Bulgaria, and a large photogravure of the Berlin Conference of 1878 with Disraeli in the foreground. To the right and left hang portraits of Alexander III of Russia and of the late Tsar Nicholas. Further reminders of the risks which kings must run are provided by the portraits of King Alexander Obrenović of Serbia and of King Carlos of Portugal, both of whom were assassinated. The desk itself is almost fenced in by a ring of family photographs and miniatures.

Opposite the desk, at the other end of the room, are two large easels which support portraits of ex-King Ferdinand and of King Boris's mother. The most interesting ornament in the room is a curious Jewish painting rather like an ikon.

It was given to King Ferdinand by the Jews of Sofia in gratitude for the Royal permission to build a new synagogue. As he told me the history of the painting, King Boris smiled.

"You see," he said, "my father was not so intolerant."

I do not imagine that King Boris has any sympathy with Nazi-ism. He is a man without excesses. In appearance he is of medium height and is rather slightly built. He is very dark. The eyes are dark; the long lashes and the small moustache are black. When he smiles, and he smiles often, the white teeth light up the whole face most attractively. He is now in his forty-fifth year and, in spite of his bald pate, does not look his age. His most prominent feature is the long, angular nose. He has a habit of stroking it.

At one moment in our conversation, when he was refuting rumours of his Fascist sympathies, he laid his long finger on his nose.

"Have I the head of a dictator?" he asked.

He has not.

At my first audience he was dressed in the regulation short black coat and striped trousers of the stockbroker. At the second he wore undress uniform. He talks colloquially, dislikes ceremony and can make friends with everyone. He is therefore popular with journalists and is the one ruler in central and south-eastern Europe who has "a good Press" everywhere.

He himself would have made a good journalist, for he can dramatise a situation. On the right-hand side of his desk there is a chair for his visitor, and directly opposite there is another small chair against the wall. These chairs have stood in this position since his father's time.

"Do you know where you are sitting?" asked the King.

I shook my head.

"On the chair on which Sir Hugh O'Beirne sat when he came to deliver Britain's ultimatum to my father. I sat here." He pointed to the small chair opposite.

The brilliant O'Beirne, whom I had known in St. Petersburg and who perished with Lord Kitchener in the North Sea, had been sent to Sofia to repair the diplomatic blunders of his predecessor and to win Bulgaria for the allied cause. He came too late, and by the irony of fate, for he understood Slavs and knew how to gain their confidence, it fell to his lot to deliver Britain's declaration of war. That was in October, 1915. King Boris was then a young man of twenty-one. The occasion was his first introduction to great events.

He has never forgotten it. He regrets Bulgaria's lost friendship with Britain and would like to regain it. More even than Prince Paul or King Carol, he realises the danger of putting all his economic eggs into the basket of one Great Power. And to-day Germany is dominant in Bulgaria's economic life, taking in 1936 fifty-six per cent. of Bulgaria's exports and sending sixty-eight per cent. of the imports.

During the last two years British purchases from Bulgaria have shown a remarkable increase. But the increase is not large enough to please the King. He wants Britain to buy Bulgaria's tobacco crop. His wish is hardly likely to be fulfilled until a nation, which now smokes "gaspers" almost exclusively, learns to appreciate the delicate aroma of Bulgarian tobacco.

King Boris is a good son. He admires his father, but he thinks that pre-war European diplomacy suffered from the deep-rooted mistrust which existed between King Edward VII, King Leopold of Belgium, and King Ferdinand. They were, King Boris told me, men of exceptional intelligence and easily the cleverest of the European monarchs. But all three disliked and were profoundly suspicious of one another. When they met, they were like poker players looking for an ace up the other fellow's sleeve. This suspicion, King Boris believes, had an unfortunate effect on the events which preceded the Great War.

The King himself is a man of peace. He is the Walter

Citrine of monarchs. He believes in the virtues of gradualness. He dislikes diplomatic surprises. His mind is firmly set
against army interference in politics. He gave me a dramatic
account of his dismissal of General Loukoff, his favourite
War Minister, for intriguing with the politicians. "I should
have acted sooner," he told me, "but I liked my man too
much."

It was a case, he said, in which the liking of Boris the
friend influenced detrimentally the judgment of Boris the
king.

He asked me my impressions of Sofia. I told him that,
although I could not help noticing the poverty, I had seen
many signs of material progress, especially during the past
twelve months.

"You are right," he said. "The country was suffering from
too much politics. After the war every peasant in Bulgaria
was a politician. You know that I have always made a great
point of going about among the people and talking to them.
I began it immediately after I came to the throne. In those
days the mayors of the smallest villages used to ask me always
what Lloyd George, Clemenceau or Wilson had been saying. Now they want to know the price of prunes and grain
and tobacco. They did not understand Lloyd George, but
they know tobacco. It is a hopeful sign."

He told me of his desire to establish democracy by gradual
stages and referred to the coming elections as a proof of his
good intentions. "If the experiment is a success," he said,
"it will prove that we have made progress. If not, there is
only one conclusion. We are not yet ripe for Parliamentary
government."

He spoke very frankly of the difficulties of the situation
and had obviously no illusions about his own position. "If
there is a good harvest," he said, "I am popular. If not . . ."
He shrugged his shoulders.

He also expressed a qualified satisfaction with the improvement in Bulgaria's relations with her neighbours, especially

with Yugoslavia. But he regretted the antagonism of Turkey and Greece and the cautious indifference of Rumania. Twenty years after the war to end war there was still no bridge over the Danube between Bulgaria and Rumania. The Balkans were behaving well just now, better, indeed, than the rest of Europe. He realised, too, that improvement could come only piecemeal. But progress could be too slow. The Balkans had powerful neighbours to the North, the West and the East. One day the other Balkan states might need Bulgaria's help. He hoped to extend Bulgaria's pact with Yugoslavia to the other Balkan states. For two years now he had been striving towards that end, but before it could be achieved there must be goodwill on both sides. In fifty years Bulgaria had fought three wars. They had begun well. All three had ended disastrously. Bulgaria had not complained. But it was unreasonable to expect the beggar always to give and the rich neighbour always to acquire.

I asked King Boris about Bulgarian re-armament and the state of efficiency of the army. He was at once on the defensive. The spirit of the troops was good. But the army was not well-equipped. All rumours to the contrary were gross exaggerations. Bulgaria, he insisted, had to move slowly. She had no money. The lack of money is certainly there, but I imagine that in re-armament Bulgaria has to move slowly or quietly in order not to arouse the suspicions of her neighbours. Re-armament, however, has had one noticeable effect.

"Our people", said the King, "have recovered their self-respect. They no longer feel themselves as Abyssinians."

As our conversation, conducted on the King's part in a brilliant mixture of French and English, drew near its end, King Boris made a dramatic defence of his country and of his people. He stated his firm belief in the healing virtues of time and his profound mistrust of all policies of adventures. He laid great stress on Bulgaria's good behaviour since the war. In that war she had suffered cruelly. To-day, the world was faced with a choice of guns or butter, but if civilisation was to survive it behoved the countries with the butter to see that it was properly distributed. The Bulgarian people were the poorest in Europe. If ever there was a country which seemed ripe for Communism, it was Bulgaria after the war. Yet it had stopped short of the precipice, because the greatest virtues of the Bulgarian were patience and commonsense.

"Foreign observers", he went on, "are always telling me that politically Bulgaria has gone too fast. I do not deny it. But they forget that Bulgaria has gone through a revolution."

"I myself", he said dramatically, "was made a king by that revolution, although in one respect I owe my throne to my father, King Ferdinand.

"Although I ought not to say it, my father was a very clever man. He had a long nose. We all have long noses."

He smiled and again laid his finger on his own nose.

"King Ferdinand saw that the odium of defeat would demand a victim. He took the odium on himself and went. By going he saved the throne for his son. At least he has saved it so far. For you never know how it will end . . ."

I rose from the O'Beirne chair, and the King came with me to the door. "Come back to Bulgaria and see more of our country. I'll give you all the help I can."

I liked that modest "our", so different from the orthodox "my" of monarchs. As I left the room, that calm and almost cheerful "you never know how it will end" still seemed to ring in my ears.

The King had said no more than the truth. I remembered how, when I was in Sofia the year before, Queen Joanna was expecting a baby. All Bulgaria was hoping for a boy. But the pessimists expected a second girl. The Coburg dynasty, they said, was associated with disaster. It had brought nothing but tragedy to Bulgaria.

The Bulgarians are superstitious, and the birth of a second daughter would have been regarded as a bad omen. But the

Boris luck held, and to-day in every house and cottage of Bulgaria you can see a photograph of Queen Joanna holding Prince Simeon in her arms with King Boris as the happy father bending down and, of course, smiling.

I believe that his luck will hold, because he has brains to back it with. He is the cleverest king in the Balkans. He has immense physical courage and his personal charm is irresistible. His moral courage is commonly supposed not to be so strong, and to his enemies his personal charm is a little suspect. The King, they say, is all things to all men.

Personally I have no doubts about his sincerity. He has come through many difficult situations not only with courage, but with statesmanlike ability. In particular, his handling of the Velcheff *coup d'état*, which in May of 1932 nearly cost him his throne and even his life, was both masterly and tactful. He kept his crown. He saved Bulgaria from Fascism, although, admittedly, the process of salvation involved the establishment of a non-Parliamentary régime.

But it is typical of the King's capacity for caution that before introducing the new régime he made a tour of Europe. Among other places which he visited he went to Balmoral. There he saw King George V and Mr. Ramsay MacDonald, who was then Prime Minister. He told them his troubles and his difficulties with complete frankness. Almost without hesitation Mr. MacDonald advised him to act.

It was on his return from this visit that King Boris laid the foundations of his friendship with the late King Alexander of Yugoslavia. The story of this friendship is a curious one greatly to King Boris's credit, and for the sake of historical accuracy I give the facts as they are known to me. Twelve years ago it fell to my lot to make the arrangements for an interview between the late King Alexander of Yugoslavia and the late Sir Peter Bark, the former Russian Finance Minister, and at that time my banking chief. At this audience Sir Peter pleaded for a better understanding between the Yugoslavs and the Bulgarians. Sir Peter made his plea as a

Slav. He had already seen King Boris and had secured his approval. But when he told King Alexander of King Boris's goodwill, the Yugoslav monarch was not impressed and replied coldly: "C'est le fils de son père"!

King Alexander's mistrust of Bulgaria was accompanied by a policy of pin-pricks on the part of the Yugoslav Government. Occasionally sword-thrusts and even gun-powder added a more sinister touch to the pin-pricks, and this policy lasted until September of 1933, when King Boris was on his way home from Balmoral. Perhaps the peaceful atmosphere of the Scottish Highlands struck some chord of sympathy in his heart. At any rate he decided to act. On his way to Sofia he had to pass through Belgrade. From the Yugoslav frontier he telegraphed to King Alexander saying that he would like very much to see him at the station. Taken by surprise and having little time to consult his Ministers, King Alexander went to the station. The two Kings, neighbours and rulers of brother races, had never met as kings, though as Crown Prince of Serbia Alexander had attended the coming-of-age celebrations of Prince Boris of Bulgaria at Sofia in 1912. Their first conversation as ruling monarchs took place, fifteen years after a war to end war and establish a League of Nations, in a carriage of the Simplon Express. The talk started badly. King Alexander was stiff and began by calling King Boris "Your Majesty" and addressing him as "vous". King Boris boldly turned the "vous" into a "tu" and the "Your Majesty" into plain "Alexander", reminding him that they were more than relations, because they were kings of brother peoples who had the same religion and the same customs and almost the same language, and recalling the festivities of 1912.

King Alexander responded generously to this advance. The train, which should have stopped for only twenty-one minutes, remained standing for nearly an hour. There and then the two Kings arranged in secret that next month King Alexander should visit Euxinograd, King Boris's Palace near Varna on the Black Sea. In October the Yugoslav cruiser *Dubrovnik* bore King Alexander and Queen Marie to Euxinograd, where they were received by King Boris and Queen Joanna. The friendship, begun at the Belgrade station, grew and flourished to the benefit of both countries. Next winter the Bulgarian sovereigns paid a state visit to Belgrade. In the summer King Alexander came to Sofia, and from these meetings sprang the Bulgar-Yugoslav Pact of Friendship.

It was King Boris's courage which won King Alexander's admiration and eventual affection. King Boris motored him all round Sofia, and at Plovdiv the two Kings left their car and walked through the streets unguarded.

King Alexander, a soldier and a brave man, was a little astonished:

"This is the first time since my accession", he said, "that I have ever walked in the streets without an escort."

"I am my own detective", said King Boris, "and to-day yours. I am a fatalist. What is written is written."

To-day, King Boris has few enemies outside the ranks of the professional politicians and the agitators, and his disinterested devotion to his country is widely recognised. He has no vices. A poor man, he makes no display and wastes no public money. In these days prophecy is a foolish indulgence, but I should say that he will go far and that he will keep his throne as long as most kings in Europe except our own.

In particular, he has a firm hold on the affections of the Bulgarian peasants. They have reason to admire him, for he has done much for them and for Bulgaria.

CHAPTER TEN

ON THE DAY after my audience at the Palace I paid a visit, with the King's permission, to Vrania, the royal estate eight miles to the south-east of Sofia. The estate is large and contains two palaces which stand side by side. They are full of indifferent paintings of the King's Coburg and Bourbon relations and with their lack of comfort look more like museums than palaces. King Ferdinand and King Boris are both versatile and talented men, but neither, I imagine, had he been put to earn his living as a modern decorator, would have prospered. The gardens, however, are magnificent. Here in summer gaily-coloured butterflies and moths of every size and kind abound and are a source of joy to King Boris who is never happier than when pursuing his entomological studies. Had he not been a king, his father would have won fame as an ornithologist. King Boris is accepted by scientists as a serious entomologist. He is at heart a country lover and is credited with the remark that cities are like antheaps but not so well regulated.

Vrania is a country microcosm of its own. The large wooded park, which contains rare timbers, is a kind of Whipsnade in which the different specimens of European deer roam at liberty. There is a large model farm on which the King studies and practises the newest agricultural developments. The whole estate is managed, under the King's personal supervision, by a German named Schacht. He is a Muenchener and no relation of the President of the Reichsbank.

In the brilliant winter sunshine I found Vrania very attractive, and the view, for which special rides among the trees have been cut, is enchanting. In all countries to-day kings have a hard life. King Boris is a lonely man. But he has his compensations, and Vrania is one of them.

The King, who likes his subjects to share what he himself enjoys, has given a park to Sofia. It is called the Boris Park, and here you may see young Bulgaria at play. In the Park itself skating in winter and tennis in summer are the two chief pastimes. Close by is the football stadium and the swimming pool. The Bulgarians, who are a fine race physically, are quite good at games and at football hold their own with the other European countries. This means that they have nearly reached the best English standard. But they do not impress you as a people slavishly devoted to sport, and walking seems to be their chief enjoyment, perhaps because it is the cheapest. On Sundays you will see them walking in the Park in stolid family groups. Even the children could not make me alter my impression that the average Bulgarian regards sport as something beyond his purse and perhaps beyond his sense of dignity.

Sofia has a passion for statues, and the Boris Park is full of little busts set on the top of short pedestals. They commemorate the names of Bulgaria's little-known great men. I also found an image of Lord Kitchener, actually, I think, the best likeness of him that I have ever seen in stone. It is almost the only British feature, except the Legation, in Sofia. But the name on the pedestal is not Kitchener's. The statue, erected by the Art-Industrial School of Sofia, is to Ivan Vazoff, Sofia's national poet.

To the sophisticated foreigner Sofia presents few recreative attractions. There is no golf course, and the chief relaxation of the diplomatic corps is riding, for which the Sofia plain offers an almost endless field of exploration. But to the average Bulgarian the real playground of Sofia is Vitosha. I approve his choice, and I shall remember till I die one afternoon that I spent on the mountain-side with the Petersons. Although it was February, the sun was warm, the sky cloudless, and the air so clear and invigorating that I raced ahead with Lady Peterson leaving the staid and dignified Maurice far behind.

First we went to Bojana, which is already halfway up the mountain and more than five miles distant from Sofia. Here in a little wooded enclosure is the curious church of St. Panteleimon. It is built in three portions and in two storeys. The upper storey which is still used as a church dates from the thirteenth century. The lower part is even older and goes back to 1100. The façade and entrance are modern.

In the little cemetery, shaded by firs, is the grave of Queen Eleanor, the second wife of King Ferdinand. Long before she died, she chose this quiet mountain retreat as her last resting-place, and the grave has been cared for by King Boris. In the old part of the church, below curious twelfth century frescos representing the ancient Bulgarian Tsars as Christs, I saw the ribbons, still carefully preserved, of the wreaths sent by the Royal families of Europe to the Queen's funeral. There was one from the Kaiser, one from the Emperor Karl and the Empress Zita, and among many others one, I think, from the King of Spain. But there was none from any member of the British Royal Family or from any of the Allied monarchs. Queen Eleanor died in 1917, and in war-time kings must hate as their subjects hate.

From Bojana we came back on our steps and took another mountain road which leads to the monastery of Dragalevzi and beyond it. Indeed, the road climbs almost to "Aleko", the shelter-hut for skiers, over 5,000 feet above sea-level. It was a Saturday afternoon, and on our way we passed the long trail of young Bulgarians, trudging on foot from Sofia to "ski" on Vitosha. Viewed from the distance, they looked like ants on a white sheet. They would not reach the ski-ing slopes till dark. They would sleep the night in a cold hut. They would "ski" all Sunday morning. Then in the afternoon they would set out cheerfully on the long ten-mile walk back to Sofia. Their perseverance and their enthusiasm were a joy to behold. Here was no softness or enervating luxury. I could not help wondering how many British boys would care to "ski" in similar conditions.

We, alas, made nine-tenths of the climb by motor-car, and I felt ashamed. Beauty should be approached with a proper reverence and demands for its appreciation a definite mental effort. In my heavy fur-coat I did climb a distance of a quarter of a mile to a natural terrace and was rewarded for my energy by a scene which left me awe-struck by its majesty. Here Zeus should have had his throne, for from Vitosha he could have looked down on a larger world than his glance ever commanded from Mount Olympus. The whole plateau, ninety miles long and fifty broad, lay open to the eye. It was like an olive-green lake surrounded by huge jagged walls of porphyry. And the beauty of the scene was intensified by a silence that was spiritual.

Only two little hills disturbed the even flatness of the plateau. Both were in or near Sofia. On one, in Sofia itself, stood the French Institute, the imposing centre of French cultural propaganda; on the other, five miles to the south-east, was the American College of Simeonovo, the only home of Anglo-Saxon culture in the Balkans.

At the invitation of Dr. Black, the President, I visited Simeonovo and inspected the College. I have no hesitation in describing it as the finest institution of its kind in central and south-eastern Europe. Here, in fine buildings superbly situated under the shadow of Vitosha, some five hundred Bulgarian girls and boys, ranging from the ages of fourteen to twenty, are brought up as Anglo-Saxons and taught the benefits of Anglo-Saxon culture.

The College has an excellent library, a theatre, a fine dining-hall, and carpentry and engineering shops. The house system is in force, and, although games are not compulsory, they are encouraged. Inter-house competitions flourish. In this respect Simeonovo bears some resemblance to an English public school. But there are many differences, in my opinion, mostly to the advantage of Simeonovo. There are no prefects or monitors. Their place is taken by house and dormitory committees. Except for a few charwomen there are no College servants. The boys and girls clean their own rooms and make their own beds. In the dining-room they wait on each other, the waiters and waitresses receiving a small salary for their services. The salary helps to pay the annual school fee of fifty pounds, which, although insignificant to the Western purse, is very high for Bulgaria.

I made a round of the classrooms and was prodigiously impressed by the fluency of the pupils. They spoke English far, far better than the English and American boys and girls in Swiss schools ever speak French. They do well, too, after leaving the College. About sixty of the hundred boys and girls who had left during the past two years were then studying abroad. Nearly all of them had won scholarships. Of the sixty half were in Germany; the others were divided among many countries.

Dr. Black believes that the giving of scholarships to foreign students is the best form of cultural propaganda in which any country can indulge, but he lays great stress on the importance of choosing the scholars from boys and girls who are likely, on their return, to play an important part in the public life of their own country.

He also gave me a graphic account of the propaganda efforts of other countries in Bulgaria. As far as expenditure goes, the Germans and Italians are the big spenders. The Germans have their own schools in Sofia. They are run by the Reich and are inspected by the Reich. Those children who are German subjects must join the Hitler-Jugend and give the Heil Hitler greeting. The German schoolmasters cannot force the Bulgarian children who visit the school to follow these precepts, but at any rate the example is there. Germany, too, gives a large number of free scholarships to enable Bulgarian students to spend a year at a German university or technical high school.

The Italian effort is no less intense, and in Sofia you can see the pupils of the Italian school walking in the streets in semi-military formation and giving the Fascist salute. Not all

M

these children are Italians. These foreign schools are popular
with the Bulgarian citizens because of the opportunity which
they offer of learning a foreign language. Free or heavily
subsidised trips to Italy are also a prominent feature of
Italian propaganda.

Dr. Black thinks that the Germans and the Italians overdo
their propaganda, but that Britain and the United States do
too little. He would gladly co-operate with us, not only because the College depends for its financial sinews on private
subscriptions from the United States and since the slump
they are not so readily forthcoming, but also because he believes in the spread of Anglo-American civilisation as the
most important factor in the maintenance of world peace.
At present he is fighting a lone battle for, in a country which
is traditionally pro-British and which still counts Gladstone
as one of its heroes, we do practically nothing to increase our
influence. Up to the spring of 1938 the British Council had
given one scholarship to a Bulgarian, and this solitary award
went to a boy violinist.

I do not criticise the British Council. In the few years of
its existence it has done splendid work. But it has no money,
for the British Government still regards propaganda, perhaps
not unnaturally, as something rather shameful, as something
akin to secret service. And the people of Britain take little
interest in this important side-line of foreign affairs. The
Alliance Française, which does a great work for French culture all over the world, is supported very largely by private
subscriptions, and these come mainly from the large French
financial and industrial concerns. The big British business
man is apathetic to cultural propaganda. He wants to
know how it will help him to sell more textiles, or more
guns.

This attitude, I think, is short-sighted. There are a hundred
institutions in Britain which could endow five scholarships
a year and not notice the cost. Two hundred pounds would
pay for one scholarship. A thousand pounds a year from a

hundred concerns would provide five hundred scholarships. It would be, I am sure, a profitable investment.

The average British reader may say: Why bother about the Balkans which have always been a source of trouble to the world? The answer is that the Balkans have changed. They represent an increasingly virile force, for they are, with Russia, almost the only part of Europe which still shows a large surplus of births over deaths. In fifty years, perhaps in twenty-five years, Rumania and Yugoslavia will have a population as large as Britain. Even Bulgaria with her six million population has approximately the same surplus of births over deaths as Britain and a surplus seven times as high as that of Sweden. Yet the population of Sweden is slightly larger than that of Bulgaria, and Britain's population is seven times as large. We can no longer afford to ignore the Balkans. They are just now in a state of rapid flux. They represent what I should call the "guns *and* butter" states. The guns of other Powers are at their gates, forcing them to spend large sums on their own defence. Yet I am convinced that their sole ambition is not war or conquest, but peace in which to develop their resources. Their cultural urge is great, yet to-day they are being pulled by the ears by various Great Powers. Their natural inclination leans towards Western civilisation and with a little encouragement they can be drawn in that direction.

When I descended from Simeonovo, I came back into the lower world, and my last two days in Sofia were strenuously mundane. First, there was the big farewell party at the Legation on the eve of Sir Maurice Peterson's departure for Bagdad. All Sofia was present, and, feeling like an intruder in a huge family party, I withdrew to a point of vantage on the stairs to watch the entry of the diplomatists. For some time I amused myself by trying to guess the representatives of the different nations. My every guess was wrong.

There was a tall, lean man with angular features, well-brushed iron-grey hair, and a monocle. He was like Sir

George Clerk without a moustache and ought obviously to have been a distinguished English actor. He was the French military attaché. There was a good-looking young man whose languid manner and faultlessly cut dress-coat seemed to indicate Eton and Savile Row. He was the Rumanian First Secretary. When I was told that a gentle and soft-spoken man who looked like a distinguished musician or poet was the Italian military attaché, I gave up my face-reading as useless and moved over to the orchestra. It was composed of Russians. They played dance music execrably. This was perhaps not surprising, for most of them had lost an arm or a leg in the war. They were, in fact, Russian invalids. The leader told me that there were 24,000 Russian refugees in the country and that out of her modest budget Bulgaria set aside fifteen million levas for their support. Slavs have the old clan spirit of the Scottish Highlander. They quarrel violently, but in adversity their generosity to the fallen brother is noble.

I was rescued from my wallflower position by Maurice Peterson who scolded me violently. "You've got to make this show go. You must dance. Pick out the prettiest girl in the room and I'll introduce you."

I did not hesitate. Early in the evening I had already picked out a radiant creature with blue eyes and flaxen hair who looked like a Nordic goddess. I indicated my choice.

"No," said the prudent Maurice, "I think you'd better begin somewhere else. She's the typist of the Consulate. Look again and choose a Bulgarian."

I looked, and, full of good intentions, made a careful scrutiny of the room. "There," I said, drawing Maurice's attention to a quiet and distinguished-looking girl with obvious Slav features, "I'd like to dance with her."

"No, you won't," said Maurice quite impatiently, "she's the Passport Office typist."

I gave up this unequal contest. The show did not require being made to go. It was going very nicely by itself both in the ballroom and in the buffet. Assigning to myself the modest but more useful task of plying Bulgarian Ministers with champagne and whisky, I withdrew to the buffet.

Halfway through the evening came the big surprise of the party. For days past the Legation ballroom had been taken over by the British Consul. At one end a stage had been erected and curtained off. There had been mysterious rehearsals from which the Minister and Lady Peterson had been rigorously excluded. Now we were shepherded into the ballroom. The lights were extinguished, and the curtain went up on an Eastern scene which drew all its inspiration from the more sensual verses of Omar Khayyam. Maurice was going to Bagdad. The Consul and the Passport Officer had written a musical review which was to show Bagdad in all its glory to the Bulgarians.

It is true that the glory belonged more to the era of Haroun Al Raschid than to the present, and in the plot I noticed generous borrowings from the Thousand and One Nights.

A harem figured in most of the scenes. The story opened with the usual Oriental pimp guide introducing an Arab trader to the Pasha's ladies. They welcome him because he brings them the latest novelties of the Parisian beauty parlour. While he is selling his wares and doing a little private business of a more romantic nature on his own account, the Pasha, attended by a giant eunuch with an executioner's sword, enters. A tragic ending is averted by the news that an aeroplane is seen approaching in the sky. All Bagdad turns out to welcome the new British ambassador.

I do not know how much the Bulgarians understood of the words, but they jostled each other in their eagerness to see the daughters of their own Ministers and of the foreign diplomatists dressed in the regulation trousers of the harem and dancing Oriental dances. Obviously Sofia was progressing. Most visitors dwell on its Oriental aspect. I cannot say that I noticed it. It is a thousand times less Oriental than Moscow. It is becoming more Western every day.

Maurice took his grand entry with his usual immobility of countenance. I could not guess whether he was pleased or vexed, nervous or completely at ease. His ability to mask his feelings is, I think, the reason for his great success with Orientals. He never loses his dignity even in the most embarrassing situation.

A few years ago he was Acting British High Commissioner in Egypt. He had then been married about nine years. During his period of office he went with his wife to Jerusalem. He visited Omar's mosque, where he was received by the head Imam. The Mohammedan priest had read in the papers that Sir Miles Lampson, the British High Commissioner, had recently married. Understanding none of the subtleties of such distinctions as "Acting", he insisted on regarding Maurice as Sir Miles and recited a long prayer for the health and welfare of the bride and bridegroom and for the fecundity of the marriage.

At this moment Mrs. Peterson, as she then was, interrupted him in her bazaar Arabic: "But I have three boys already."

The Imam beamed with delight. Obviously he thought that Sir Miles Lampson was a hell-of-a-fellow to have had three boys in less than nine months, and the taciturn Maurice, untiring in his seal for the maintenance of British prestige, did nothing to disillusion him.

On my last evening, as the Petersons had to go to another farewell party given in their honour by the Bulgarian Prime Minister, I dined at the Diplomatic Club with our First Secretary and our Consul. I spent a pleasant evening comparing notes with them on the Diplomatic and Consular services of yesterday and to-day. I reserve my judgment about the Diplomatic service, although I think that the intellectual standard is higher to-day than it was before the war. But I am quite sure that the Consular service is far more efficient than it was in my time. In bygone days the Balkans were a snare and a temptation for many young Consular officers. The removal of Anglo-Saxon restraints and the loneliness of the life seemed to undermine their moral resistance, and the tale of mismarriages and alcoholic breakdowns is quite a long one.

There is one Balkan hotel where the porter still points out the hooks to which a certain Consul, after throwing all his whisky bottles out of the window, used to chain his wrists, in order to prevent himself from going out again to buy more drink. He is long since dead, but there was a certain heroism in these desperate measures of self-defence which in my weaker moments I sometimes envy.

Since the war, both Balkan life and Consular life have changed. The new type of British Consular Officer is a man of wide knowledge and culture. Very often he has missed the Diplomatic service by only a few marks, and it is not always the Diplomatic service which gets the better man. To-day, a Consular Officer's duties leave him little time for leisure and temptation. His work brings him into contact with every stratum of the population, and to a Minister who knows how to use him his expert knowledge can be invaluable. In the Balkans I am especially grateful to Consuls like Mr. Cecil Rapp of Zagreb and Mr. Boyd Tollington of Sofia, not only for their hospitality and kindness, but also for much inside information which I could not have acquired elsewhere.

Britain is the only Great Power which still makes a distinct cleavage between its Diplomatic and Consular Services. I hope to live to see some form of amalgamation between the two services. Both, I feel sure, would benefit, and we shall never have a really first-class foreign representation until the dams are broken down and the gates of promotion opened wider.

After our dinner we went on to the raspberry fool theatre to see a Bulgarian presentation of Chaikovsky's ballet *The*

Sleeping Beauty. The orchestra was good and the *décor* surprisingly attractive. I found an old friend in the producer, Max Frohmann, the brother of Marguerite Frohmann, the Moscow ballerina. But in spite of some Russian assistance the dancing was a heavy and rather laboured imitation of the Moscow classical school.

We had to leave before the end. We had persuaded Maurice Peterson that it was part of his education to visit a Sofia *Nachtlokal* before he left the Bulgarian capital. He had promised to meet us there after the Prime Minister's party, and on pain of his displeasure he had charged us to be there before him. The adventure was one of my less successful experiments. The place was called L'Etoile, but there was nothing star-like about its site. It was, in fact, little more than a cellar, and the entrance was situated at the foot of a long stair of stone steps. It was the most break-neck descent to Avernus that I have ever seen.

We sat in a kind of horse-box with low partitions, and very soon we were joined by Maurice. His arrival created a mild curiosity. I doubt if a Sofia *Nachtlokal* had ever before been graced by a guest in white tie and dress-coat. Certainly the other guests were not distinguished either by their personal appearance or by their dress. They were not numerous and they were, I think, all foreigners. There were Jew traders and German commercial travellers. They did not sit together. But they showed no signs of hatred. *Nachtlokals* are great levellers, and in the smoky atmosphere of L'Etoile the Germans neither drew their robes aside nor showed any fear of racial contamination. There was a fat and ugly Turk who, our Consul told me, was a rich tobacco merchant. On a raised dais a nondescript orchestra played a blaring jazz music, and every now and then a hard-faced and angular soubrette came to the loud-speaker and sang the words of the tune in a guttural English.

We sat down and ordered whisky. In Sofia the *Nachtlokal* exists only for the more civilised foreigner, and he is rightly made to pay for his civilisation. For a weak and watered whisky we were charged seven shillings a glass.

A variety programme was in progress. It was surprisingly good, but not good enough to make a success of my evening. There was an embarrassing arrangement which I was unable to alter. The artistes and the dancing girls sat at a round table at the end of the dancing-floor. Unfortunately, their table was alongside ours, and very soon, scenting wealth in Maurice's stiff shirt-front, they began to ogle us and to ask for drinks and cigarettes. It was obvious that here they combined two rôles and that their salaries were only a small part of their means of subsistence.

I looked at Maurice's face. It was as hard as Aberdeen granite. In vain I tried to refill his glass with whisky. In vain Tollington, our Consul, tried to create "Stimmung" by dancing on the small revolving table which was the one modern feature of the place. Maurice became more dignified, more solemn, more taciturn. We left early. As we climbed the long steps which led us back into the fresh air, Maurice gave a "phew" of relief. It was the first time his lips had moved for nearly an hour.

I left Sofia the next day. The year before, I had made my way to the station in a misty dawn with the Legation villas gradually emerging through the greyness from their gardens. During the short drive I had seen the sun rise like a ball of fire until it dispelled all the clouds. The picture lived in my memory as a symbol of Bulgaria's post-war struggles.

On this occasion I left a peaceful city under a starlit night. Maurice came to the station to see me off, and as we said goodbye I wondered rather sadly if ever I should be able to afford the journey to Bagdad. His promotion had been rapid, and I was glad for his sake. But selfishly I wished that he could have remained in the Balkans.

I liked these Slav countries. There was something in my nature which could not resist the Slav appeal. Perhaps it sprang from my Russian experiences. But I doubted this.

Beyond a natural curiosity I had no particular desire to return to Russia. But I meant to go back to the Balkans, and during these last two years I had been fortunate in having old associates there. I had begun my career in the Foreign Office in the same room with Sir Ronald Campbell, our Minister in Belgrade. I had shared a house with Maurice in Prague. In Russia, in 1918, I had lived for some weeks with Sir Reginald Hoare, now our Minister in Bucharest. In their different ways they are exceptionally talented men.

Such a happy combination of circumstances, I reflected, could never occur again.

CHAPTER ELEVEN

THE JOURNEY FROM Sofia to Bucharest is one of unexcelled beauty. The railway line runs through the deep gorge of the Isker valley. There are few signs of habitation, and the mountain scenery is wild and romantic. As for the Isker, it is the Queen of highland rivers, faster than the Spey, more desolate than the Morar or the Gruinard. I have often seen the Bavarian Iser which inspired Campbell's well-known line "and Iser rolling rapidly". He could never have seen the Bulgarian Isker tearing its rugged course through the rocks and boulders of the narrow defile. It looks like the ideal salmon river. But I should not care to wade it. Nor should I like to risk my life on the narrow bridges, made of brushwood stretched across four wires, over which the Bulgarians walk and even drive their sheep with an easy nonchalance.

I have always enjoyed this journey, but I confess that it is unnecessarily long. The distance is only four hundred kilometres. Yet the train takes fourteen hours, and there is a four hours' wait at the Danube frontier. I can, therefore, sympathise in an acutely personal sense with King Boris's desire for his bridge across the Danube. Not that I had any personal grounds for complaint. Thanks to the intervention of M. Krucescu, an old Prague friend, and at that moment the Rumanian Minister in Sofia and an ardent advocate of a Bulgarian-Rumanian understanding, I was given every facility by the Rumanian authorities and was piloted through the customs and across the river by the Rumanian Consul. Other travellers, however, are not always so fortunate, and the Danube bridge should and must be built.

Alas! there are few foreigners to agitate for its construction, and no one makes this journey unless he is compelled by dire necessity. There are very few British visitors to Bulgaria. Sir Maurice Peterson was Minister in Sofia for nearly two years. During his period of office there were only twenty-four entries in the Legation visitors' book, and among these my name figured twice.

In the past it was, I am convinced, Rumania's fixed policy to isolate Bulgaria. More recently the policy of good neighbourliness has begun to operate, and Rumania has now placed an order for a train-ferry which will be ready in 1939. It will not be so convenient as a bridge, but it will certainly be a welcome improvement.

During my four hours' wait between Russe and Giurgiu, the Bulgarian and Rumanian frontier stations, I found plenty to occupy my time. I am never bored beside a river, and here there was the Danube. It is not blue. I do not suppose that it has been blue for centuries. But it is always immensely impressive, especially at dawn and at sunset. The horizon seems to stretch to the end of the world. On the north bank a graceful line of poplars harmonises admirably with the gentle flow of the great river. To the west there is an island covered with low willows. On week-days fleets of barges and tugs ply a busy trade. But on a Sunday they are tied up alongside the wharves of Giurgiu. Town and river seem asleep, and the silence is broken only by the whirr of a gaggle of geese as it spreads its arrow flight across the sky.

The barges carry oil, for Giurgiu is connected by a pipe line with the great Rumanian oilfields at Ploesti. Most of the barges fly British flags, and I saw two splendid new motorbarges which also flew the Red Ensign of Britain. They take Rumanian oil up the Danube. Much of it goes to Germany. I have no strong political convictions. I belong to no political party. But there are some things which I find difficult to reconcile with the peace aims to which I suppose every civilised man and woman subscribe. We democratic peace-loving peoples live in fear of armed aggression. With sound reason we dread the ambitions of certain nations. There is a grave danger of Europe being divided into two warring groups. Yet each group helps the other to equip itself with the weapons of war. Britain supplies Germany with much of the raw material for her re-armament. British Malaya, populated mainly by Chinese, sends much-needed iron ore to Japan. Italy makes warships for Russia. If this is the essence of capitalism, there is something wrong with the capitalist system.

The traveller who crosses over from Russe to Giurgiu must be struck at once by one contrast. He is leaving a poor country for a rich one. Russe looks asleep and poverty-stricken. You feel the wealth of Rumania the moment you set foot on the wharf of Giurgiu. Since my last visit, only twelve months before, there had been a vast transformation. Everywhere were signs of building activity. Already the foundations for the new train-ferry pier had been laid. A new Customs House had begun to raise its head. Given efficient and honest administration, Rumania will be one of the richest countries of Europe and, if the present birth-rate is maintained, its population of twenty millions will double itself in fifty years.

On arriving at Bucharest I found a breathless Legation chauffeur on the platform to meet me. Sir Reginald Hoare had kindly sent his car to Giurgiu to save me the tedious railway journey to Bucharest. The chauffeur, who had been delayed on the road, had missed me at Giurgiu and had raced the train all the way back, giving it half-an-hour's start and a beating.

It was pleasant to stay at the British Legation, although as a house it is small and hardly worthy of the might, majesty and dominion of the British Empire. On my 1937 visit I had been there in a semi-official capacity. I had been officially shepherded. I had been entertained by the Rumanian Government. There had been speeches and other formalities which always unnerve me. Now my time was more or less my own and, without wishing to appear ungrateful to a very hospitable nation, I must admit that I preferred my freedom.

There are obvious advantages in being the British Minister's guest. You are given every opportunity of meeting the high officials of the country to which the Minister is accredited, and in the privacy of the Minister's study you have the invaluable advantage of being able to compare your own impressions with the inside knowledge of an experienced diplomatist. As hosts Sir Reginald and Lady Hoare were perfect. In the evenings they took me everywhere they went themselves. They arranged luncheon and dinner parties for me. They put me into touch with everyone that I wanted to see, and in the mornings and afternoons they allowed me to do what I liked.

I lived a strenuous life. In the normal course of Nature Bucharest should have been under a mantle of snow at the beginning of March. But the winter of 1938 was a freakish one, and for weeks the sun shone from a cloudless sky. The air was warmer than the average temperature of an English June, and my fur-coat was merely an unnecessary piece of luggage.

In these ideal conditions Bucharest was an enchanting city, and I spent many happy hours in admiring the modern American architecture, of which the new telephone building is the outstanding example, and in exploring the fast disappearing old corners. For the city is changing its physiognomy with startling rapidity, and already the Bucharest of 1938 is as different from the pre-war Bucharest as is the modern San Francisco from the wooden shacks of the first gold-diggers.

If Bucharest is changing, so, too, are the Rumanian people. In the past, I was, like many of my countrymen, prejudiced against the Rumanians, mainly because I thought them less virile than the Yugoslavs and the Bulgarians. I think that most Englishmen make the mistake of judging Rumanians by the mundane world of Bucharest. On the surface, Bucharest society is pleasantly easy-going, mildly vain, and slightly effete. But generalisations are dangerous, and you can match every volatile member of Rumanian society with a serious one.

Prominent among the titled leaders of Rumanian society are the Cantacuzenes. You could find no more serious intellectual than the tall, ascetic-looking Prince George Cantacuzene. He recently spent three months roughing it in the deserts of Syria, Irak and Arabia in order to paint. He has a studio in a high flat overlooking all Bucharest, and here he works twelve hours a day. He is a painter of distinction, but he has a higher claim to fame. He is one of the leading architects who to-day are altering the face of their country. He does not stand alone in his seriousness. But there are other types whose ultra-worldliness leaves an impression of frivolity. And these contrasts you will find throughout Rumanian society.

Tact and a guard on one's tongue are essential in Bucharest. The Rumanians are sensitive. They resent very much being stigmatised as Balkan. They regard their country as the Eastern outpost of Western civilisation, and in some respects they do not exaggerate. Their culture is mainly French. Most Rumanians of good family have studied at a French university. They are excellent linguists and are very well-read. On the whole I think that it is fair to say that their culture is higher than their character. In the past the big families have run Rumania, and the administration has not been good. The cultural mind of Rumania may be Western, but the methods of government have always been semi-Oriental.

Even to-day it would be easy to write a book on Bucharest scandals, beginning with the currency smugglers and ending with Madame Lupescu. It has been done by other writers, but I shall not follow their example if only because these scandals are merely the froth on the surface of a Rumanian life which is changing very rapidly. In recent years there has been a strong reaction against corruption in public life and against low moral standards. With all its objectionable features of pro-Nazi-ism amd anti-Semitism the notorious Iron Guard was a manifestation of this reaction. I met some of its members. They had all taken a vow of abstinence and asceticism. There was one young man who used to set aside weekly a hundred lei (about two English shillings!) from his salary in order to visit a brothel. He took the Iron Guard pledge and saves, or perhaps I should say used to save, his money, for the Iron Guard has now been disbanded.

The ascetic cult has been adopted by other young Rumanians who have no Iron Guard sympathies. They train religiously for football, and they play "rugger". It is true that there are only eight or nine Rugby clubs, but the keenness is only less remarkable than the results that have already been achieved. In the international match against the picked strength of France in Paris, Rumania was beaten by only ten points. Association football, however, is the popular game of the people. There is a League run on British lines, and crowds of 50,000 turn out to watch the big matches.

During my visit I met Rumania's "rugger" captain. He was the son of a rich banker and had been educated in England. His manliness and his modesty impressed me greatly. He was a natural athlete, had only recently taken up golf, and was already one of the best players in Bucharest. I played with him and Sir Reginald Hoare on the course just outside the city. A long, winding lake divides most of the holes, and one side of the course abuts on a large aerodrome. The greens are more sand than grass, and putting, already difficult, is not made easier by the aeroplanes, which, piloted by learners, swoop down perilously near one's head before landing.

These young Rumanians will undoubtedly have an all-important effect on the development of the new Rumania. And so, too, will the young Rumanian women, for in Rumania woman is superior to man, and the modern young Rumanian girl is full of initiative. At dinner one night I sat next to Princess Marina Stirbey, who is Rumania's Amy Mollison. Her composure was everything that I had imagined

wholly un-Rumanian. No Englishwoman could have been
more phlegmatic. She talked of flying to Africa or to Australia as calmly as I should talk of taking the train to Inver-
ness. She expressed a restrained regret that today there were
no new fields to explore. She told me one fact which illustrates very graphically the state of tension in central and
south-eastern Europe. She could fly, she said, in six hours
from Bucharest to Paris. It took her six weeks to obtain the
necessary permits to fly over the intermediate countries!

I met numerous virile types among the writers and journalists. The most attractive was Mihail Sadoveanu, a fine, big
fellow, and a disciple of Sir Walter Scott. He made Scott
popular throughout Rumania, and, while I was in Bucharest,
one of Scott's novels was being published as a serial in one of
the leading Bucharest newspapers. Sadoveanu is one of the
great novelists of Europe, and his works have been translated
into nearly every European language except English. He has
the additional merit in my eyes of being a passionate angler,
and I hope next spring to accept his standing invitation to return to Rumania to throw a fly on the trout streams of the
Bukovina.

I met two newspaper men of a different type, for they represented the editor-politician. These were M. Lugoseanu
and M. Gafencu. Both are what we should call young men,
for they are still well on the right side of fifty. M. Lugoseanu
was for some years Rumanian Minister in Rome. Then he
married the daughter of the proprietor of the *Universul*, the
Rumanian newspaper with the largest circulation, and became an editor. He, too, forced me to revise my war impressions of the Rumanians. His conversation was severely practical and devoid of the flamboyant mannerisms of the elder
Rumanian politicians. But his dispassionate analysis of the
European situation was masterly. His culture and his sympathies were Western, but his period of office in Rome had
impressed him with the strength of the Italian effort. He
thought that the British made a mistake in under-estimating

N

the armed force of Italy and in thinking that economic collapse would curb the Duce's ambitions. Lack of money had
never stopped a war; it might easily cause one. There was
to-day a new Italy which would not die with Signor Mussolini. That was a fact with which Rumania had to reckon.

Personally, I have always believed that the Berlin-Rome
axis will be broken not by Anglo-French diplomatic over-
tures, but by the logic of events in the Balkans. Italy has a
rôle to play there. In particular, Rumania has more to fear
from Germany than from Italy. In her struggle to escape
from economic domination she will look to everyone who
can help her, and among the potential helpers Italy may
figure prominently.

M. Gafencu looks British and is pro-British. He is, in fact,
Scottish by origin. His great-grandfather was a Scot called
Saunders who, at the invitation of the Tsar, went with his
wife from Scotland to St. Petersburg to arrange the art
treasures of the Hermitage. He remained in Russia, and there
a son was born to him. The son, who became a Russian subject, was banished to Bessarabia for being a freemason. His
son, M. Gafencu's father, crossed over into Rumania, and
tacked the Rumanian name of Gafencu on to the original
Saunders.

M. Gregory Gafencu is a man to watch. Still young, he is
more vigorous and more ambitious than M. Lugoseanu. He
fought in the war as a young aviator, and for his gallantry in
the air was given the British Military Cross. He has been
Under-Secretary for Foreign Affairs. Fifteen months ago he
became owner and virtual editor of a newspaper called *Tim-
pul*. Under his energetic guidance it has already nearly caught
up with the circulation of *Universul*. Early in 1938, when King
Carol was looking for a new administration to replace the
maladroit Goga Government, M. Gafencu put forward the
idea of a government of "les hommes de quarante ans". He
himself would, of course, have been one of the quadra-
genarian ministers. He is an advocate of M. Stojadinović's

"politique de bon voisinage", and favours a Central European economic *bloc* which would include Poland, Czechoslovakia, Yugoslavia, Hungary and Rumania. He believes that, if this *bloc* is not created, Germany will deal piecemeal with all the smaller states and reduce them to economic vassalage.

With M. Gafencu I met M. Ghelmegeanu, another of "the men of forty", and also a man whose future career is worth watching. M. Ghelmegeanu is a member of the Maniu Party, but is inclined to chafe under his leader's lack of iniative. M. Maniu, as the leader of the Transylvanians, holds much the same position in Rumanian political life as M. Maček, the Croat leader, in Yugoslavia. The two men have something in common in their caution and in their obstinate attachment to ideological theories. And like M. Maček, M. Maniu, now an elderly politician, is criticised by his younger followers for his inactivity.

M. Ghelmegeanu, who is now Minister of Communications, told me very frankly how difficult was the position of Rumania between Germany and Russia. Every Rumanian, he said, who attached himself to a foreign Great Power inevitably committed political suicide. Carp and Margiloman had ruined their careers by their pro-German sympathies. To-day, the star of Titulescu had been eclipsed, probably for ever, by his pro-Russian policy. M. Ghelmegeanu was yet another supporter of the policy of good neighbourliness.

I think that in one respect the views of these three clever Rumanians coincide. They believe that the smaller states of central and south-eastern Europe must rely on themselves and co-operate as far as possible in order to maintain their independence. In particular, they are convinced that Rumania must play her cards very carefully in the game of European power politics. She must wait and watch while the European drama unfolds itself. There must be no repetition of the tragedy of 1916. In other words, Rumania must adapt her policy to the preponderance of Great Power strength. She will not fight, if she can help it, for any ideo-logy. She does not want to see either Russians or Germans marching through her territory.

M. Lugoseanu, M. Gafencu and M. Ghelmegeanu are out-standing examples of the young Europeanised Rumanian. A more purely local type is M. Pamfilio Secearu, the owner and editor of *Currentul* and the possessor of the most vitriolic pen in Europe. Dark as a gipsy, broad-shouldered, self-made, vigorous, violent, pro-Italian and anti-Semitic, he gave me one of the most amusing, if slightly exhausting, mornings in my life. For an hour he harangued me on the decadence and deficiencies of Britain. Were we blind to what was happen-ing in Europe? Were our young men so pappy that they still talked platitudes of pacifism to an armed world? As he jerked out his short, staccato sentences, he stumped his room, his fists clenched and his thick, black hair bristling. Historical allusions flew from his mouth like sparks from an anvil. Athens, Carthage, all the vanished empires of the past were marshalled to show the inevitable fate of peoples who grew soft through luxury. I stood up to him as best I could, telling him that if we were slow to bite we never let go. His white teeth flashed beneath his burly black moustache.

"Why do you neglect and despise us?" he said vehem-mently. "Can't you feel the new life that is pulsing here? In fifty years, in twenty-five years—bah!—in ten years, Ru-mania will be one of the great countries of the world!'

"Come," he said. Then he seized me by the arm and drag-ged me off to inspect his new office, built at great expense and superlatively modern. As *Currentul* is not a big money-maker as newspapers go, many Rumanians wonder if cer-tain foreign reactionary states have not something more than an academic interest in its fortunes. As we went from room to room Pamfilio's pride swelled with every step. And every few seconds he turned to me with a "Can you beat this in London?"

I said confidently that we could—but I was not sure. Such

grandiose surroundings were rare in a London newspaper office.

Slightly overwhelmed, I crawled back to his editorial room. He should have been out of breath, for he is plump. But his energy was not exhausted. He took me out on to a balcony. All Bucharest was at our feet.

He swept a pugilistic arm towards his own magnificent new building. "This is the new Rumania in which I believe," he shouted. Then he pointed to a low, dirty quarter beneath us. "That's the old Rumania. That has to be destroyed; that's Jewish. That's why I hate Jews. They cling to the East."

The quarter was not Jewish. But Pamfilio's stream of words had something of the magnificence of a mountain torrent. I do not know how far he will go. He is too tempestuous, too extreme, and I imagine that like most politicians he can change his opinions with the wind. But if the young generation has but a hundredth part of his dynamic energy, Rumania will indeed be a great country.

I had not been able to follow the trend of Pamfilio's argument. All that I could deduce from his violent abuse was an obvious desire that Britain should be strong. And this is less curious than it seems. During the past two years I have been amazed not only at the number, but also at the different types, of people abroad who want Britain to be strong. I should not exclude even Signor Mussolini from these different categories. It is true that the desire springs mainly from fear and self-interest. But it is also prompted by other considerations. There are many Europeans who see the unfolding of the present European drama as the approach to a second Punic War, with Britain and Germany in the rôles of Carthage and Rome. They want us to win for two reasons. They are satisfied that we have no territorial ambitions in Europe. They realise that, although we are Imperialists, we are reasonably tolerant and do not bully overmuch. The Germans want their subject races not only to respect the mailed fist of Germany, but also to feel it.

Curiously, too, the Anglo-Rumanian Society in Bucharest is almost the most active and best-organised in Europe, and I have had first-hand experience of many of these societies. It is run almost single-handed by a young Rumanian called Mateescu. His enthusiasm is sometimes irritatingly overwhelming, but he deserves a gold medal for his work. In a country where British influence has been small in the past and where British culture is little known he has done marvels. English lessons are now immensely popular, and from small beginnings and with little help from Britain the English school in Bucharest has now over a thousand pupils.

In Cluj, the attractive university town of Transylvania, I found a similar progress and a more democratic spirit. Here the excellent Professor Grimm has taught a class of some two to three hundred young Rumanian students not only to speak fluent English, but also to appreciate the British conception of life. I talked to many of them. I inspected the University and the students' hostels, which are run on somewhat similar lines to our English colleges at a tenth of the cost. I lunched and dined with the professors. I was impressed by the sane and healthy outlook of the students. Their eagerness and their faith in life were enthusiastic. Their ambitions were already defined. Every student to whom I spoke knew already what he or she wanted to do in life. I was surprised by their implicit trust in Britain's power to keep the peace of Europe, and their belief in the League of Nations was stimulating and a little pathetic. I think that we all must alter our preconceived notions about the decadence of the Rumanian people.

It is true that one can still find many examples of the old Rumania, especially in Bucharest. Moral standards are still low. Political corruption and commercial dishonesty are still rife. It is still difficult for a pretty typist to obtain employment without surrendering herself to her employer. British Consuls still warn British girl artistes against accepting an engagement in any Rumanian town. In Bucharest itself there is more carmine to lip and nail space than in any other capital in Europe, and woman in her fleshiest sense is still the main attraction of the middle-aged Bucharest citizen.

During my 1938 visit I did not go to any low night haunt, but I was taken to the Melody Bar, the fashionable dancing place of Bucharest. It was crowded to its full capacity. It was eminently respectable. The women were smart and expensively dressed. The men, most of them over fifty, looked tired, as though they had had to work too hard to pay for their partners' clothes. The hard work I suppose, was a figment of my own imagination, and the tired and heavy eyelids probably were the result of too many sleepless nights. I found the place boring, and, as I always do when I am bored, I could not help contrasting the display of wealth inside with the poverty in the streets.

On the surface, at any rate, Bucharest is a city made for women. Its shops and its amusements cater for women. In the Calea Victoriei, the Bond Street of Bucharest, you sometimes see two women walking together, but rarely two men.

Moreover, the average Bucharest male of over forty is lazy. He prefers a job in a government department to a business office. Bucharest is a city of barbers' shops. No government official shaves himself. He goes to his Ministry early, reads the newspapers till ten, and then strolls over to his favourite barber's shop. It is his club. He meets his friends here and spends a pleasant hour in discussing politics or the latest Bucharest gossip. In the afternoon he spends a similar hour in his favourite café, which is his second club.

Doubtless, there are many Rumanian officials who work long hours on end, and perhaps I am guilty of exaggeration. But I owe one back to Pamfilio, and in any case it is an exaggeration with much truth in it. The result of this easy-going indifference is that the commerce of Rumania is largely in the hands of the Jews, and, if they were expelled, the economic life of the country would come to an immediate standstill. As things are, the happy-go-lucky inefficiency of the Bucharest Rumanian is mainly responsible for the periodical waves of anti-Semitism which submerge the country.

This contrast of the old Rumania and the new obtrudes itself on the foreign visitor wherever he goes. Both pictures are true. To-day, Rumania stands at the cross-roads of her history, and her rate of progress depends on how quickly the energy of the new Rumania can overcome the inertia of the old. Personally, I am prepared to put my money on the new Rumania and the new generation.

CHAPTER TWELVE

I ARRIVED IN Rumania at a most exciting moment in her political life. Only two months before, the Tatarescu Government had been defeated at the elections, and a Government defeat in a Rumanian election is sufficiently rare to make a political crisis inevitable. The minority Government of M. Goga had taken the place of the Parliamentary administration of M. Tatarescu. A distinguished dramatist, M. Goga was a clown as a politician. His anti-Semitism, as rabid as that of the notorious Herr Streicher, was not confined to the Jews of his own country, and from a prominent Englishman in Bucharest I received a first-hand account of his conversation with the new Rumanian Prime Minister.

M. Goga, whose anti-Jewish mania made him pro-German and anti-French, was fulminating against M. Blum, who was then Prime Minister of France. Blum was a Jew. Rumania could have no dealings with a Government of Jews.

The Englishman thought fit to remind M. Goga that the British Secretary of State for War was also a Jew.

"That is quite different," said the fanatical Rumanian. "In Britain a Jew rises to power by his own merits. In France he is put there by a combined conspiracy of the Jewish group which dominates French finance and French politics."

Holding these views, M. Goga had little chance of political survival. On achieving office, he had dissolved Parliament and had promulgated a series of anti-Semitic decrees which had caused panic among Rumania's 900,000 Jews, and which had had the inevitable result of reducing the country's industry and finances to chaos. Then the King had stepped in, had dismissed the Goga Government, and had proclaimed his new semi-authoritarian Constitution.

The voting for the new Constitution took place on the day of my arrival. I have little faith in plebiscites that are held in any country east of the Rhine and south of the Baltic. The result is always an inevitable victory for the powers who conduct the plebiscite. In Rumania it gave a favourable vote of ninety-nine per cent. Yet in Bucharest, and, doubtless, all over the country, many voted "for" who spoke more or less openly "against". One high official told me that he was opposed to the new Constitution because he was a monarchist. The King had now taken the last emergency measures. He had removed all the buffers between himself and the people. If to-morrow there were dissatisfaction, it would fall on the King's head. When I asked this official why he voted for the Constitution and yet criticised it so strongly, he replied: "My pen belongs to the Government of the day; my tongue is my own."

In spite of these criticisms I was struck by the fact that the voting took place without any disturbance. Indeed, the only excitement was provided, not by domestic politics, but by another extraordinary diplomatic incident in a Bolshevik Legation. A few days previously, all Bucharest had been thrilled by the story that M. Butenko, the local Soviet Minister, had disappeared. From Moscow M. Litvinoff had thundered accusations of kidnapping against the Rumanian Government. Now came the news, later fully authenticated, that Butenko had fled to Rome in order to escape the murderous intentions of the Moscow Ogpu agents in his own Legation.

Otherwise, voting day was more of a national holiday than a political occasion, and I formed the opinion that among the rank and file of the population there was considerable enthusiasm for the ideals of the new Constitution which were expressed in the slogan: "honest administration and less politics."

There was, too, some admiration for the astuteness of King Carol, who was credited with letting the pendulum, personified by M. Goga, swing to the extreme Right with the deliberate intention of preparing public opinion both at home and abroad for his own new Constitution. If this is true, King Carol certainly achieved a large measure of success.

I was in London when the Goga Government came into power, and I saw one very high British official who was seriously perturbed. He predicted the worst, including the entry of Rumania into the German orbit of influence. He was vastly relieved when the Goga Government went and King Carol's milder régime took its place. Had Rumania gone straight from the Tatarescu administration to the new Constitution, the transition would have been too abrupt, and many people both in Rumania and abroad would have been shocked.

No visitor can remain for twenty-four hours in Bucharest without realising the dominating influence of the King. He occupies a position halfway between that of a dictator and a constitutional monarch. His power is great. Yet it is circumscribed by the necessity of placating the politicians, by an inborn respect for the decencies of kingship, and by a natural caution.

I did not see him during my 1938 visit. But in 1937 I had a long audience with him. The Royal Palace, which is situated in the heart of the city, is much more like the English idea of a king's palace than King Boris's converted Pasha's house in Sofia, or even the new Yugoslav Palace on Dedinje. Its large courtyard always reminds me of Buckingham Palace, and the ceremonial changing of the Royal guard adds to the resemblance. The interior, too, looks and is English. When I was there, the whole palace was being modernised inside and re-decorated by the London firm of Maple's.

King Carol surrounds himself with more kingly pomp than any other Balkan monarch. King Boris is ultra-democratic in manner. Prince Paul of Yugoslavia sits down beside you and offers you a cigarette from his own case. King Carol sits rather stiffly on a throne-like chair behind a high desk. He smokes innumerable cigarettes in a long holder. But he does not offer one to his visitor, not even to foreign diplomatists, including His Britannic Majesty's Minister. His manner is slightly nervous. He lacks much of the personal charm of

King Boris and Prince Paul. But he is shrewd and extremely intelligent, and he understands the politics of his country and the character of his people. He has two desires: to make Rumania prosperous and to keep his throne. He may do both. He reminds me forcibly of the Prime Minister's remark about King Magnus in Mr. Bernard Shaw's *The Apple Cart*: "One man who has a mind and knows it can always beat ten men who haven't and don't."

In appearance, too, King Carol is not unlike Sir Cedric Hardwicke's make-up as King Magnus. He is fair and has very blue eyes with long, fair eyelashes. He looks fit and robust. His cheeks glow with the healthy pink of the English hunting man. He is at his best in the open air, and prefers his country palace at Sinaia to Bucharest.

When I saw him, he was dressed in a uniform of British Air Force blue. I opened the conversation by congratulating him on having accepted the honorary post of Patron of the Anglo-Rumanian Society. At once he began to expatiate on the necessity of improving Anglo-Rumanian relations. He seemed a little hurt by Britain's indifference to Rumania.

"I realise," he said, "that the Hungarians are very successful propagandists with the British ruling class. They give the English a good time, they speak English, they like the same things: sport, shooting, a country gentleman's life. We Rumanians are not so advanced. But Rumania is worth cultivating. The possibilities of her future are immense."

He asked nothing more than that the British should come to Rumania and see the country for themselves. He told me that of all the many foreign books on Rumania that he had read only one had succeeded in capturing the spirit of the Rumanian people. This was Mr. D. J. Hall's *Rumanian Furrow*. He expressed to me his own fervent desire to visit Britain.

I am sure that he spoke from his heart and not merely as a compliment. Hitherto, however, ill-luck has dogged his steps. He was to have paid a state visit to London in the late autumn of 1935. On the eve of King Carol's departure King George contracted his fatal illness. Another visit arranged for the autumn of 1936 had to be postponed owing to King Edward's abdication. Yet a third postponement, again on the eve of the King's departure, was caused by Herr Hitler's dramatic coup in Austria.

I should say that, where Britain is concerned, King Carol has an inferiority complex. Certainly he has been cruelly treated by the British Press. Many of the stories that have been written about him are totally untrue. Admittedly, there is or was Madame Lupescu. But the King is hard-working and abstemious, and he is not the only monarch who has had a mistress. His tastes are simple. He likes a game of bridge and is fond of classical music. But for six days of every week he is at his desk from early morning till late at night.

Once again I must stress the folly of antagonising potential friends, especially when they are as well-disposed as King Carol. For the King has strong pro-British sympathies. He would not be his mother's son if he had not. Moreover, he regards Britain as the bulwark of the monarchical system, and in so far as the different stage of development of his country allows he tries to model himself on the British ideal of kingship.

In order to destroy the popularity of the Iron Guard the King had to embody in the new Constitution some of the more popular features of the Iron Guard programme. The country was tired of the wide-spread corruption which flourished under the Rumanian parliamentary system. The new Constitution curbs the activities of the politicians. But this is no excuse for branding King Carol as a Nazi or Fascist. He is not. Nor has he any wish or intention to put his neck under the heel of any dictator. He is essentially a man of caution.

I spoke to him about foreign affairs. I referred especially to the unsatisfactory state of Rumania's relations with Bulgaria. He was more guarded in his replies than King Boris or Prince Paul had been, but he spoke shrewdly and with more freedom than I had been warned to expect. Relations with Bulgaria, he told me, were improving. He referred to the new train-ferry across the Danube as an example of the improvement. But he was against territorial revision.

"You cannot tell where it will stop," he said with some truth.

His general attitude was much the same as that of M. Stojadinović. Rumania, he said, would not join any pact or make any pledges which might involve her in an attack on Germany. The Little Entente served a useful purpose so long as it was limited to keeping an ambitious Hungary in her place. It would not operate if Czechoslovakia were attacked by Germany. He was in favour of good relations with all Rumania's neighbours, including Russia. But there must be no Russian interference in Rumania's internal affairs and, above all, no Russian armies marching through Rumanian territory to the aid of anyone. In a sentence, the King is a supporter of the "politique de bon voisinage" in the sense that small nations must face geographical facts, and that peace, so necessary to Rumania's progress, is not to be sacrificed light-heartedly for an ideological adventure. Rumania came into the Great War too soon and suffered cruelly. She will not repeat her mistake.

The King is fond of sport and, as I took my leave, he said he hoped that I would come back to Rumania to fish and shoot. He himself is a good shot, and his eighteen-years-old son, Prince Mihai, is even better. King Carol would like to play golf, too, but he remembers M. Briand's disastrous game with Mr. Lloyd George at Cannes, and he is afraid of making himself ridiculous in the eyes of his people.

The British Minister once asked him to play on the Bucharest course.

"No," he said regretfully, "that would be all right in England. It won't do here."

I think that the British picture of King Carol is out of focus. He has certain weaknesses of character. He may lack the graces of Prince Paul, and the wide erudition and disarming frankness of King Boris, but he is their equal in political intelligence. I should say that he was the shrewdest politician of the three. He made on me the impression of a hard-working and thoroughly capable ruler, who had his finger on the nation's pulse and knew as well as any of his ministers how to prescribe for its various diseases, including its occasional epidemics of German measles. I think that expert opinion in Bucharest will agree with this view.

Although Rumania is divided almost equally into two political camps, the one democratic, the other semi-authoritarian, the King's cautious attitude towards foreign affairs meets with considerable support. It is an attitude which is not properly understood in Britain. It is condemned by Russia.

In the summer of 1938 M. Litvinoff expressed his opinion in the hard-hitting sentence: "For a small and weak country to speak now of neutrality means to declare that she refuses the assistance of the League, friends and allies, and invites all those who wish to rape her to do so."

This is, of course, an *ex parte* statement and does not represent the real situation. Neither Rumania nor the other Balkan states have any intention of refusing the assistance of the League or of potential allies. But they are in the position of soldiers in the front trenches. They want to feel sure that the assistance of their friends will arrive before disaster overtakes them. They have seen the fate of other nations who have relied on the League. They suspect its strength. They are tired of being told that "moral force" is the determining factor in all wars. They know what "moral force" did for Abyssinia. Above all, they are suspicious of Russia's assistance. For if they fear Germany, the Balkans have no love of Russia.

If Rumania or, say, Yugoslavia were faced with the alternative of hostile violation by Germany or friendly violation

by Russia, many of her people would consider German violation as the lesser of two evils. But neither Rumania nor
Yugoslavia has the slightest intention of allowing herself to
be raped by anyone. Both countries will resist economic
penetration to the best of their powers. They will certainly
fight if their frontiers are invaded. But they seek to postpone
the evil day as long as possible, relying on the democratic
Great Powers to increase their own strength and that of the
League to an extent that will make aggression anywhere in
Europe impossible. It is a policy of "safety-first", but if its
armchair critics abroad were Rumanians or Yugoslavs most
of them, I think, would approve the Carol or the Stojadinović policy.

To some extent the political divisions in Rumania are
divisions of age. On the whole, although there are some notable exceptions, the older men lean towards democracy in
the circumscribed form in which democracy is to be understood in the Balkans. They have been brought up in the
parliamentary tradition.

During my visits to Rumania I have now met a goodly
number of the leading Rumanian politicians, and at the
house of the genial and talented M. Tatarescu, the former
Prime Minister and as much as anyone the confidant of King
Carol, I was introduced to several members of the new semi-
authoritarian Cabinet. All were professional politicians, but
in their morning coats and striped trousers they looked more
like professors at a colleague's wedding. My left-hand neighbour at luncheon was a poet. On my right sat M. Comnen,
the new Minister for Foreign Affairs. He talked learnedly
and moderately on Rumania's position in Europe, but I was
so busy admiring his beautiful French that I listened only fitfully to his well-reasoned argument. He spoke with the precision and easy grace of a French academician. He looked
French. I put him down, I hope not mistakenly, as a man
soaked in French culture and therefore as a Francophil. In the
gathering I saw no potential dictators. These men were as far

removed from Fascists as the gentle Mr. Maxton is from Stalin.

The younger men are admittedly different. Their ideas are still in a state of flux. But I think it is true to say that, on the whole, they are more open-minded than the older generation, more critical of democracy. Some are frankly pro-Nazi and anti-Semitic. A larger number is pro-Fascist. Many, probably the majority, do not see their way clearly. They fear the aggressive Imperialism of Germany. But their fear is mingled with a varying degree of admiration for German thoroughness and German efficiency.

In this confusion of opinions it behoves the foreign diplomatist to move carefully and to rid himself of pre-conceived notions. There is, I think, a tendency in London and Paris to bank too heavily on M. Titulescu, to assume that he is indispensable to Rumania and that his return to power is inevitable. I should be the last to deny the capabilities of M. Titulescu. He is only fifty-five and, while there is breath, few things are impossible. But I think that the assumption of his indispensability is probably an illusion. He has already had two long innings. There is no third innings in cricket and only very rarely in politics. In Rumanian eyes he is the foremost champion of the Franco-Soviet pact. It does not fit in very well with the new policy of good neighbourliness. At the present moment he is certainly out of favour.

There is another factor which militates against the likelihood of his return. During the election of December, 1937, he lost ground heavily. He came back to the country, threw in his lot with the Maniu Party, and promised to deliver an election address to the peasants. He did not deliver it in person but sent a gramophone record of his speech. This record did him harm.

Owing to the clashes between democrats and anti-democrats the political situation in Rumania often looks ugly. But it is, I think, never quite so serious as it appears. The Rumanians are sometimes violent in speech, but as a people they

o

are easy-going and good-natured. They are, too, great sticklers for good manners, and in politics as in any other walk of life good manners are an excellent brake on hot tempers. The Rumanian workman is civil. Politeness comes naturally to the Rumanian peasant. The Rumanian "social-ite" bends himself double. After a long round of official dinners in Bucharest I could hardly refrain from giggling. Every night it took nearly half-an-hour to get the male guests into the dining-room. Everyone stood back, bowing and saying, "After you."

The scene reminded me vividly of an old French song which I used to hear in the *cafés-chantants* of Paris over thirty years ago. In a long series of couplets the song told the life-story of two men who were so polite that they missed all their opportunities: their promotion, the girl of their heart, their official honours. Each couplet ended with the refrain: "Après vous, mon cher Alphonse; après vous, mon cher Emile." In the end the two men die and go to Heaven. St. Peter is so bored by their eternal *après vous* that he locks the gates and consigns them to Hell. And there the devil, who has no use for politeness, tumbles them into the flames with his pitch-fork.

With all this politeness, the Rumanians have a keen sense of humour, and Bucharest lives on its anecdotes. It was an anti-Semite who asked me the riddle: "Why was the anti-Semitic Goga dismissed?" When I could not guess it, he replied: "Because of the 'syn-a-goga', of course."

Every cultured Rumanian is a born raconteur, and this anecdote, a true one, about Prince Antoine Bibescu may appeal to English and American readers.

A few years ago a high Rumanian official was sent hur-riedly on a special mission to Washington. On his first night he was invited to an official dinner. His heavy luggage had not arrived, and he had only a dinner-jacket with him. He put it on, hoping for the best, but when he reached the house at which he was to dine, he found to his horror that every man was wearing a dress-coat. He dashed to the Rumanian Legation, found a Poole-made dress-coat belonging to Prince Antoine Bibescu, who, of course, had several, borrowed it without permission, and succeeded in getting to his destination without being unduly late. After dinner Prince Bibescu, two inches taller and much stouter than his colleague, came up to him, looked him over and said: "Who made your coat?"

"Oh, it's one of Poole's," said the colleague rather nervously.

"H'm," said the Prince, "so's mine. He doesn't seem to make so well for you as he does for me."

Then he beamed with satisfaction, as he added: "I expect he takes more trouble over me."

I do not think that we shall have a revolution in Rumania just yet awhile. Good nature is the mother of tolerance, and like most easy-going peoples the Rumanians are learning the art of giving six inches before Discontent takes six yards for itself. Twenty years after the war Hungary is still a feudal country, and its feudal barons look with hungry eyes to Slovakia and Rumania for an opportunity to recover their lost estates. The big Rumanian landowners have had most of their acres clipped from them by the post-war agrarian reform. They have taken the clipping, perhaps not gladly, but, at any rate, with that resigned shrug of the shoulders of which Prince Bibescu is the chief exponent.

CHAPTER THIRTEEN

THE MORE THE foreign visitor sees of Rumania, the more likely he is to conclude that it is a country of contradictions. As he strolls through the broad, well-kept streets of Bucharest and admires the imposing public buildings, he says to himself: " The Rumanians are right; this is indeed a Western capital; a Brussels if not a Paris." While he muses, he is jostled by a hawker dressed in home-spun peasant clothes and carrying two baskets of fruit suspended Oriental-wise from a pole balanced on his shoulder. The hawker salaams in apology, and the visitor wonders if he is in Singapore. He asks a Rumanian policeman the way, and a smartly dressed constable directs him with the good nature and courtesy of a London "bobby". The next day he opens his newspaper and reads some revolting story of Jewish villagers being rounded up and beaten by the Rumanian police.

You find these contradictions and contrasts everywhere you go. Surprising as it may seem, it is nevertheless true that foreign military experts rate the work of the Rumanian General Staff higher than that of the Yugoslav or Czechoslovak General Staffs. Yet there are no proper cranes to land the munitions and guns which arrive from abroad and very few roads on which to move them to strategic points. The attention of the General Staff has been drawn frequently to these defects, but little or nothing is done. In this pleasant land which is being so rapidly Westernised time still moves with Oriental lethargy.

If you are a British visitor, every Rumanian business man you meet tells you of his desire to do more trade with Britain. Yet economically Rumania is bound to Germany who now that she has annexed Austria dominates Rumania's foreign trade. Owing to the currency difficulties which afflict all the states of central and south-eastern Europe, Rumania has clearing arrangements with her foreign customers. The object of these agreements is to maintain a certain fixed proportion in the trade between two individual countries. It is a thinly-disguised return to barter. You buy with what you sell. Rumania has all the worst of her clearing arrangement with Germany. The Reich takes from Rumania grain and petroleum products. With Austria she is by far the biggest individual buyer of these products. But she does not pay Rumania in cash. The money for these goods is deposited in blocked marks in Berlin. For these blocked marks Rumania wanted certain raw materials which she needs. When the arrangement was made, Germany promised the raw materials. But now Germany cannot deliver them. Instead she tries to force on Rumania textiles which Rumania does not want and arms which she would rather buy elsewhere. When I was in Bucharest in March, 1938, Rumania had close on £2,000,000 locked up in Germany. She needs this money for re-armament and for the payment of the interest on her foreign-loans. Yet she is unable to free herself from her economic shackles.

When you talk to an educated Rumanian, he seems to you, that is if he is not an Iron Guard sympathiser, the most tolerant person in the world. Yet Rumania has the reputation of treating her minorities worse than most other countries do. I am not greatly impressed by the argument that, because a country treats its minorities well, the minority should be satisfied. Everything depends on the nationality of the minority. If the minority is composed of members of a proud, imperialist race and is discontented, it will be discontented under the best treatment. A long experience of central Europe has made me realise the difficulty of drawing any fair ethnological division. But I think that the Versailles peace-makers blundered in laying so much stress on the importance of geographical frontiers and in including such large minorities in the new states of central and south-eastern Europe. Large minorities are a nuisance to any state. To a small state they may be a disaster. And Rumania has large minorities: 1,500,000 Hungarians, 900,000 Jews, 790,000 Ukrainians, 725,000 Germans, and 290,000 Bulgarians. Of these minorities the most dissatisfied are the Hungarians, and the dissatisfaction is fomented from outside. In Budapest Hungarian Irredentist propaganda never ceases.

Mr. Beverley Nichols is not the only Englishman who has heard the story of the charming old widow who, having lost her all, saves up enough money to return to her lost home in Transylvania in order to scatter a handful of Hungarian soil on her dead husband's grave. At the frontier the Rumanians discover the packet of soil and take it away from the old lady. This story has been going the rounds of Europe for many years. The Hungarians have other ambitions in Transylvania than the scattering of Hungarian soil on graves. They are essentially an attractive race. But they are proud. Like the Germans they regard themselves as a Herrenvolk. They look down on the Czechs and on the Rumanians, and herein lies the root of the whole minority problem.

Personally I should be in favour of returning to Hungary the solidly Hungarian parts of Transylvania and Slovakia. But few Hungarians would be satisfied with this revision even if it were offered to them. The ruling class in Hungary wants the old frontiers with all the large minorities.

The Rumanians, who in the past suffered under Hungarian rule and who understand these Hungarian ambitions much better than the British do, are only human. They react unpleasantly. The Hungarians in Rumania have their rights, but it would be absurd to pretend that they are liked or that they are well-treated.

Another Rumanian contrast is provided by the bourgeoisie and the peasantry. The peasants are hard-working, full of endurance, and infinitely patient. Their physique is splendid, and nowhere in Europe will you find men who, with good leadership, would make better soldiers. Not that they have strong martial instincts. Like the great mass of the people in every country, they have no wish to fight anyone, and all that they ask from life is: a good harvest, a good wife, a roof to cover their heads, and a little extra money to buy a new hat-ribbon for the holidays. When one compares their homely fare and simple faith with the café life and material sophistication of the bourgeoisie, it is hard to believe that the two classes are of the same race.

Collectively, Rumania makes on me the impression of a country with growing pains. It is, I think, a healthy child. With ten years of good nursing in the form of honest administration—and if King Carol can provide the years and the honesty, he will go down to history—I have no fears for its future.

Apart from the richness of her natural resources, Rumania is also a most beautiful country. The scenery is extraordinarily varied. The very name of Transylvania suggests pixies and witches and beautiful princesses whose long hair becomes entangled in the trees. The Carpathians are the Rockies of Europe, and the Transylvanian Alps the Blue Mountains of our fairy-tales. There is the coast of the Black Sea, rocky but not barren, for here there is a wealth of subtropical flowers and vineyards which have yielded wine since the days of the Romans. "See Balcic and live" is the Rumanian's invitation to the most picturesque of her Black Sea resorts. And the monotony of the great plains, richer in soil and softer in colour than the Russian steppes, but giving the same impression of boundless eternity, is relieved by the picturesque and sometimes bizarre churches and monasteries which are dotted over the whole countryside.

For over three hundred years Rumania has been a country of architects, and, although the Byzantine influence is strong, Rumanian architecture has a charm and originality of its own. Some of the finest churches and boyars' houses are to be found in Bucharest and its environs, and with the Baedeker bug in my blood I devoted all my spare time to sightseeing. My cicerone was the excellent Mateescu. Alas! I had also to make use of him as an interpreter. Although Rumanian should come easily to anyone who knows Slav and Latin, I have never learnt it. I have already begun to remedy this defect, for without some knowledge of the language it is impossible to hold any conversation with the people. And it is from the people, and not from the politicians, of a country that one learns the fundamental truths.

The most curious of the churches near Bucharest is the tiny Fundenii Doamnei constructed nearly two hundred and fifty years ago. It is an Orthodox Church, but the outside walls are decorated with frescos in Persian style. The ceiling and inside walls give the pictorial history of Christ's life. In the porch are grotesque pictures of the sufferings of the martyrs and of the punishment awaiting sinners. One fearsome fresco shows a "spate" of mortals being swept into the cavernous mouth of a waiting leviathan. These mural paintings reminded me vividly of the punishment pictures which decorate the ceiling of the Regent's Court at Kloeng-Koeng in Bali.

The most beautiful boyar's house is the Palais Mogoșoaia about four miles from Bucharest. It is the home of Princess Marthe Bibescu, the well-known Rumanian authoress. The palace has a Venetian effect, and from the graceful loggia on the first floor you look down on the placid waters of the lake below. A superb stone terrace leads down to the lake, and on a still, sunny day the reflections are so vivid that it is hard to tell whether the house is in the water or on dry land. Mogoșoaia is one of the show homes of Europe.

As for monasteries surely no religious sect has had such a partiality for them as the Orthodox Church. Near Bucharest there are so many that to-day they have been put to odd uses. If I give first place to the Vacareşti monastery, it is because of its magnificent site on a small hill overlooking Bucharest and the surrounding plain. It belongs to the type of fortress-monastery, and I had to obtain a special permit from the Rumanian Government in order to visit it, not because it is a military fortress, but because it is now the chief prison of Bucharest.

The architectural glory of the monastery is its church, which is regarded as the finest in the Bucharest district. The interior is richly decorated. It contains a valuable collection of ancient ikons, and the approach to the ikonastasis, guarded by eight magnificent stone pillars, is majestic. But I was more interested in the floating human wreckage than in the standing stone. Rumanians are said to treat their prisoners badly. But I saw no sign of harshness. Indeed, inside the huge quadrangle with its gardens and grass plots there was considerable liberty. Although it was early March, the sun beat down fiercely on the sheltered ground, and some two hundred prisoners, comically dressed in brown striped pyjamas, were doing forced sun-bathing in the open. I saw other prisoners reclining on the cloistered balcony of the Abbot's house. One man was lying flat on his face with his feet crossed and his arms stretched out. He looked like the back view of a crucifix. I wondered what he was thinking of and if his attitude betokened remorse. Probably he was only enjoying the sun. For these prisoners were convalescents, and the Abbot's house is now the prison hospital.

I strolled about among the prisoners. I confess that my curiosity was even stronger than my sympathy. Yet I felt ill-at-ease, not through fear, but from shame lest I might seem to be prying on the humiliation of others. My apprehension was unnecessary. The prisoners paid little attention to me. They showed no resentment, nor did I notice any pronounced criminal types among them. Most of them looked as if they would not have hurt a fly. One prisoner, detailed to carry the warder's keys while I made my round, bowed and smiled good-humouredly every time he opened a door. Yet among them, the warder told me, were many old " lags " who were no sooner released than they went back to crime.

The warders themselves were not obtrusively in evidence, and during this morning hour of exercise supervision was relaxed. I saw only one sign of unnecessary discipline. The first time that I walked past the group of sun-bathers, the warder grunted an order. The prisoners sprang to their feet, shuffled into line, took off their caps, and waited at attention until I had passed. I felt embarrassed and humiliated.

It was visitors' day at the prison. I left before they were admitted. But as I passed through the main gate, I saw them waiting at the grille. They were mostly peasants, and for every male visitor there were ten women. One woman stood apart beside a large private car. She was young and beautiful. She was dressed in black, but it was a fashionable and expensive black. The peasant women chatted briskly with each other. But the other stood like a statue, the rouge on her lips contrasting vividly with the pallor of her cheeks.

Another former monastery has been converted into the Controceni Palace, and here, amid idyllic surroundings lived Marie, former British princess and Queen-Mother of Rumania. During my 1938 visit she was ill and had gone on a vain journey to Italy and Germany in order to seek relief from the incurable disease which ended her life a few months later. But in 1937 I had a long and memorable audience with her. The Palace was the home of Carmen Sylva, Rumania's poet-Queen and mother-in-law of Queen Marie. As I drove through the old monastery-gate, I remembered the early romance of Queen Marie's husband who wanted to marry Mademoiselle Vacarescu, Carmen Sylva's lady-in-waiting. Carmen Sylva, who had an artistic and romantic temperament, favoured the marriage, but her husband forbade it.

Queen Marie herself was artistic and romantic, although not romantic enough in 1937 to approve Madame Lupescu. She was an attractive and highly intelligent woman, and, when I saw her, her face still bore the traces of her former captivating beauty. Her personality was stamped on every square inch of the Palace. As I went up the main staircase, I passed portraits of Queen Victoria and the Prince Consort, who were her grandparents. And at the top I was confronted by a delicate Lazlo painting of Queen Marie herself.

In the large drawing-room where I waited for five minutes was a huge Byzantine fireplace. Above it hung a black ebony crucifix. There were crucifixes everywhere. On a large table stood rows of animals in Royal Copenhagen china. The long windows looked out on to the park and gardens. Then I was taken to an upstairs room with a vaulted beam ceiling and a carved stone fireplace. The atmosphere was heavy with the scent of flowers. From the rafters hung a large wooden model of an old sailing-ship. There were more crucifixes, and conspicuous in its wooden frame was a large ikon. The room, lit by a dim-religious light, was so dark that for a moment I thought that it was empty. Then two Pekinese sniffed at my heels, and from the background I heard a soft, pleasant voice call my name.

Queen Marie was half-sitting, half-reclining on a divan. Half-a-dozen books and a copy of the *Revue de Paris* were lying by her side. As I came forward, she rose and took a chair beside a small tea-table. And while she poured me out a cup of tea she talked with an easy fluency on many subjects. She told me that she had read my book on Russia, and I felt a momentary embarrassment as I tried to recollect what I had written about her, remembering suddenly a remark which her daughter, the Queen of Yugoslavia, had made to an English friend of mine: "Mamma is not very pleased with Mr. Lockhart."

Queen Marie, however, made no reference to her displeasure. She was too pre-occupied with the political situation in Russia. She was anti-Communist, but was sure that the Rumanian peasant would never go Bolshevik. He was too practical, too full of commonsense, too attached to his own plot of land.

From Russia we entered the field of foreign affairs. The Queen, who was very pro-British, was worried by our inactivity in Rumania. The German propagandists were working night and day. Why did Britain do nothing? The Germans knew how to play on the feelings of hate and mistrust which the young Rumanians felt for Russia. Britain seemed to regard Russia as a desirable and useful ally.

She was interested, too, in the latest news of the Duke of Windsor, for whom she had a great affection. She told me that she had written six articles on the Coronation, all concerned with King Edward VIII. Then she had had to alter them.

From the Duke of Windsor to King Carol was a natural step. Queen Marie had a mother's desire that her son should do well. She was distressed by some of the King's moral failings. But she praised his intelligence and told me not to believe the rumours that he was influenced politically by Madame Lupescu. Such rumours were ridiculous and showed complete ignorance of the King's character. She was very eager that he should go to England and that he should make a good impression. She talked with complete frankness.

Then, leaving foreign affairs and politics as though they were the curse of a troubled world, she turned to books. Her manner changed. She became witty and vivacious, laughing at the foibles of most authors including herself. She liked authors. She would sooner have been praised as an artist than as a Queen. She herself was an artist in the real sense of the word. She painted; she sculpted; she was a genius as a landscape gardener. But I think she derived most enjoyment from her writing. She told me that she was writing another volume of memoirs, but that, as she had now come down to the present, her difficulties were almost insurmountable. Restraint and reticence were imperative, and restraint and reticence were obstacles to a writer.

Queen Marie was everything that was feminine except in one respect. She had no stupid vanity in her character. Only once did she show any trace of pride. This was when we were comparing notes about lecture tours in the United States.

"The Americans told me", she said, "that I was the only European who has ever stood the rigours of a tour without showing a trace of fatigue, and who did everything he or she was asked to do."

I expect her temperament and superabundant nervous energy carried her through. In that winter of 1937 she looked too frail to stand any fatigue.

She talked, too, of her English literary friends: Barrie, Sir Ronald Storrs, and Sir Stephen Gaselee, the learned librarian of the Foreign Office. Especially Sir Stephen Gaselee, whom she looked up to as her literary mentor. She used to send him her literary articles to read and to criticise. The highest praise she ever received from him, she told me, was when he returned a series of articles with the comment: "Even I learnt something from them!"

The world is rightly suspicious of royal talents which are written up beyond their merits. But Queen Marie was one of the most remarkable women of our times, and I do not think it an exaggeration to say that, if she had been born in a peasant's cottage, she would have risen above her surroundings and made a name for herself. She reminded me forcibly of Millicent, Duchess of Sutherland. Indeed, in their unconventionality, in their romanticism, in the wide range of subjects which interested them both and, not least, in their love of aggressive little Pekinese, the two women had much in common.

At the end of our long conversation she showed me over her special apartments: the huge bedroom with its private little chapel in the alcove, the library with its masses of English books, and even the dentist's room with its marvellous modern chair and electric fittings in white china. There was nothing English about the dentist's chair, and I doubt if there is its like in London. It was the latest product of the German firm of Siemens, Halske.

In recent years Queen Marie had perhaps lost a little of the public favour by her alleged tendency to interfere in politics. And here is yet another Rumanian contradiction. Although Rumania is essentially a country in which women not only are honoured but also are in many respects superior to the men, feminine interference in politics is not tolerated. There has never been a Rumanian Zenobia. There is to-day no provision for a Queen in the Rumanian constitution.

Nevertheless, Queen Marie was still immensely popular, and to the ex-soldiers she was a legendary figure. She had experienced many tragedies in her life, but the one that lived with her was the death of her youngest son. He died as a child during the war and is buried in the Cotroceni church in the quadrangle just opposite the main-door of the Palace. He was the only one of her sons who caused her no trouble, and with the passing of the years her love for him grew. At the time of his death she was distracted, and, in order to forget, she threw herself into her nursing work with complete abandon. Typhus was then raging throughout Rumania. But the Queen paid no attention, going everywhere and exposing herself to the dangers of infection with a reckless bravery which probably drew its strength from the streak of mystic fatalism in her character. In every town and village stories are told of men whose lives she saved by her nursing.

I met one Rumanian whose brother was stricken with typhus. He was in a military hospital near Jassy, and the doctors had given up all hope of saving his life. The Queen visited the hospital, saw the wasted figure, and was told that the man had lost all will to live. She sat with him through the night, and he recovered.

Now that Queen Marie is dead, the legend of these stories will grow. Her weaknesses will be forgotten, and she will become a national heroine. Her apotheosis will not be undeserved, for in the creation of the Greater Rumania she played a nobler and a more efficient part than any Rumanian politician or general.

My stay in Bucharest was all too pleasant. As the days passed, the round of hospitality increased, and in an atmosphere which has often proved fatal to the powers of resistance of British and American diplomats the self-discipline which I had imposed upon myself began to relax. The kindness of Sir Reginald and Lady Hoare was overwhelming, and the official dinners which they arranged for me at the Legation brought with them a glut of political conversations which sometimes lasted until far into the night. Of these conversations, two stick in my mind.

One was with an Austrian ex-naval officer who is to-day the Rumanian representative of a vast American motor-car concern. He was a charming man, progressive, intelligent, humanitarian and impartial. He said that if he were dictator of Europe he would not allow a gun or an aeroplane to be constructed until roads, schools, and hospitals had been built to his satisfaction in every country. He was, perhaps not unnaturally, too prone to measure civilisation by the number of motor-cars. He gave me the approximate figures for Central Europe: 5000 cars in Bulgaria, 12,000 in Hungary, 15,000 in Yugoslavia, 35,000 in Rumania, 65,000 in Austria, and 90,000 in Czechoslovakia. In other words, there is one motor-car to 100 Austrians, to 160 Czechoslovaks, to 571 Rumanians, to 725 Hungarians, to 933 Yugoslavs, and to 1200 Bulgarians. The figures do not represent the potential wealth of Rumania or Yugoslavia. Nor are they a proof of a higher civilisation and culture. But they do represent fairly accurately the present state of what we are pleased to call modern progress in the countries concerned.

The other conversation was with M. Antonescu, the former Rumanian Foreign Minister. He was a fine, cultured old gentleman with charming manners and the mentality of a good European. Although Austria had not yet fallen, Nazi aggressiveness was already raising its ugly head, and M. Antonescu was anxious about the fate of the smaller Central European and Balkan States. He favoured the closest economic relations between Poland, Hungary, Czechoslovakia, Yugoslavia, and Rumania. When I told him that I was going to Prague, he said to me: "Tell Beneš from me that he must make his peace with the Poles at any price."

Without doubt M. Antonescu spoke words of wisdom. But I knew what Dr. Beneš would say. He would shrug his shoulder, express his full agreement, and explain *privatim et seriatim* that he had done his best. And up to now his best had not succeeded. Even during those weeks of relative calm I had seen the figures of the Polish minority in Czechoslovakia swell in the facile imagination of Colonel Beck, the Polish Foreign Minister, from 80,000 to 250,000. Even allowing for the awkward situation of Poland with regard to Germany, I found it hard to understand the Polish hostility to Czechoslovakia except on the ground of the most reprehensible opportunism.

Incidentally, these numerous conversations with Rumanian politicians afforded me a proof of Sir Reginald Hoare's popularity with every class of Rumanian. He is another example of the taciturn diplomatist, and in a country where talking is almost perpetual motion taciturnity is a valuable asset. Sir Reginald speaks rarely and then slowly. He is very English and very gentle and is loved by everything that has life. Yet he nearly made a false start to his Rumanian career.

Soon after he arrived at his new post, he went to luncheon with Queen Marie at the Cotroceni Palace. As he was sitting down, he knocked over his chair. It hit and hurt rather badly the Queen's favourite Pekinese. The Queen was upset, rushed to the dog, and picked it up, comforting it with such soothing expressions as: "did the nasty British Minister hurt you?" On that day Sir Reginald's luck was out. But it returned next week in full measure. He had to go to the Palace to see the Queen, and, as he was shown into her room, the Pekinese rushed to him, jumped up on his lap, and enlisted him as its chief friend.

From that moment all went well, and when Sir Reginald says anything the Rumanians take notice. When I was in Bucharest, every Rumanian was convinced that it was the British Minister's influence which had induced King Carol to get rid of the unpopular Goga Government. The story was probably quite untrue, but it added to Sir Reginald's prestige and popularity.

Twenty years ago he had Labour sympathies combined with political ambitions. But his true *métier* is diplomacy, and he has, I think, no reason to regret the lost possibilities of a Parliamentary career. He has done excellent work in Rumania, for he is shrewd, full of understanding, and infinitely patient. In times of crisis his imperturbable calmness acts like a well-oiled brake on the Rumanian tendency to excitability.

I enjoyed my conversations with Sir Reginald, but, fearing to outstay my welcome, I took a sudden decision. In so far as I had a plan, I had intended to return to Transylvania, to revisit my friends at Cluj, and then to stay for a week or two in Hungary on my way to Vienna. Quite suddenly, and without much consideration, I made up my mind to go back to Zagreb at once. I had, it is true, an instinct that something was going to happen in Vienna sooner than the politicians expected, and to Vienna Zagreb was a convenient stepping-stone. Throughout my journey I had been obsessed by a premonition that this might be the last of my Balkan jaunts for many years. In Bucharest I was a stranger. In Zagreb I had friends of many years' standing with whom I was on terms of what the Germans call "per Du." I wanted to steal a few days of assured enjoyment before moving into the troubled atmosphere of Vienna, Prague and Berlin. Somewhere, too, before my eyes floated the picture of Tania, the young Russian girl, whose beauty and charm and courage had impressed itself so vividly on my mind.

These were the three vague reasons which influenced my decision. As events turned out, it was a fortunate decision,

P

for it gave me an opportunity which I should never have forgiven myself for missing. I take no credit for any prescience. My decision was made on impulse, and, if I am to be honest with myself, it was the third reason that prompted it.

CHAPTER FOURTEEN

THE DISTANCE FROM Bucharest to Zagreb is more than twice
as long as that from Sofia to Bucharest. Yet the train journey
takes only twenty hours as against fourteen. I left Bucharest
in the morning, partly because the morning train is the best,
but mainly because I wished to see the Iron Gates again.

For the first part of the route the train crosses the vast
Wallachian plain. I like plains. They instil in me a melancholy longing. But I do not find them monotonous, and I
am never happier than when I am alone on the treeless moorlands of the island of Lewis in the Hebrides. The Wallachian
plain bears little resemblance to the Hebridean *mahair*. It is
rich and gay with well-tilled fields and luscious grass. Slender
poplars and drooping willows afford a pleasant shade to the
oxen and sheep, and pigs are everywhere, fat, grey-black,
big-tusked, and more like boars than our British pigs. Far
more even than the other Balkan States, Rumania is a pig-
land, and in 1937 she was still exporting pigs by the hundred
thousand to Austria.

But I did see one typical Scottish scene. As I passed a tiny
village with its white-washed houses glistening in the sun, I
saw a rough stretch of grass with goal-posts at each end. They
were crazy goal-posts, made of branches and all askew,
just as you see them in the Scottish Highlands to-day, and on
the sward lusty young peasant boys were kicking a football. In a few years perhaps, the Arsenal will be importing
Rumanian professionals to make a football holiday for
London, and the Arsenal show-men will owe a debt to Scotland. For, if England discovered football, it was Scotland
who taught it to Europe.

I found a continuous diversion in the railway stations.
Peasants carrying live-stock and still wearing their heavy
sheep-skin coats, although the weather was summer-like, got
in and out and, as in Russia, a crowd of villagers stood on the

platform to watch the passing of the train. Conspicuous in the throng stood the Rumanian station-master, resplendent in double-breasted blue coat with gold buttons and a blue uniform cap with scarlet crown. Rumanian station-masters are imposing fellows. They look like a cross between an admiral and the hall-porter of the Waldorf-Astoria in New York.

As we approached the Danube, the scenery changed. The land became undulating and less fertile; the temperature dropped. On leaving Turnu-Severin, where the ruins of the famous Trajan Bridge are still visible, we entered a narrow gorge with high mountains on each side. Our train ran so close to the Danube that at moments we seemed to be on a bridge without parapets. We had reached the passage of the Iron Gates.

As a European Niagara they are disappointing. A chain of low rocks, mostly submerged, with here and there a jagged point showing, spreads itself across the river, and between them the stream swirls slowly and without much foam. Below the rocks I saw green humps which looked like the up-turned keels of wrecked fishing-boats. A French-speaking conductor told me that they were artificial supports on which the Danube fishermen stretched their sturgeon nets.

The Gates acquired their name because formerly they were a bar to all navigation. But for more than forty years now the traffic has been open, and ships pass by a narrow canal which has been cut through the defile on the opposite side of the railway. I saw two long black barges awaiting their turn. They were being drawn by an old-fashioned paddle tug which reminded me of a Mississippi show-boat.

If as rapids the Gates are less imposing than many a Scottish salmon-pool, the mountain scenery is magnificent, and a mile or two higher up the river I had an enchanting view of the tiny island of Ada-Kaleh with its old Turkish fort and minaret standing proudly above the poplar-ringed village.

The population is still Turkish, and here, too, I saw a football ground so close to the river that, when a match is played, the services of a boatman are required to rescue the ball from the Danube.

When we came out of the gorge the mountains receded, leaving a wide plain of grassy marsh-land between them. It was deserted. The only living creature that I saw was a heron, his figure elongated by the shadows of the sunset and his wings pressed round him like a well-fitting morning-coat, as he stood motionless by the side of a narrow stream. The sense of peace was wonderful, and under its influence I spent the rest of the evening in reflection. My Balkan tour was nearly ended. When and in what circumstances should I see these Balkan States again?

During the day I had interspersed my sight-seeing with the reading of F. L. Allen's *Only Yesterday*. It is a history of the prohibition and gangster period in the United States, and the reading of it made me wonder if, morally, political life in the Balkans was worse than, or as bad as, political life in Western Europe and the New World. I came to the conclusion that of all the changes that I had noticed during the last twenty years the most important and the most hopeful had been the civilising process in the Balkan States. It was true that, after the war, they had adopted with more rashness than foresight the ultra-modern forms of democratic government. Since then there had been an inevitable reaction, and the Western democracies had been disappointed. But the greatest mistake the West had made and was still making was its foolish attempt to urge the Balkan democratic foal to gallop before it had learnt to walk. In due time the Balkans would find their own form of democracy. The spirit was there; the rate of progress would depend on the example set by the Western democracies.

After all, less than a hundred and fifty years ago the total electorate of Britain was only a few hundred thousand, and political corruption was on a scale to which the Balkans had never been able to climb. Yet at that time we considered ourselves the most progressive country in the world and were thus regarded by the other nations.

Nor was the boast of "The Peaceful Peninsula" mere figment. The impact of a strong, aggressive Germany had forced the Balkans to look to their defences. But they had no ambition to loose off their guns because they liked the sound. Their desire for peace was universal. If we wanted to make friends in the Balkans, it was time that we stopped writing such inaccurate clichés as "getting over one war and getting ready for the next is their whole life".

The threat to European peace did not come from the Balkans. The danger of the new situation lay in the fact that with the weakening of the general forces of peace the Balkans were once more exposed to the intrigues and machinations of imperialist Great Powers. The foreign secret agents were already there, and they were even more pernicious than the secret police of the local governments, because they were disruptive, whereas the local secret police existed principally to maintain order and to keep individual governments and ministers in power.

Owing to the title of my first book, *British Agent*, many people think that I was engaged in secret service. This is quite incorrect. Still, I have seen something of its workings. During the Great War I was more than once inside the holy of holies near Whitehall from which it was conducted, and I have met some of its chiefs and of its agents. I have the greatest admiration for the courage of secret service agents. I believe in the value of concrete information of the kind procured during the Great War by our Naval Intelligence Department, which was remarkably well-informed about the movements of the German Fleet. But I am profoundly suspicious of the political intelligence supplied by secret service agents, few of whom have had any previous experience. It is absurd to imagine that a secret service agent has reliable sources of political information which are not available

Meeting Notes

to the diplomatic ambassador or minister. If he has, he should be made the minister, and the minister should be sacked.

As for bought information, it is nearly always worse than useless. Sir William Wiseman, who ran our political intelligence in the United States during the Great War, once told me that of the many millions of pounds we spent, eighty per cent. might as well have been poured down a drain. From my own experience I can say the same about the money spent in Russia in 1918.

Secret service, as distinct from naval and military intelligence, is, I suppose, a necessary evil during a war. But in peace-time I should like to see it abolished except for contre-espionage purposes.

My hopes of a few peaceful days in Zagreb were rudely shattered. No sooner had I made my arrival known to the Šverljugas than I received a telephone call from an old Slovene friend. He wanted to talk to me about the Slovene minority in Italy. As he is an Italian subject, it would be unfair to give his name, but among the Slovenes who are Italian subjects, his is a big and honoured name. The minority problems of Europe are complex, and few experts agree how they are to be solved, or if, indeed, they can be solved in any way except by force. But all experts are unanimous in their view that the German and Slovene minorities in Italy are worse treated than any other minority. In particular, the lot of the Slovenes is desperate, for they have no champions in a world which reacts only to fear and force. There are nearly 350,000 of them, concentrated mainly near the frontiers of their own homeland, and they are being subjected to a ruthless process of nationalisation.

Like the Roman emperors on whom he models himself, Signor Mussolini believes that language is the basis of all nationalism, and he is bent on forcing the Italian language on his minority subjects. For sixteen years he has been trying to stamp out Slovene by methods which include the obliteration of Slovene names on Slovene gravestones.

I asked my friend how far the Italian policy of forcible nationalisation had succeeded. He spoke more with bitterness than with anger. He made no attempt to conceal the truth. Among the older Slovenes, he told me, the policy, so far from succeeding, had merely stiffened the Slovene resistance. But with the children it was another matter. In school they were taught nothing but Italian. They had to do their preparation in Italian. Only at home could they learn their own language. Like the Polish mothers during the long years of Poland's partition, the Slovene mothers taught their children to pray in Slovene. But the Duce was more ruthless than Kaisers or Tsars, and from the Slovene point of view the results were not satisfactory. The new generation, my friend said, knew neither Slovene nor Italian correctly. He showed me some letters that he had received from young Slovene soldiers who had been serving in Abyssinia. They were written in a Mumbo-Jumbo of Italian and Slovene, and were incomprehensible to anyone who did not know both languages.

I asked him what hopes he had for the future. He shrugged his shoulders. A warm supporter of the League of Nations, he did not mention Geneva. "If the Germans annex Austria," he said, "Mussolini will have to treat his German minority very differently. Perhaps we may benefit indirectly."

It seemed a slender hope. As we talked, the sun streamed through the open window. The trees in the gardens outside were already heavy with leaf. The birds were singing. What the good people of Zagreb called spring but I called summer was already here. It had come much earlier than usual. If the year 1938 will be famous in history for its diplomatic surprises, it will also be remembered for its freakish winter. "Hitler weather" the incorrigible German romanticists called it, but to me it seemed as if Nature, taking pity on a crazy world, had advanced her seasons in order to comfort oppressed humanity. And certainly the world was crazy at that moment.

The Moscow trial was then at the apogee of its absurdity, and every day the newspapers gave in full the confessions of the accused. Only that morning Rakovsky, whom I have never seen, had referred to a clandestine meeting with me, and the sight of my name in print brought back to me a past which I would gladly forget and filled me with a vague uneasiness. In Austria Herr Schuschnigg, having capitulated to Herr Hitler at Berchtesgaden, seemed to be reasserting his authority. He was going to hold a plebiscite—a plain yes or no for Austria's independence. In Zagreb the local politicians were sure that he would have a large majority. They knew how plebiscites were conducted in Central Europe. I was not so sure.

Restless and unsettled, I refused all invitations with the excuse of tiredness and spent the evening with the Russians. But I was in no mood either for laughter or for tears. The place was crowded, and the noise jarred on my nerves. Even Tania was irritating, not understanding my apprehension and, indeed, having nothing but contempt for politics and politicians. She tried to win me from my black mood and, failing, gave up her efforts with complacent good-humour. "You're tired," she said. "Why not go to bed, and tomorrow. . . ." I laughed. I knew these Russian tomorrows. But I took her advice.

The next day was Friday, March 11. Early in the morning I went to the Ban's Palace to meet the Vice-Ban whom Stanko Šverljuga had suggested that I ought to see. I found there Viktor Ružić, the Ban, and Mažuranić, and they showed me over the Palace. It reminded me of the Governor-General's house in Moscow in pre-war days, and, as we strolled through the countless reception rooms, I saw in my imagination the bright uniforms of vanished empires. We joked and laughed. Mažuranić made Ružić send for a bottle of "slivovica," and we pledged each other in a glass. On that morning all seemed as well with the world as it ever is in these days of perpetual crisis. With the Vice-Ban, who was no linguist, I had my first long political discussion in Yugoslav. He is a Serb, full of political wisdom, very fair-minded and patiently optimistic. But we spoke about Croatia and Serbo-Croat relations. No one seemed anxious about Austria. No one even suggested that Herr Hitler might take his own measures to stop the plebiscite.

That evening the Šverljugas gave a large dinner-party for me. The other guests included the chief Zagreb notabilities: the Ban, the Vice-Ban, ex-ministers, and leading lawyers and bankers. Before dinner there was more "slivovica" while we waited for the last guest to arrive. At eight o'clock Stanko Šverljuga was called to the telephone. We were to start without the Vice-Ban, who had to wait at his office for a telephone-call from Belgrade. Everyone laughed and made jokes about Father Korošeć, the Minister of the Interior. Apparently he had a habit of ringing up from Belgrade at night, and the Ban and Vice-Ban were always missing their dinner. Ours was a gay meal. The Šverljuga cellar is one of the best in Croatia, and the conversation light, sometimes slightly malicious, and often brilliant, flowed freely. Never, I think, have I enjoyed a more care-free meal.

We were already back in the drawing-room when the Vice-Ban arrived. He was calm like most Serbs. He shook hands with everyone.

"Belgrade must have been busy to-night," said Madame Šverljuga.

"Yes, Belgrade is busy."

Then he told his story very quietly. Hitler had acted. Schuschnigg had resigned. German troops had crossed the Austrian frontier. Belgrade was already taking dispositions to guard her own frontier and to prevent the inrush of Austrian refugees. It was the end of Austria.

The gaiety went out of our party like a fused lamp. The male guests formed themselves into little groups and withdrew into the back room. For a moment all conversation seemed to stop. Then there was a confused buzz of low-pitched voices. The bankers began to add together Germany's and Austria's trade with Yugoslavia, and saw at once that Germany would now hold a dominant position in Yugoslavia's economic life.

As the individual opinions began to sort themselves, I realised that these cultured Croats regarded Vienna as a provincial Englishman looks on London. It was their cultural Mecca. The general sentiment was one of concern. There was regret for the pre-war past, regret for the post-war mistakes. I remembered how many times in bygone years Stanko Šverljuga had warned me against the unrealities of French policy in central Europe, and, although no one uttered a word of blame, I seemed to hear, perhaps mistakenly, a kind of "I told you so" note in the general comments.

There was anxiety, too, about the new situation. These Croats were rich. All had something to lose from the uncertainties of the future. Yet behind the anxiety more than one showed a resigned, if resentful, admiration of Germany, who understood the value of action and who carried out so efficiently the precepts of the old French maxim: "voir, c'est savoir; vouloir, c'est pouvoir; oser, c'est avoir." No one mentioned Britain. Everyone seemed to realise that she would or could do nothing.

I made up my mind to go to Vienna at once. But, as always happens in these moments of turmoil, there were irksome difficulties to overcome, and the next two days were spent in confusion.

On the Saturday morning I walked to the British Consulate to seek the Consul's information about passports, money and trains. On the way I passed the Austrian Consulate or, to be accurate, the former Austrian Consulate, for the Germans had already taken it over, and a huge German flag with the swastika rampant flaunted itself exultingly from the flagstaff. At our own Consulate I found Rapp as cheerfully helpful and efficient as always. He gave me some English pounds, which in these days of currency restrictions are invaluable because they can be changed anywhere. But his efficiency had not been able to discover what ban, if any, the Germans had imposed on travel into Austria. Nor could any other official in Zagreb supply me with this information.

From the Consulate I walked up to the old town to the house of M. Pusilović, an Anglophil Zagreb barrister whom I have known for many years, and who was giving a luncheon party for me. On my way a newsboy ran past me, flaunting a special edition of a local newspaper and shouting raucously, "All About the Vienna Revolution." I bought a copy and took it with me to the house. While I was showing it to Pusilović, the local Government censor came up and, after being introduced to me, said with a smile: "Where did you buy that paper? It has been confiscated."

I had read the paper, which was only a single-page news sheet, and told him that I could see no reason for its confiscation.

He pointed to the huge headlines: "The Beautiful Blue Danube Flows with Blood and Hitler Marches Resound In The City of Waltzes."

"That's why," he said.

I understood. The Yugoslav Government was being careful. The "politique de bon voisinage" was already being applied to Yugoslavia's new and powerful neighbour.

At the luncheon I met a most attractive and cultured Yugoslav diplomatist and had a long conversation with him. He was a man of ripe judgment, a Croat, and a democrat. He knew Nazi Germany well and had met all the leading Nazis. He told me of a conversation that he had had with General Goering, to whom he had suggested tactfully that Nazi "diplomatic surprises" might one day provoke a serious clash.

"Bah," said the General with supreme confidence, "you have only to bang your fist on the table. Then the democratic countries make a few speeches in Parliament, and nothing happens."

My new Yugoslav acquaintance was profoundly disturbed by the German coup in Austria, not so much because of the *fait accompli* as on account of the manner of its execution, which he regarded as an irreparable breach in the delicate post-war structure of peace by negotiation.

Our conversation ran mainly on the probabilities of Italy's reaction to the Hitlerian coup. My Yugoslav, who knew his Italians, was convinced that, however much she might juggle with the cards of diplomacy, Italy was bound to feel resentment, because her turn would come sooner or later. The Sudeten Germans in Czechoslovakia might be freed first. But, even if he wanted to, Herr Hitler dared not leave the Tyrolese Germans in Italy to their fate. The Pan-German movement, he said, was now stronger than its Fuehrer. He had a map which he had bought in Germany two years ago. It showed the future German Reich as ambitious Nazis wanted it to be. The new frontiers extended beyond Slovenia and a part of Croatia. They included Trieste.

The Germans, he went on, did not trust the Italians, and to illustrate his point he told me an amusing story. He had sat next Herr von Papen at a dinner at which the German diplomatist had made a speech praising Germany's great new ally. At the end of the speech the Yugoslav twitted Herr von Papen, a soldier who had assuredly not forgotten the Great War, on his new love for Italy. And then he reminded him of the experience of Major Furlong, an American who came to Zagreb after the war as a member of some international Commission. When the American arrived in Zagreb, he had an expensively fitted suit-case. At once a man rushed up and offered to carry it to the hotel, which was only three hundred yards from the station. The Major agreed. But when he reached the door, there was no sign of the porter. The suit-case was never seen again. Three months later the Major left Zagreb. Again he walked to the station, but on this occasion he was accompanied by a number of important Croat officials. In his hand he carried a superb new suit-case. Seeing it, a Croat official at once called a street porter.

"Here, Major," he said, "let this fellow carry your bag."

But the Major protested. "No, gentlemen," he said quietly, "you see, it's this way. The first time I trusted one of these guys. When I lost my bag, that was the porter's fault, for I was new to the place and didn't know the ropes. But if I trust him again, then it's my fault if anything goes wrong."

Von Papen saw the point of the story and laughed.

On the Sunday I made an abortive attempt to depart and was actually in the train, when the station-master warned me that I might be turned back at the frontier. Monday was a day of farewells. In the morning I went to say goodbye to Šverljuga, who had been untiring in his efforts to obtain reliable information for me, and who had helped me to arrange my money matters. I found him closeted with Professor Frangeš, a former Minister and Yugoslavia's greatest economist. Frangeš, vigorous and brimful of optimism, was walking up and down the room, waving his arms and talking like lightning. During the week-end he had worked out a comprehensive scheme to free Yugoslavia from the dangers of German economic domination.

"We must look to the Mediterranean," he said. His plan envisaged new markets in Malta, Cyprus and Rhodes. His *exposé* was magnificent in its lucidity. But it sounded to me a little unreal.

In the late afternoon I drove Tania out to Samobor, a picturesque village with a ruined castle about twelve miles west of Zagreb. As we left the Štrossmayer Square, the sun beat down on the Archbishop's Palace, turning the red roof to the colour of flowing blood. Against the clear skyline the Sljemme mountain stood out with the sharpness of a silhouette. At Samobor we had a five o'clock dinner in the village inn beside a running stream. We looked at the hills, shimmering with the virginal green of spring, and talked of the future.

I asked her if there was anything that I could do to help her to leave the nightmare life which she was forced to lead.

Her face lit up, and she talked eagerly of her hopes and ambitions. Her dream was a career on the films, but she had no illusions about its reality.

"There are not many opportunities in this country," she said. "If I could get an engagement in London or Paris, there might be a chance. As things are, I have to carry on. Now I live solely for the short summer season on the Dalmatian coast, where I can bathe and lie in the sun."

She turned her face away for a moment. Then she took a cigarette and smiled bravely. "I've had six years of this life. You know its temptations. So far I've withstood them. Anyone will tell you that I'm the most unapproachable woman in Zagreb. In three more years I'll either have the strongest character of any woman in the world or go under altogether."

I looked at her. I did not doubt her determination. What I feared was her power of resistance in so irregular a life. With a Russian woman you must insist on absolute method in order to avoid absolute chaos. Tania was a child of the sun, and the nature of her life deprived her of it. Already under her eyes, large, luminous, and as dark as a ripe plum, were lines which spoke of long nights spent in an atmosphere of smoke and foul air. Yet her courage was magnificent.

Only a few days ago I had received a letter from Freddie Cunningham, my old Malayan friend. 'I am still a bachelor," he wrote, "but you may be amused to hear that I have a share in a wife." Then he went on to tell me that he had taken a ticket in a lottery. The prettiest Chinese girl in Malaya was raffling herself in an attempt to raise £10,000 for the Chinese War Fund. She had undertaken to marry the holder of the winning ticket.

The story, true in detail and successful in its conclusion, had impressed me as the most remarkable example of woman's courage that I had ever heard of either in the New World or the Old.

Tania's courage was of the same stamp. She, too, belonged to the new young women who, knowing life, faced it more boldly than many men. They had been steeled in the furnace of the last war. Then they had driven motor-cars. In a future war they would drive aeroplanes. They would be attacked and would defend themselves. It was a shattering thought. Yet if the call or the opportunity came in time, I knew that Tania, for one, would answer it without hesitation.

I drove her back to her work, and before the garrish stucco entrance of the restaurant we said goodbye. We shook hands very gravely. Then, without looking back, she slipped through the swing door. I wondered if I should ever see her again, if her strong character would triumph over these grim surroundings. I knew that the odds were a hundred to one against.

I went back to the hotel, paid my bill, and, sending my luggage on in advance, walked down to the station. It was a beautiful night. The air was cool and bracing, and the Gothic towers of the cathedral stood out in black relief against the clear, moonlit sky.

Rapp and Sejk came to see me off. The Consul, who had won an M.C. in the last war, was pleasantly cheerful, but my old fishing-friend was full of forebodings. He brought a fresh alarm. Half-an-hour ago he had heard a radio message sent out from Vienna warning all travellers that no one could leave or enter Austria without a special pass from the German military authorities.

I was, however, tired of waiting, and without more ado I boarded the train. It was almost empty. I was the only passenger in the sleeping-car.

As I stood waiting at the window, Sejk made an effort to be gay. "If you come back in the autumn, don't forget to bring your fishing-rods." Then he shivered apologetically. "I can't help it," he said, "this reminds me of 1914."

But in 1914 there had been the blind enthusiasm of ignorance. To me the atmosphere seemed more like that of 1916 and 1917 when, in Russia at all events, men went unwillingly to a war that had no attractions.

And to that generation both Sejk and I belonged.

Q

BOOK III

"WHERE THE GUNS SPEAK"

"If indeed Athens can remain at peace and if the choice rests with us, I personally feel that we are bound to do so . . . But if there is another person concerned, with sword in hand and a mighty force at his back, who imposes on you with the name of peace but himself indulges in acts of war, what is left but to defend ourselves?

"If you choose to follow his example and profess that you are at peace, I raise no objection. But if anyone mistakes for peace an arrangement which will enable Philip, when he has seized everything else, to march upon us, he has taken leave of his senses, and the peace that he talks of is one that you observe towards Philip, but not Philip towards you. That is the advantage which he is purchasing by all his expenditure of money—that he should be at war with you, but that you should not be at war with him."

CHAPTER ONE

A BRITISH PASSPORT still possesses many advantages, and, as I made my entry into Austria on the Tuesday morning of March 15, mine acted like an Open Sesame. The forebodings of my Croat friends proved groundless. At the frontier I was not even roused from my sleep. When I awoke to a rose-pink dawn, I was near Gloggnitz and well inside the new German territory.

The Semmering hills were still crested with snow, but the early morning frost on the fields was already melting in the sun. At Payerbach, where in years gone by I had fished so often, I saw numerous advertisements in English. In recent years the district had become a playground for British tourists. Now, I reflected, they would not be so numerous. Yet the countryside looked Austrian; that is, peaceful and asleep. On the neat villas I saw few Nazi flags.

It was not until the train approached Vienna that I noticed visible signs of the change which had shaken the world. At Liesing I saw the first German troops. They were encamped beside a factory. A company was on parade. In a field close by, a group of soldiers was playing a miniature football match with a tennis ball.

All the way from Liesing to Vienna the symbols of the Hitlerian triumph increased. German aeroplanes, glistening in the bright sunshine, circled over the outskirts of the city. Swastika flags were everywhere. Most houses were content to fly two flags, but on the famous workmen's blocks, built by the Socialist Municipality of Vienna, a swastika banner hung from every window. I wondered if the Socialist occupants of these model dwellings had hung them there by military command or by a natural precaution.

I have had more than my share of luck in revolutions. I have been an eye-witness of many tumults, and I have never suffered serious inconvenience. The same good fortune attended me in Vienna. My arrival at the station was normal. As I drove by taxi to the Bristol Hotel, I was unmolested. It is true that the streets were crowded. But there was little noise. Youth predominated in the crowd, but it was a cheerful, laughing youth. The only unpleasant sign of aggression was the presence of small bands of young men, scarcely more than boys, who, without uniforms, but wearing a swastika red armlet and carrying a rifle or a hunting knife, swaggered along the pavement. These were the Austrian Nazis. They reminded me of the first Red Guards in the early days of the Bolshevik Revolution. Some were, undoubtedly, bent on revenge. Others, I suspected, were more concerned with looting.

As I turned into the Kaertnerring, I found a huge throng standing patiently outside the Imperial Hotel. The sides of the street were lined with the grey-coloured motor-cars and military lorries which had brought the German troops with such dramatic speed to Vienna. German soldiers, pink-cheeked and good-humoured, stood by the cars and fraternised quietly with the crowd. They showed no signs of exultation. They were doing a routine job. Their discipline and their behaviour were exemplary.

The hotel itself was draped with swastika banners. Herr Hitler had arrived on the previous evening. Young Vienna was in the street to catch a glimpse of the Fuehrer to whom it had surrendered its independence with obvious enthusiasm.

The Imperial Hotel was the Fuehrer's Vienna headquarters, and to make room and safety for him the civilian guests had been evicted. Some of them were old clients who had lived there for many years. Others were foreign diplomatists. They, too, had been bundled into the street at a minute's notice. They disliked this treatment.

With some truth a senior foreign Minister, who had spent several years in Prague before being transferred to Vienna, might exclaim: "The Czechs are a people whom one may not like but must respect; the Austrians one likes but cannot respect."

But diplomatic protestations were useless. Austria was now part of Germany. In one night foreign Legations had lost their standing.

As my taxi crawled the hundred yards to the Bristol higher up the Ring, I seemed to be passing through a cordon of German troops. Their field-grey uniforms dominated the whole scene. Two sentries stood on duty at the hotel door, and for a moment I was in despair. The Bristol, too, had obviously been taken over by the military. Once again my luck held. I walked as boldly as I could through the door, crossed the hall full of German staff-officers, and went up to the reception-desk.

"You have a room for me engaged by the British Consul," I said. The clerk shrugged his shoulders and looked at his book. He seemed tired and ill at ease. And well he might be, for the Jewish managers had been dismissed, and he was now under the orders of the German General Staff. Twice he was interrupted in his search by German officers demanding rooms. At last he found my name and smiled faintly. "You're fortunate", he said, "the military have left your room free."

Silently I blessed Captain J. W. Taylor, our Consul, who had performed this good deed for me. I had known him for many years, and had always admired his courage and his energetic ability. During the Vienna troubles he showed both these qualities in the highest degree, and I hope that our Foreign Office will not overlook his merits.

Although I was relieved, I felt subdued. Memories of the past surged in my mind. How often had I crossed the threshold of this hotel to be greeted with deferential bows by friendly Austrian servants! Here I had dined with Sir William Goode in the early post-war years and had discussed a hundred schemes for the reconstruction of Austria. Here, too, I had made merry with companions of another sort on more frivolous occasions. In those days the best was always reserved for the British. These good times—good for us if not for the Austrians—had lasted almost to the final hour.

Only a year ago I had seen the Duke of Windsor dancing in the tea-room, while the same crowd, which now stood so patiently before another hotel to welcome another idol, waited outside to cheer Prince Charming when he left. There was still a photograph of him in the large ante-room, but now no one looked at it. Then we British had been gods. To-day, we were less than nothing. Where once I had been on terms of intimacy with hundreds, I was alone in a friendless city.

With a slight malaise in my stomach I went upstairs to the breakfast-room. My embarrassment increased when I saw that every table was occupied by German officers. They took no notice of me. All were dressed in sober field-grey. The fine uniforms of the pre-war era had disappeared, and with their disappearance had gone much of the old swagger. After standing stupidly for what seemed an age, I noticed a table at which one officer was breakfasting alone. I walked up to him, bowed, and asked if I might sit down. He was polite and even friendly, commenting on the weather which was radiant and presently paying his bill and leaving me with the excuse that he had a busy day before him.

I ordered my coffee and bought a bundle of the various morning newspapers. The *Neue Freie Presse* was still dressed in its old garb, but its soul had been Nazified. The front page gave fulsome details of the Fuehrer's arrival in Vienna. The leading article contained an obsequious eulogy of his services to Deutschtum. But the sport and theatre pages were unchanged. I scanned the theatre and cinema programmes. Among the performances billed for that evening were *Green Pastures*, *Tovarish*, *A Midsummer Night's Dream*, and, at the Opera itself, *The Bartered Bride*, Smetana's great Czech opera. It seemed a strange programme for Hitler Day, and, indeed, before the evening came the performance of *The Bartered*

Bride was cancelled. Nevertheless, the programme was a reminder that Vienna was not Austria but an international city with more mixed blood than any other capital in the world. What was a Viennese? A mixture of German, Slovene, Czech, Hungarian, Rumanian, Croat, and Jew. Each of these nationalities was represented in the list of football teams given in the sporting pages.

Only the day before I had read in my Zagreb newspaper an article claiming that Chiang Kai-Chek, the Christian general of China, was a direct descendant of the Slovene monk called Kaishek who went to China as a missionary three hundred years ago. Be this as it may, Schuschnigg himself, the Austrian Chancellor, whose foolhardiness had brought his own house tumbling down on his head, was of pure Slovene origin. All this jumble of Viennese nationalities was intermarried to an extent which made racial definition impossible. Now it was to be Germanised with ruthless German efficiency. The German newspapers left no room for doubt regarding the Fuehrer's intentions. Quoting Arndt's famous dictum that Austria, on account of her burden of foreign peoples, had only half the German spirit and quarter the German strength, they demanded the expulsion of 200,000 Jews. But if the Nazis intended to apply the Aryan grandmother comb to Vienna, it was not 200,000 Jews who would have to be immobilised, but nearly three times that number.

I took a taxi and drove to our Legation. As I passed the Ballplatz, my chauffeur had some difficulty in making his way through the huge crowd which stood outside the old Austrian Foreign Office. The waiting throng was there to greet Herr von Ribbentrop who at that moment was taking over the seals of office from his Austrian predecessor.

Later in the day, a Nazi journalist who had been present gave me a first-hand account of Herr von Ribbentrop's inspection. The ex-champagne merchant had spent the morning going through the rooms, sitting at Metternich's table, examining the great globe which has stood there since the

Congress of Vienna. He had done his job with quiet dignity, and the Austrians had fawned on him. One of the first Germans to stake his all on Herr Hitler's fortunes, he had won that day the triumph of his loyalty.

It was curious that Ribbentrop, a Reichs German, should be interested in Metternich. For Metternich was essentially an Austrian hero. The Viennese had called Dollfuss the Millemetternich, and the Nazis had murdered Dollfuss. The name, intended as a compliment, had brought no luck to the diminutive Austrian Chancellor. Metternich himself had not fared too well. Exactly ninety years ago, in that same month of March, he had been forced to flee from Vienna and to seek refuge in Brighton in just the same manner as the Jewish victims of the Nazi triumph were now struggling to escape to England.

Herr von Ribbentrop was not the only Nazi chief who had accompanied his Fuehrer to Vienna. Every extra edition of the local newspapers announced the arrival of some prominent Nazi. The advent of Dr. Schacht was heralded with headlines containing an illuminating admission of Germany's ambitions which the financier had made in an exuberant speech: "the road of the Niebelungs is now open to the East." Only General Goering was absent. He had remained in Berlin to hold the fort for his Fuehrer and to push on the production of Germany's air force.

When I reached the Metternichgasse, it was deserted. The big gate of our Legation was shut, and, as the porter admitted me, he spoke in a low voice. Here there was no exuberance. Michael Palairet, our Minister, had already been recalled to London. I knew that he would not come back. Only capital cities had Legations, and Vienna was no longer a capital. The atmosphere was depressing. A hundred years ago, I reflected, the Emperor Ferdinand was being crowned in Vienna, and former ambassadors including the envoy of His Britannic Majesty had added a colourful presence to the pomp and majesty of the ceremony. In 1938 Vienna was celebrating a different triumph to which the diplomatic representatives of foreign Powers were not invited.

With increasing gloom I thought of the many happy meals and talks I had had within these walls with British diplomatists: Sir Francis Lindley, Lord Chilston, Philip Nichols, and the gifted and lovable Allen Leeper. In those days, not so long ago but now infinitely remote in their irrevocability, the Austrian Government had taken no step without consulting the British Minister. Even during my visit in 1937 Sir Walford Selby had been pleasantly optimistic. Everything was going as well as could be expected. Schuschnigg was doing splendid work. The presence of the Duke of Windsor had stimulated British prestige. Austria was struggling to rid herself of German influence.

Now Schuschnigg was imprisoned in the Belvedere and even his closest collaborators were cursing him for his mistakes. German influence had made Austria a part of Germany.

At the Legation I found Harold Mack, the First Secretary, in charge. He looked tired and worn-out. For three days he had been working night and day. Yet his work was now of no avail. He was shut off from all communication with the new official world. The Legation was neither beleaguered nor molested. It was merely ignored.

Not wishing to waste either my own time or the time of the Legation staff, I made my way back to the Bristol and, paying off my taxi, set off on foot to the Consulate. My way led me past the Hofburg. It was the identical path which I had trod daily for six months, when, fourteen years ago, I was an official of the Anglo-International Bank.

The Consulate itself was in a former portion of my old bank. The building, known still as the Giesmueller Palace, had great traditions. In 1798 it had housed the French Embassy, with Bernadotte, Napoleon's marshal and founder of Sweden's royal line, at its head, and from its windows the soldier-ambassador had watched a mob, infuriated with

Germanic patriotism, tear down the French tricolour from the Embassy flagstaff. Here, too, Beethoven and Schubert had given concerts, and in the room in which our Consul now sat Bismarck had stayed when he attended his nephew's marriage. The same room might have been the scene of a more historical marriage. When I called on Taylor in 1937, I found him busy with plans for the marriage of the Duke of Windsor and Mrs. Wallis Simpson who at that time were considering being married in Vienna. Had their original intention been carried out, the ceremony would have been performed in the Giesmueller Palace.

If the Legation had been like a deserted house, the Consulate was alive with human activity. The large ante-room was crowded with Viennese Jews seeking such help and advice as the British Consulate could give them. John Taylor, our Consul, handled them magnificently, and his calm, unruffled manner and quiet efficiency made me proud of a brother Scot. He had a word of comfort and good counsel for each victim, and his soothing influence did much to chase the terror from many eyes. But there were tragic scenes, and one prominent Jew who had befriended many English people in Vienna fell on the ground, seized Taylor by the ankles, and begged him to help him to leave the country. In other circumstances the position might have seemed ridiculous. But now pity fought with violent indignation for the uppermost place in my emotions. The Nazis wished to eliminate these unfortunate people. Yet no Jew was allowed to leave the country.

Taylor took me into his private room, and in half-an-hour I had another picture of the Nazi *coup d'état*. Taylor confirmed my impression of the excellent behaviour of the German troops. Even the Jews welcomed their presence, for the troops represented discipline, order and certain standards of decency. But working behind them were the Gestapo, the dreaded agents of Herr Himmler. They were already present in large numbers, and they had instituted the Schnellgericht, the lightning court which, like the old Ogpu in Moscow, carried out sentences in a few minutes.

Taylor was still in touch with the authorities and offered to arrange an interview for me with Seyss-Inquart, the puppet Austrian Chancellor who had invited Herr Hitler to take control of Austria's destiny. But I refused. I was no longer a journalist. In any case there was only one place to study a revolution, and this was in the streets. I remembered the first day of the Russian Revolution. Then I had been in the streets when the trouble started and had been carried along by the singing mob, who forced their way into the town Duma in Moscow. What had happened in Vienna was also a revolution. I would see it in the same way. And I walked the streets till my feet were sore.

At every corner beggar-women were doing a brisk trade in swastika badges and photographs of "Our Fuehrer taken since his arrival in Vienna." Nearly everyone including the few foreigners wore in their button-hole some badge of identification. Only the Jews were forbidden to wear any emblem, and with an obstinate pride I accepted voluntarily the same ban. But, although the Inner Town was densely packed with exultant joy-riders, no one asked me a question or interfered with my free passage. The first Russian Revolution had been a people's holiday characterised by much kissing and flag-waving and frequent repetitions of the popular slogans: "Constitution" and "peace without annexations and contributions." True, to most of the ignorant mob "konstitutsia" was a grandmother and "anneksi and kontributsi" distant provinces akin to Alsace and Lorraine. But they represented in the heart of the people both relief from the long strain of war and the promise of a better future.

The Vienna revolution was a soldiers' joy-ride, and outwardly it bore the same evidences of good humour and exultation. But there was one difference. In referring to British criticisms of "the rape of Austria", Mr. Ward Price, who had entered Austria with the German troops and had been received by Herr Hitler, had said "if this was rape, never have I seen a more willing victim." There was truth in the observation, but only a half-truth. Those who lined the main streets and who cheered and flag-waved so lustily were young men and women under twenty-five. In the side streets I saw unmistakable signs of distress on the faces of the older people.

Nazi-ism is, above all, a youth movement, for youth, bewildered by the ferment of post-war ideas, wants jobs and hopes to get them from an omnipotent Fuehrer. In all countries the men and women over forty want security, and in Vienna on that day there were many men and women of over forty who would lose their all and were already conscious of the impending loss. But they would vote for Herr Hitler in the plebiscite which had just been announced with typical illogicality by the Nazis who had turned out Herr Schuschnigg for daring to suggest a similar plebiscite. The "safety first" instinct is strong in most of us, and nearly every revolutionary movement is made by a small but violent minority. The Bolshevik revolution was certainly the work of a minority, and in the Civil War minorities represented both sides, the masses changing over more than once as the fortunes of war swung in the balance.

Sir George Ogilvie Forbes, who was in Madrid during the Spanish Civil War, told me that a similar reluctance to be drawn into the struggle was evident among the majority of the Spanish people. Until Herr Hitler made his dramatic coup, probably twenty-five per cent. of the Austrian population was actively pro-Schuschnigg. Perhaps twenty-five per cent. was violently pro-Nazi. The other fifty per cent. represented the sheep who wanted only to be left in peace. Had Herr Schuschnigg been allowed to hold his plebiscite, they would have voted for him. Now they would vote for Herr Hitler.

As I passed down the Graben and up the Kaertnerstrasse, the signs above the shops still revealed the international character of Vienna. All were open. Scores of tourist agencies proclaimed the merits of Austria as a happy home for holiday-makers. A shop, probably Jewish, still flaunted in bold lettering its sign of "Old Bond Street". But already on a few of the more obviously Jewish shops the signs had been obliterated, and a red poster proclaimed that the concern had been taken over by the Nazis. The bookshops, too, had transformed their windows. The works of Jewish authors had been removed. A huge photograph of the Fuehrer, draped in Nazi colours, filled the centre of the lay-out, and round it in serried rows were piled copies of *Mein Kampf*. In every background hung a map showing in deep red lines the frontiers of the new German Commonwealth.

I turned aside to enter the great cathedral of St. Stephen where I had so often prayed in the past. To-day, it was deserted. All Vienna, including the priests, was in the streets. Rather morbidly I began to look for the old night-haunts where in bygone years I had wasted my substance. Many of them had been owned by Jews. Already there had been many changes since my time. Now there would soon be more. Where was Haupt, the king of *Nachtlokal* violinists, who had initiated me into the intoxicating charms of Viennese Lieder: "Von Sekt sind die Geigen berauscht", "Wien, Wien, nur Du Allein", "Ich weiss auf der Wieden ein kleines Hotel", "Im Prater blühen die Bäume", and "Es gibt Dinge die muss man vergessen"? There were many things now that one would have to forget: the champagne and the violins, the Viennese girls, the gayest, the bravest, and the least mercenary of all the lost tribe of Liliths, the little hotels in the Prater. There were little hotels nearer than that. They were there quite close to me in the little side-streets off the Kaertnerstrasse, dingy, dirty rabbit-warrens to which the street prostitutes brought their clients at all hours of the day and night. Now they, too, would be cleared away, and the cleansing would be one entry on the credit side of the Nazi book of deeds.

Still prompted by a vain desire to resurrect the past, I went across to Meissl and Schadn's, the old hotel in which I spent my first night in Vienna more than thirty years ago. In those days it was much frequented by Austrian officers. Here was enacted the grim tragedy of Colonel Redl, a senior officer of the Austrian General Staff, who not long before the Great War sold the Austrian secret war plans to the Russian Government. When his treachery was discovered, four of his brother officers called on him at Meissl and Schadn's and, having explained the situation, said goodbye, leaving a loaded revolver on the table. They waited downstairs until the sound of a shot told them that the Colonel had taken the easiest way out. It was a typical soldier's *dénouement*, very gentlemanly and very Austrian. To-day, the Nazis would use different methods. But, I reflected, there were few cases in history of a German officer betraying his country.

From Meissl and Schadn's I went to the Drei Hussaren, a restaurant which had been made fashionably popular by the Duke of Windsor. A year ago almost to a day I had dined here with Hans Simon, a former Austrian Treasury official well-known in the higher British financial world. For hours we had discussed the Austrian situation. Simon was then mildly pro-Habsburg, not for sentimental reasons but because the Habsburg solution was the only effective barrier to Nazi penetration. The movement, he had told me, was growing. I thought then that an attempted restoration was more likely to provoke Nazi intervention than to give peace to Austria. But I did not say so. Now the hopes of the monarchists were extinguished—perhaps for ever. And I had Simon on my conscience. He was a Jew. Would it embarrass him or me if I went to see him? Later in the day I discovered that he had already left for London. He had foreseen the end when Herr Schuschnigg paid his fateful visit to Berchtesgaden.

As I made my way back to my hotel in a roundabout fashion, I passed Sacher's or rather what once was Sacher's.

Here, too, I had often stayed, had taken part in conferences with Bank of England directors, and had listened to Ralph Hamlyn pleading for the salvation of the Austria which he loved so passionately.

At Sacher's I had spent many nights in frivolous entertainment with young sparks of the Austrian aristocracy and in a private room had seen them, as the last bottle was opened, raise their glasses to the young Archduke whom they called their Emperor. There was no place reserved for them in to-day's celebrations. Some of them would seek to curry favour with the new régime, but for the majority this German holiday was an Austrian day of mourning.

As I stood hesitatingly before the dark-grey building, a band of young boys and girls, holding hands and shouting Heil Hitler, came running round the corner and in their mad dash nearly knocked me over. They were rushing to gain a place on the Ring where already huge crowds were assembled for the great military parade in which the Fuehrer himself was to take part. These young people symbolised the spirit of the new Vienna. The old Vienna, which I had known, was a shadow city of ghosts.

R

CHAPTER TWO

IT WAS AFTER two o'clock when I found myself back in the Bristol. I had had to struggle for the last two hundred yards of my walk, for both sides of the Ring were lined twelve deep with people. This was the Fuehrer's hour. Since his arrival on the previous evening he had been closeted in his hotel. Now he was to show himself to the Austrian people.

I was hot and tired, but already I had begun to regret my refusal of Taylor's offer to provide me with a journalist's seat at the Heldenplatz, where the Fuehrer was to speak. Now I should not even see the march-past. The window of my room looked out on a backyard. The serried rows on the Ring were an impenetrable barrier. As I walked through the wall, I had a stroke of luck. I ran into the officer with whom I had breakfasted in the morning. He recognised me with a smile.

"Are you not going to see the parade?" he asked.

I told him that I had no place.

"Ho," he said, "we'll soon mend that. Come with me."

He took me upstairs to a large room on the first floor. It was comparatively empty. At the open windows sat a score of rather dowdily-dressed women. They were, I imagined, the wives or friends of the German officers staying in the hotel. But only two or three officers were present. The others were taking part in the parade. Fortunately, for me, my new acquaintance was on the Air Staff and had a free afternoon. He found a corner for me at a window from which I had a clear view of the Ring.

Herr Hitler was already at the Heldenplatz, and loud-speakers relayed his rough, harsh voice to the waiting crowd below. When he had finished his speech, a dull throbbing sound of engines filled the air. I saw the crowd below bend back their heads like one man to scan the sky. In a few seconds a great host of aeroplanes—two hundred and fifty my officer friend told me—sped gracefully across the clear, blue sky. Then down the street came the sound of marching feet. The procession had begun. The German troops had been only forty-eight hours in Vienna; yet forty thousand men were taking part in the parade.

As the first platoon came into sight, the crowd cheered itself hoarse. The troops marched well. Their physique was good, but not so impressive as that of a pre-war German battalion. They looked very young. Most of them were born in the last year of the Great War, and in all European countries the 1918 generation is below standard. They were rather dirty-looking. Indeed, their tramping feet raised small columns of dust, for Vienna was enjoying Hitler weather, and the sun beat down on crowd and troops alike with almost summer heat.

As the soldiers passed, girls in the crowd threw garlands of wild flowers at them. The soldiers smiled good-humouredly, but they never relaxed their discipline for a second. Their rifles and their grey steel-helmets, glinting in the sun, moved forward with machine-like precision. Only their pink and sweating cheeks distinguished them from an army of Čapek's Robots.

I made a close study of the crowd. It was composed of all classes. For once workers and bourgeois stood side by side with undivided enthusiasm. My predominant impression was of young faces and rather shabby clothes. This was no host of reactionaries assembled to greet a reactionary triumph. Whatever their motive, it was the people of Vienna who lined the streets. And they behaved with typical Viennese good-humour and light-heartedness, relieving the solemnity of the occasion with a touch of comedy which a Berlin crowd would never have attempted. Every regiment that passed had its band. But the bands were silent. Perhaps they were too tired to play. More probably there had been no order from a higher source, and in its absence no regimental officer dared to give the command. Then a sturdy workman in the street below me started a rasping shout of "Musik". The joyous crowd took up the refrain, and at once both sides of the Ring resounded with an insistent chant of "Mu-sik, Mu-sik". The troops smiled. But they did not play.

I turned to my friendly officer. "Their enthusiasm is wonderful," I said politely. "Yes", he said nonchalantly. "But the Fuehrer will make them work soon. They won't like that so much."

There was no arrogance in his voice. But he spoke with a quiet assurance which indicated his implicit belief in German superiority and in the German virtues of order and discipline. I remembered previous conversations with Austrian officers and diplomatists who had served in Berlin during the War. There was not one who had not made some complaint of his treatment by the Prussians. Back to my mind flashed the memory of a remark made to me in 1920 by a high Austrian official who had played a leading part at the peace negotiations.

"I was forced," he said, "to be present at a surgical operation on my country. But the British surgeons were so kind that some of the pain at least was alleviated. It was, of course, humiliating to have to beg for charity and mercy, but not so insulting as the humiliation which was felt by every Austrian who had to deal with Prussians during the war."

After all, there was a world of difference between the Austrian and the Prussian. It is not the great invasions which cause the political transformations of history, but the changes in the ideas of peoples. Vienna might rejoice to-day over a Hitler holiday, but, unless the German Messiah could change or had already changed the mentality of Austrian youth, there was much in the new régime which would soon prove distasteful to the easy-going Austrian.

I had time enough for reflections of this nature, for the military parade seemed to last interminably. By now it was becoming monotonous. In their field-grey the troops looked too much alike, and even in the street there was a noticeable decline in the enthusiasm as when a Cup Final degenerates into a stalemate of poor football.

Then suddenly the atmosphere becomes electric. The crowd stiffens, and from higher up the Ring swells the sustained roar of thousands of voices. The Fuehrer is approaching.

Presently his open car comes into sight. He stands bolt upright, like a dummy figure, holding the windscreen with one hand. His face is almost hidden beneath his clumsy uniform cap, and all the power and the might and the glory seem to be concentrated in the grotesque Charlie Chaplin moustache. Behind him sit the unpleasant-looking Himmler, the Derjinsky of the Nazi movement, and two generals.

The car crawls at a snail's pace. There may be scores of Gestapo agents among the vast crowd. But they are not visible. There is no double cordon of troops or police to overawe the would-be assassins, or even to keep the straining mob in its place. Anyone could have thrown a bomb with almost certain success. From the windows of the houses anyone could have fired two or three shots with an odds-on chance of killing his man.

I am impressed almost against my will. Even the bitterest anti-Nazi, I say to myself, must admit that Herr Hitler has courage. And if the Fuehrer thinks, as think he must, that all Austria is on his side, he has some justification for his belief.

As he passes, the crowd surges forward in an ecstasy of emotional fervour. The women beside me at the open window spring to their feet. Their breasts are heaving. Their eyes are wet with tears of excitement. Thousands of hands shoot out at a rigid right angle, and to a series of roars of "Sieg Heil! Sieg Heil!" as rapid as machine-gun fire, the little man passes on his way.

This Tuesday of March 15, 1938, was Hitler's greatest triumph, and to find its parallel one has to go back to the days of Rome when illiterate privates became emperors.

The procession was not yet over. After the troops and the great man had passed, came lorries with Austrian Nazis and proletarian representatives from the big Viennese factories. They looked shoddy and unreal, and their presence was an anti-climax. Long before the last lorry had thundered past, the Fuehrer was already on his way back by aeroplane to Germany.

Slightly enervated by my own emotions, I went downstairs to the inner hall to order some coffee. Presently in came crowds of German officers who had been taking part in the parade. They sat down quietly at the tables. The largest group was round a little, dapper, bemonocled general. Again I was impressed by their behaviour. They were tired and very sober. They drank tea or coffee, smoked cigarettes, and spoke in low voices. These were not "the sons of Belial flown with insolence and wine" of my pre-war student days in Berlin. When, five abreast, they passed you on the stairs, they made a gap. They were polite and dignified. They looked impressively, almost alarmingly efficient.

As I sat watching them, I felt sad and depressed. During the day I had talked with several British officials who, like John Taylor, had lived with the Austrian situation for many years. They were full of regret for what they regarded as an historical tragedy. I tried to see the events of the day in their true perspective. For some years past the British had looked on Vienna as a second home. Austria had become almost a colony, an adopted daughter to be addressed in terms of "poor-dear Austria". Yet we had done little for our foster-child. True, we had lent her money. But recipients of doles regard them as a necessity and not as a favour. We had been mildly sentimental, but against this sentimentality could be set the post-war mistakes for which we all were responsible.

Immediately after a war for the self-determination of peoples, Austria had wanted to attach herself to Republican Germany. The French would not hear of it, and we had acquiesced. Yet morally it was just as wrong to refuse self-determination to a people who wished to be dependent as it was for Signor Mussolini to violate the liberty of a people who desired to remain independent. If this was not strictly true, it was at any rate the point of view of all Germans and many Austrians, and, inevitably, it made our moral indignation over Abyssinia very suspect to Central European eyes. Sentiment has its place in international relationships, but sometimes it acts like a film over the eyes of reality.

Again, the French had vetoed the later proposals of Dr. Curtius and Herr Stresemann for a Customs Union between Germany and Austria. And again we had done nothing. And to-day what would Britain and France not give to put the clock back to the days of Stresemann? Yet again, if we were against the Anschluss, surely self-interest demanded that we should have given to Austria the means of economic existence. In the early post-war days diplomatists like Sir George Clerk and Sir Francis Lindley had urged some system of economic co-operation between the Danubian States. But the effort had been poorly sustained. And because the effort was half-hearted, and because they believed that France and Britain would never permit the re-armament of Germany, the Czechoslovaks, the Rumanians, and the Yugoslavs had followed the example of their Great Power allies and had held on obstinately to all that they had won, delaying the concessions whose only chance of success depended on their being made in time.

The folly of this policy or lack of policy had helped to make Hitler and to rally to his standard Germans living outside of Germany. A re-armed Germany had now intervened to right in her own way wrongs which we should have rectified when we were strong and Germany and Austria were weak. And a considerable proportion of the Austrian people had acquiesced willingly, both in the method and the result of the intervention. The rule of force had been established. It was recognised not only by Austria, but by all Austria's neighbours. Everywhere there was fear of Germany, but there was also the caution and the respect which fear imposes. The post-war prestige of France and Britain had sunk. There were, of course, many other considerations and difficulties about which one could wrangle and argue interminably. But here was the whole conclusion of an unpleasant matter.

I was still hot and footsore, but I was too restless to feel tired. I had to make my plans. Now that the Fuehrer had left Austrian soil, there would be an inevitable lull. The process of Nazifying Austria would take many weeks to complete. I could not afford the time to stay and watch it. In any case, with Germans pouring into Vienna with every train, it was uncertain how long I could keep my room. Now that the annexation was an accomplished fact, Prague would be even more exciting than Vienna. A leading article in the *Deutsche Allgemeine Zeitung* that afternoon made this quite clear. The article dealt with the unfulfilled aims of Nazi policy in regard to German minorities in other countries. It pointed out that minorities were a curse to every country, that treaties which allotted large minorities were not peace treaties but only armistices, and that Germany had no further ambition than to reclaim the Germans at present living outside the Reich. There was a specific reference to the Sudeten Germans in Czechoslovakia.

Moved by these considerations, I made up my mind to go to Prague at once. I telephoned to John Taylor, our Consul, and within half-an-hour that great little man had obtained a sleeping-berth for me on the Prague train. Engaging a "sleeper" sounds a simple matter, but at a time when all is confusion and when even those in authority are not sure what is going to happen, it represents stout work and the possession of that powerful local influence which is the hallmark of every efficient Consul.

After packing my things, I took a taxi and drove out to Grinzing, the little suburb at the foot of the Kahlenberg. It is surrounded by vineyards, and here in summer the Viennese gather to drink the "Heuriger" or new wine and to make merry with song. It figures in one of the scenes of the film *Congress Dances*, and has given inspiration to all the Viennese song-writers from Schubert to Benatsky. Every Englishman who has been to Vienna knows it either from a personal visit or from the song:

> "Ich moecht' einmal wieder in Grinzing sein,
> Bei Wein, bei Wein, bei Wein."

The place had always been a favourite resort of mine, and, wondering if I should ever visit Vienna again, I came here to spend a quiet hour before going back to the Consulate to say good-bye to Taylor. In my desire for seclusion I had chosen the right spot. Citizens of Chicago lived through the worst period of gangsterdom without ever hearing a shot fired or once setting eyes on Al Capone. And here at Grinzing, with-in a mile or two of all the hubbub and cheering in the Ring, I found absolute peace. The place was deserted. The gardens of the little restaurants were a wilderness of winter-grass and neatly stacked tables. I found a small restaurant open, and talked to the Wirth while I drank a glass of wine.

"I hope that you are going to have a good season," I said politely.

He shrugged his shoulders. "God grant," he muttered fer-vently. "But with all these political changes who knows. There will be fewer tourists."

To the post-war Austrian "tourism" meant money and a profligacy of expenditure to which the local Viennese could not aspire.

I left him and drove up to Kobenzl where in bygone sum-mer days I had lain in the cool grass and read my book or tried to write. Here, too, was a satisfying solitude. From here Loti would have written a poetic farewell to Vienna. A superb description of the descending night would have sym-bolised the fallen greatness of an empire, now remembered only by the tombs of its Kaisers and the empty palaces of a once proud aristocracy. But my own thoughts were still busy with the honest Wirth that I had left down below. How much, I wondered, did revolutions and political convulsions help the small man. Future generations might benefit, because by the time they grew up revolutions were stabilised to a new normal. But the present generation always suffered.

Soon I was lost in the dark passages of futile speculation. But I lingered on, waiting on the wooded hill until the first lights began to twinkle from the Danube city. At first there was no sign that the night had fallen on a new Vienna. Slowly the stars came out, very bright in the clear atmosphere. Then suddenly a stream of yellow-electricity shot up from the centre of the city. The Rathaus had sprung into flood-light in honour of the Nazi triumph.

On my way back into the city I passed a group of Austrian Nazis. They were marching in military formation, and singing the words of the *Horst Wessel Lied*:

> "Die Strasse frei den braunen Batallionen,
> Die Strasse frei dem Sturmabteilungsmann!
> Es schaut auf uns voll Hoffnung Millionen;
> Der Tag fuer Freiheit und fuer Brot bricht an."

> [Make free the way for our brave Brown battalions;
> For gallant storm-troops sweep the broad road clear.
> On us are fixed the longing hopes of millions;
> The Day for Freedom and for Bread draws near.]

In St. Petersburg I had seen another revolution carried out to a similar slogan of bread—"bread and peace". But Russia had found no peace. Herr Hitler would bring bread to Vienna. German efficiency would see to that. But would he bring freedom?

It was strange to hear the German Nazi Lied sung by Austrians in a city which had won universal fame for Lieder of a lighter sort, and which even in the difficult post-war years had given to the world artists and singers like Paula Wessely.

Yet even in its death-agony anti-Nazi Vienna could still smile bravely, and find in the *Horst Wessel Lied* the inspiration for the first Viennese jest on the Hitlerian *coup d'état*. On the first day of the new régime the little daughter of an anti-Nazi Austrian family came back from school.

"Well, Liesl," said her anxious father, "how did you get on?"

"Oh, not so bad," said the little girl, "the teacher made us sing the *Paula Wessely Lied* all the time."

It was after seven before I reached the Consulate. But John Taylor was still working at full pressure. His day had been full of incident. An English business man with a Jewish name had been arrested and nearly beaten up by Austrian Nazis. Taylor had secured his release. On the Consular desk lay a sheaf of telegrams from England seeking news of English girls who were studying German and art in Vienna. One signed by Lord Halifax requested the Consul to send home at once Miss Ormsby-Gore, the daughter of the former Secretary of State for the Colonies. Taylor had answered all the telegrams and made the necessary arrangements for Miss Ormsby-Gore's departure. Yet his work was not over. The queue of Jewish suppliants seemed as large as ever.

I sat down and waited. At last everyone had been dealt with, and I helped Taylor to clear up. In the outer room we found a narrow, oblong tin. For a second I half-wondered if it might be an infernal machine. Taylor unscrewed it. It contained a packet of rubber sheaths. Under Nazi law the sale of contraceptives is a serious offence. Presumably, some anti-Nazi visitor, afraid of being beaten up if he were found with such a tin in his possession, had discreetly left it in the Consulate.

When all was ready, I went off to dine with Taylor before catching the night train to Prague. His house was on the outskirts, and to reach it we had to drive through the city. Strangely enough, the streets, full all day, were now almost deserted. The vast crowd, worn out by three days of over-enthusiasm, had at last gone indoors. Even the street-hawkers, who had reaped a rich harvest from the sale of swastika badges and photographs of the Fuehrer, had disappeared. In the stillness of the star-lit night Vienna looked bewilderingly beautiful.

Dinner was an interrupted meal, Taylor being called away to the telephone every few minutes. But he gave me a graphic account of the situation as he had seen it. Behind the scenes of enthusiasm in the street, things were moving fast. The thousands of Himmler's Gestapo agents had already been busy. The Schnellgericht had claimed its first victims. Arrests were being carried out ruthlessly. Several British subjects had been threatened. Others, employed by Jewish firms, were already bemoaning the almost certain loss of their jobs.

These were the commonplaces of a Consul's daily round. He recounted them without any display of nervousness or excitement.

He asked me if I had heard any news of Douglas Reed, *The Times* Vienna correspondent and subsequent author of *Insanity Fair*. Reed, who had written a previous book on the Reichstag fire, was in the Nazi black books and had wisely taken his departure as soon as the Gestapo agents made their first appearance in Vienna. Taylor had provided him with a new British passport on which there was no mention of his profession. News had reached the Consulate that Reed had been searched at the aerodrome and that his money had been taken from him. No one knew whether he had been arrested or allowed to leave the country, and it was not until I reached Prague that I learnt that he had arrived safely in Switzerland.

There was another guest besides myself at the Consular dinner-table. This was a Jewish lawyer, who had done much excellent work for the British authorities in Vienna. He was leaving for Prague that night, and would have the sleeper next to mine. Taylor, who had provided him with special papers, begged me to keep an eye on him and to help him in case of any trouble. I gave my promise at once, but not without a feeling of uneasiness which increased when Taylor warned me that I could not expect to cross the Czechoslovak frontier as easily as I had entered Austria from Yugoslavia.

At the station, however, all was normal. Tired and leg-weary, I entered my sleeper. I had not rested for nearly twenty hours, and we were close to Prague before I awoke. Once again I had crossed the frontier without a German even entering my compartment.

In the grey dawn, with a smoke-pall hanging over the city, I felt a twinge of conscience regarding the fate of the Jewish lawyer. I should have been awake and vigilant at the frontier. I opened my door, and there he was, standing in the corridor, a wan smile of relief on his face. My own relief was almost as great. He was safe, even if he had been deprived of all that he possessed.

The British Legation servant was on the platform, and soon I was being conveyed in a comfortable car to the Thun Palace, where formerly I had spent so many happy years. At the great archway gate stood Rosenbaum, Sir George Clerk's former butler and now the occupant of the Legation porter's lodge.

It was not yet seven, and I was taken up to my bedroom on the third floor. I opened the big windows and looked down on the city below me. The fog had lifted, and the dull dawn had become a clear spring morning. Slowly I took in the huge expanse of vista from Kramař's villa on the left, across the new town, over the waters of the Vltava river, shining like silver in the sun, to the green cupolas of St. Mikuláš beneath the shadow of the Petřin hill on the right.

I lingered over the old landmarks: the roof of the National theatre, the statue of Jan Nepomuk, and the towers of the Karluv Most. My emotions were mixed. I felt a nostalgic regret for the past. Never again should I see President Masaryk sitting erect on his horse and riding in the Stromovka in the early hours of the morning before riotous young secretaries had gone to their bed. He was the noblest figure and the fairest-minded man that I had met in any country since the war. I thanked God that the seventeen years of his presidency had been blessed with peace, that he had died in the knowledge that his work had prospered, that he had been spared the grim present and the perhaps grimmer future. Kramař, embittered nationalist, but full of charm, was also dead. Švehla, too, was gone, and many others besides, and their passing marked the milestones in my own life.

But there was also happiness in my heart. I was in a city in which I had many friends. Above all, there was an air in which one could breathe freely. In Vienna the hedge of rifles had seemed to choke me. Here I was in a democratic country which, unlike some of my countrymen, I had always liked and which since its creation had made more rapid progress than any country that I had ever visited. And in that work of progress towards a better civilisation I was proud to have been even in the humblest way a participant.

CHAPTER THREE

I FOUND PRAGUE under the emotional domination of the events in Austria. One had only to look at the map of central Europe in order to realise that the prevailing anxiety was inevitable. Czechoslovakia had built a series of almost impregnable Maginot lines to the North. Now she had a new danger in her rear. With 100,000—or was it 200,000?—German troops spread over Austria, she was nipped between the pincers of a huge German nut-cracker. When and how would it close?

This was the question which agitated the mind of every Czech. Many wondered what Britain and France would do. Some had high hopes; others, disillusioned by unfulfilled promises, were pessimistic. Most people were prepared for far-reaching concessions to the Sudeten-Germans. All were determined to fight to the bitter end, if Germany, as many feared, intended to annex their country. It was this determination, combined with the admirable calm of the whole population, which made the strongest impression on me.

My time was fully occupied in seeing old friends. In Vienna it had been difficult to establish contact with the authorities. The Austrians had ceased to count. The chief actors in the drama of annexation were Germans, and all of them had been engaged in staging the pageant of the Fuehrer's triumph. Here in Prague my difficulty was to avoid seeing too many people. I was glad that I was staying at our Legation. My position as a guest provided me with an adequate excuse for evading embarrassing questions.

The Legation staff was working overtime, but I had, of course, several long talks and walks with Basil Newton, our Minister. He had come to Prague from Berlin where he had been Counsellor of Embassy, and he knew both the Czech and the German points of view. A descendant of Cochrane, he has much of that great admiral's phlegm. I had worked

with him in London for a few months after the war and
never once had I seen him flurried or impatient. Shrewd in
judgment and tactful in manner, he possesses an almost judi-
cial impartiality, a quality valuable in a diplomatist, essential
in a country like Czechoslovakia, and, unfortunately, not
possessed by all previous British Ministers in Prague. Basil
Newton, I felt, was a sound man for a delicate and most difficult situation.

My first contact with Czech officialdom prepared me for
the barrage of questions which were to be fired at me from
all sides. On the night of my return to the city where I had
spent so many years I dined with an official of the Czech
Foreign Office. He was a fine fellow, big, strong, intelligent,
and a brilliant linguist. He had been an officer in the former
Austrian army and had spent two years in Russia as a war-
prisoner. He had re-visited that country after the war as a
Czechoslovak subject and spoke Russian with an easy
fluency. His views on Russia represented a fundamental
difference between Czechoslovakia and her Little Entente
partners, Yugoslavia and Rumania. The Yugoslavs and the
Rumanians have a wholesome dread of Bolshevik Russia.
Many Czechs believe in the efficacy of Czechoslovakia's pact
with the Soviet Government.

My friend was one of them. He had no sympathy with
Bolshevism. He was not perturbed by the Moscow trials, nor
was his faith shaken by the crude elimination of the Bolshevik Old Guard. He regarded these purges as inevitable and
even desirable. He saw in them a proof of the growing
strength of nationalism in Russia.

What he did rely on was the new generation which knew
nothing of the outside world, but which was strong and
conscious of its power. The fundamental and lasting effect of
the Russian revolution had been, not the establishment of a
new political system, but the transformation of the old, slow-
witted, bearded "mujik" into a smart, clean-shaven young
man who was already more air-minded than most western

Europeans. Nor was my Czech friend worried by any doubts regarding the efficiency of an army whose commanding officers could never be certain whether they were going to be promoted or executed. Russia had men enough, and there were scores of good officers to take the place of traitors.

His views were perhaps extreme, but I also met more highly-placed Czechs who were convinced not only that Russia was much stronger militarily than in 1914—and this I was prepared to believe—but also that she would honour her pledges without hesitation.

Probably to many Czechs the wish is father to the thought, although I am bound to admit that the Czechoslovak Foreign Office is exceptionally well-informed about Russia. I could not help feeling that this faith in Russia was perhaps the gravest complication in a situation that bristled with a thousand difficulties. For, whatever might be Herr Hitler's objectives in Czechoslovakia, his main aim was certainly to to make it impossible for Czechoslovakia to be used as a jumping-off ground for a Franco-Russian attack on Germany.

We dined in a new fish restaurant under the shadow of the huge statue of King Wenceslaus, and after dinner my host offered to take me round the night haunts of Prague. But my heart was not in *Nachtlokals*. I had re-visited them completely and thoroughly the year before with some friends that I had met at Karel Čapek's. And I had seen ghosts, phantoms of once brilliant pianists who had never emerged from the morass of night-life, and of a talented operatic tenor who had slid down into Avernus. The girls of yester-year had disappeared, their short tinsel reign over. Only the proprietors and the head-waiters remained.

I wanted to talk politics, and we went to a quiet little wine-cellar in a sixteenth century house. The cellar roof was vaulted. On a shelf old-fashioned bottles stood between sets of medieval armour. A rough slab on the wall bore the signature of an Imperial hangman who had plied a busy

s

trade after the battle of the White Mountain, where in 1620 Bohemia lost her independence. A radio set, relaying pre-war gipsy songs, from Moscow of all places, provided the only touch of modernity. And here we sat until late into the night, while my friend tried to cross-examine me on what Britain would do in certain eventualities. Were we blind to our danger? Did we not realise that the future of the British Empire might be lost or won on the battlefields of Czecho-slovakia?

I thought that this was not impossible. Even more than Belgium Czechoslovakia had been the cockpit of Europe's long list of wars. During the seven years of my more or less permanent residence I had fished near or shot over a dozen battlefields, including Austerlitz, Hochkirchen, Turnau, Kolin and Koenniggraetz.

But what could I say? I was ignorant of the intentions of my Government. In all probability they were still unformed, for the German problem in Czechoslovakia had as many sides as the facets of a diamond. In my heart I felt that, if the Czechs were to fight alone, the venture would be tanta-mount to suicide. If Hitler only wanted, as he had always stated, to safeguard the three-and-a-quarter million German minority, could there be a European war over the fate of the Sudeten Germans? That would be illogical, because at the end of the war, if Germany's opponents were victorious, the problem would still remain. If the Fuehrer intended to incor-porate the German minority in the Reich, could we go to war? The answer was more difficult. There was a fairly solid mass of Germans living on the Northern frontier of Czecho-slovakia, but there were other enclaves of Germans extend-ing deeply into the country. In many places the two races were hopelessly intermingled. The very nomenclature stressed the absence of clear-cut divisions. The three German Ministers who had been members of the Czechoslovak Cabinet were called Czech, Spina, and Zahiček, all three pure Czech names. One of the leaders of the Czech Socialists was

Pan Nemec—Mr. German. My late friend and former Czech Finance Minister bore the German name of Sonntag. But Britain, I felt, would not go to war to prevent a partial incorporation of the German minority, more especially as the issue was never likely to be presented in the form of an external aggression. The Fuehrer liked to work from the inside.

There was another alternative. Shakespeare had set a seaboard to Bohemia less ignorantly than most people supposed, for at one period of her history Bohemia extended to the Adriatic. What frontiers would Hitler fix? If he intended to annex all Czechoslovakia, would we fight? This was the most difficult decision of all. With control of the great Škoda works and of the powerful Czech industry, Germany would be immensely strong. Yet my instinct told me that, if the British people had to choose between a preventive war now and the possibility of a war against a more powerful Germany later on, they would prefer the possibility to the certainty.

There remained the question of concessions. Could and would the Czechoslovak Government go far enough? Concessions were necessary. They should have been made in the easy and now irrevocable past. It was true that the Czechs treated their minorities better than the Italians or the Poles or the Hungarians treated theirs. The Germans of Czechoslovakia had their full share of schools. They were well represented in the judiciary. But they had legitimate grievances. They had been official-ridden. There had been aggravating pin-pricks by the local Czech police. There was also the unpleasant fact that North Bohemia, where the Germans were concentrated, was a distressed area. Above all, there was the feeling of every German in Czechoslovakia that he belonged to a Herrenvolk, a master race, and that the Czechs and the Slovaks were a cattle folk or, at best, a race of servants. For fifteen years the feeling had been suppressed. The advent to power of Herr Hitler had fanned it again into a roaring flame.

In my replies to my Czech friend's questions I concentrated on the concessions. I pointed out that, in order to ensure even temporary peace, the new Germany had to be reckoned with, her wrongs, real or imaginary, examined impartially, and her suspicions of wilful frustration removed. Compromise was difficult, but it must be tried. . . .

My friend agreed, but in every argument he always came back to the same question: "What if Germany wants more than the utmost concessions that any independent state can make? What will you do then?"

Once again I "hedged", saying that I was sure that the British Government would make every effort to promote and assist a fair compromise. I knew that my answer would give little satisfaction.

I had heard other Czechs, much more important public figures than my host, say bluntly: "What are you going to do? If only you will tell us plainly, we shall know what to do ourselves. If you will do nothing, then we must go to Berlin and make the best terms we can before it is too late."

I realised that compromise with Germany at other people's expense might prove a dangerous policy and might merely hasten the day when, without friends, we should have to face a Germany with whom no compromise was possible. Yet I knew that there were powerful influences in Britain which were working for peace at any price. Already they were conducting a shameful propaganda describing Czecho-slovakia as a ramshackle state unfit to govern itself.

These were the two postulates. A show of firmness would pull Germany up sharply. She probably did not want war now. On the other hand, dictators dared not risk a diplomatic defeat, and a rigid attitude might easily provoke a cataclysm. To anyone who knew the East it was already clear that, whoever might win the war between Japan and China, the white races had lost it. A European war would mean the eclipse of Europe and the transfer of civilisation to the New World.

A reluctance to pledge Britain to premature commitments had always been the traditional feature of British diplomacy. In the past it had proved a sound policy. Even since the war British patience had more than once acted as a brake on a Europe which had been in danger of running away with itself. To-day, patience was more necessary than ever even if at times it seemed to aid the exponents of blackmail diplomacy. It was, however, a comfortless anodyne to a nation which was living on the edge of a volcano. If only we had been stronger, less torn by internal dissensions, there would have been less need of patience. . . .

I went to bed tired and slightly pessimistic.

There were sufficient grounds for pessimism, especially in the newspapers which were full of accounts of suicides of anti-Nazi Austrians in Vienna. On my first day in Prague Major Fey, the former military collaborator of Dollfuss, shot himself after first killing his wife and his nineteen-years-old son, and a prominent Austrian lawyer threw himself out of a high window. On the same day I saw in Prague the long funeral cortège which accompanied the coffin of Ottokar Fischer, the gentle Czech poet and director of the National Theatre, to its last resting-place. He had died of excitement on reading the news of the arrival of the German troops in Austria.

Very soon, however, the fine weather and the cheerful aspect of the Prague streets revived my spirits. A nation which is on the verge of disaster betrays its anxiety by a false gaiety. Its mind is animated by the spirit of "eat, drink and be merry, for to-morrow we die." It prepares itself for the inevitable by sitting up late, drinking champagne, and spending its money recklessly in a feverish desire to squeeze the last juices of enjoyment from a fruit that is to be stolen from it.

I found none of these signs of nervous collapse in Prague. I saw no traces of dejection on the face of the Czech people. Men and women went about their business with a quiet confidence which was good to see. Young clerks made a flying jump at moving tramcars and grinned when they landed safely. Plump business men drank their Pilsener with philosophic calm in the crowded cafés. Urchins played football in the street corners with a rag ball when the policeman's eyes were turned away. The bookshops were full of books in every language. Here were no wares of war such as I had seen in Vienna. Side by side with the novels of authors like Wells, Galsworthy, Somerset Maugham, Sinclair Lewis, Martin du Gard and Thomas Mann, were numerous works on art, sociology, architecture, and history in striking testimony to the culture of a nation which has been taught by Masaryk that the cure for educational ills is more and better education.

I went to see my old fishing friend, Vladimir Rott, who has always placed his delectable fishing waters at the disposal of every English angler who visits Prague. I do not say that I found him cheerful. But at any rate he was undismayed. We talked, of course, of the situation. That was inevitable. But he asked no awkward questions, and soon we were back on the Ottava, the silver Spey which flows beside the old Castle of Raby where Žižka, the Czech Cromwell, lost an eye.

"You will come again in June, yes?" he said. "If all goes well, we shall go together to Raby."

Only the "if" betrayed the anxiety which every Czech must have felt at that hour.

I called, too, on my publisher. Like everyone else he had been affected by the uncertainty of the political situation. When the Hitler stroke fell on Vienna, he had been on the point of getting married. Now he had postponed his marriage until the horizon cleared. But he was cheerful enough. Trade was good. Up to now the book market had prospered. He asked me many questions about my new book. Our conversation was brisk and business-like.

On his desk lay a pile of thin paper-covered books. The

outside cover was silver-grey with a design of a weeping woman dressed in black with five silver swords in her breast. The books were copies of Karel Čapek's latest play *Mother*. It is the whole drama of post-war civilisation concentrated in the life of a mother whose husband and four sons have been killed in foreign wars or civil wars. One son, the youngest, remains. In the last act the wireless breaks the silence of the tragic household. "Calling all the world. Calling all the people. This morning the enemy's aeroplanes attacked the village of Borzo and bombed the village school. Machine-guns shot down the school-children. Eighty were wounded. Nineteen killed. Thirty-five blown to pieces . . ."

The dazed mother gives a little cry: "Children! Someone is killing the children."

Then she turns to the wall, takes down a rifle, and puts it in the hands of her last remaining son. "Go," she says.

Czech soldiers, and officers too, I saw in plenty. The men looked stolid and, in their deep brown khaki, rather sombre. The officers made an impression of quiet efficiency, but their appearance was slightly unsoldierly. Their general manner was unobtrusive. They lacked the "Schneidigkeit" and hard exterior of the typical German officer. The truth is that the Czechoslovak army is well-trained and splendidly equipped, but that the Czechs are soldiers more by necessity than by natural instinct. A race which looks to Masaryk as its national philosopher has no love of fighting for fighting's sake. If aeroplanes soar daily over Prague, they are there for defence and not for aggression. More than most nations, the Czechs believe in the civilisation of butter and not of guns. And a wise administration has made the butter go round liberally.

There is one aspect of Prague which always pleases me. It is the general well-being of the whole people and the absence of contrasts between poverty and wealth. On most afternoons I took a car and drove out into the country, partly to revisit old haunts and partly to note the changes. I was astounded by the prosperity of the peasantry, the vast extension of the building programme, the neat villages with their new houses, and the well-tilled fields. These changes represented a progress which was not confined to the Prague district.

A year ago I had made a tour of Slovakia. I had first visited the country in 1920 and had been moved to pity by the backwardness and wretched poverty of the people. In 1937 I saw a new province with fine roads, new villages with new churches and schools, and a regenerated peasantry which was receiving good prices for its grain and from the new tobacco industry. One house in every four was new and had been built during the last ten years. There was electric light everywhere. I had a long talk with M. Jančak, the Director of Public Works. He impressed me by his efficiency and his eagerness to realise an ambitious programme. I met the leading Slovak political leaders, the chief business men, and the most prominent writers. I found everywhere one prevailing opinion. In the first years of the new republic the Czechs, flushed with the unaccustomed enthusiasm of bureaucratic power, had made mistakes. But the mistakes had been rectified. Every Slovak was pleased with the present and looked forward eagerly to the future. Every Slovak was proud of the fact that he could claim both Masaryk and Milan Hodža, the present Prime Minister of Czechoslovakia, as a compatriot.

Admittedly, there were Slovaks who desired a fuller measure of autonomy, just as there are Scots who demand a fuller measure of self-government for Scotland. There was the aged Father Hlinka who gave such indiscreet interviews to foreign journalists. But no one who knew Hlinka had any doubts of his broader patriotism.

I had met him in the early post-war years. He impressed me as a man obsessed with his self-chosen rôle of a martyr. I remembered when he had been seeking a martyr's crown with more violence than usual. It was, I think, in 1920. The

Czechs had been forced to put some restraint on him. He had been arrested and taken, much to his disgust, to the splendidly equipped Czech sanitorium in the Podol district of Prague. Here he had been installed with every comfort. The Masaryk family sent him flowers and fruit. One day M. Jan Masaryk, the present Czechoslovak Minister in London, came to see him, and the old gentleman exploded.

"Look here, Jan," he said, "this is too bad. I thought you were my friend. I want a real jail."

That was Hlinka. He had been a rebel all his life, an Irish Slav whose hand was against every Government. For forty years it had been against the Hungarian Government. If sometimes his passion for oratory led him to compare the errors of the Czechoslovak Government with the sins of Magyarism, did that mean that he wished to return to the past? No. Not even for a front page in the foreign press. Hlinka, and every Slovak, knew that across the frontier were proud Hungarian magnates who dreamed of the return of their lost acres and who hoped to fish successfully in the troubled waters which Germany was now creating. Was it thinkable that an awakened peasantry would return willingly and without a struggle to the feudalism of the Middle Ages? A schoolboy could give the answer. Yet in Britain there were men—peers and members of Parliament—who believed that such a return was not only possible but even necessary to the peace and progress of Europe. There were others who even pretended that it was desired by the Slovaks themselves. British peers had had a soft place in their hearts for Hungarians ever since Montrose had rewarded a Hungarian poet for "writing some verses to my lord." By all means let Hungary's wrongs be righted, but not to the extent of demanding that a people who had been freed should be put back under Magyar yoke.

One afternoon I drove out to the Star Palace, from which the ill-fated Frederick of the Palatinate and his Stuart Consort, "The Winter Queen", had watched the Battle of the

White Mountain. In 1920 it was completely in the country. To-day, the new Prague comes almost to its fringe. In the early sunset the little wood in which the Palace stands looked very peaceful. Doubtless, the sun had gone down on as peaceful scenes during the Thirty Years' War when half-Europe was in arms. I could not help wondering how soon the graceful harmony of these leafless trees and brown fields might be destroyed by the bombs of attacking aeroplanes.

That evening I had my first reunion with the Bubelas. Ctibor Bubela was the first Czech secretary of the British Legation in Prague and in that capacity gave invaluable assistance to our first Minister, Sir George Clerk. He is now one of the managers of the huge coal and banking concern of Pechek. His wife was my former secretary, and at their marriage I made my first speech in Czech. They are a charming couple, and Bubela himself, fair-haired and blue-eyed, is one of the most broad-minded, cultured, and reliable men that I know.

They introduced me to their two boys, fine, upstanding youngsters with an excellent knowledge of English. They had been brought up on English, for Mrs. Bubela has a deeper knowledge of English literature than most English-women and has made a special study of the works of Mr. Somerset Maugham.

Bubela was calm and restrained as he always is. His business took him almost weekly to Berlin, and, whatever he may have thought of Nazi ambitions, he had nothing but praise for the German officials with whom he came into contact. They were correct and even friendly in their business dealings. They carried out their contracts with a punctiliousness which was rare in other Central European countries. As for the political future, the Czechs would be as conciliatory as possible. But of course there were limits beyond which no people could go.

I was glad to listen to so much common sense from Bubela. I heard similar views expressed by nearly every

responsible Czech in Prague, and this, too, in the midst of a
propaganda campaign conducted from Berlin with a violence of language and a wilful perversion of the facts that
were revolting to decency. Even the Narodni Democrats,
the followers of the late Dr. Kramař, the chief Czech Chau-
vinist and a bitter opponent of Masaryk and Dr. Beneš, had
lost much of their sting, and in Dr. Hochman, Kramař's
political executor, I met a man who was not only intelligent
but also fair-minded and ready for a compromise which was
dictated less by fear than by the knowledge that, whatever
happened, Germans and Czechs would have to live side by
side. Indeed, in Prague I found more tolerance than I had
met with in any other European capital east of the Rhine
and south of the Baltic. This is no more than the truth. It has
been true since 1932. It is true to-day and is in one sense a
justification of Czechoslovakia's right to an independent
existence.

If Bubela was reassuring, I could see that Mrs. Bubela was
worried.

"What is going to happen to us, Mr. Lockhart?" she said.

She made a brave face, but there was a note of anxiety in
her voice. I knew that when she said "us" she meant what
was going to happen to her boys. My feelings were tugged
in two directions. Reason ranked me on the side of caution
and compromise. Yet I could not be blind or indifferent to
the dangers which threatened a people who had always
treated me with kindness and consideration. All my personal
sympathies were with these Czechs and Slovaks, whose
virtues had never received their just appreciation in Britain
and whose administrative failings, minor compared with
those of most European nations, had been wilfully exaggerated by interested parties.

CHAPTER FOUR

I FIND IT difficult to convey to the English reader who has never been abroad an accurate impression of the atmosphere created in all the smaller states of Central Europe by the events of March 11, 1938. In a night frontiers, which had been accepted willy-nilly as stable, became suddenly fluid. The flood-gates were open to ambitions long nourished in secret.

In some cases the ambitions were evil. Poland, unable to resist the dangerous temptations of opportunism, did not hesitate to bully and embarrass a sister Slav people by putting forward extravagant demands on behalf of her small minority in Czechoslovakia. Hungary, with a far larger minority to reclaim, had more legitimate grievances. But even in the countries where ambitions were strongest, hopes were tempered by fears. Hungarian magnates might wish to regain their lost estates in Slovakia, but they could hardly regard with equanimity the new situation in their own country. They were monarchists. Now their hopes of a Habsburg restoration had been shattered. Henceforth they would have to look to Berlin for the satisfaction of their claims. It was not a pleasant prospect. A proud aristocracy had little in common with Nazi upstarts, and in Hungary itself there were young Hungarian peasants who hated the maintenance of feudal rights, and who were ready to embrace the Nazi faith with much of the fervour and romanticism of its original exponents.

There was another factor which was far more disturbing. Was it not an old German boast that a German could drive a horse and cart from the Bavarian frontier to the Black Sea and sleep every night of the long journey in a German village? The boast might be exaggerated, but it had been resurrected, and in all the Central European and Balkan states there were German minorities, varying in size and compactness, but unpleasantly alike in their demands for a place under a German sun. They were the outriders of the Nazi drive to the south-east. As the orbit of Germany's influence extended, their demands and claims were certain to become more vocal and more insistent.

Although, as Dr. Goebbels had said with menacing bluntness, the Nazis had a Henlein in every country, the diplomatic energy of the Reich was concentrated on Prague. Perhaps the best idea of the prevailing tension can be conveyed by the presence of the large number of foreigners who had suddenly descended on the Czechoslovak capital. The city, once neglected by all except the business man and the tourist, was now full of English men and women. Many of them were journalists.

Kennedy of *The Times* was staying at the British Legation; a shrewd, intelligent man, with a cultural background and a first-hand experience of British diplomacy. The experience had not been acquired in journalism. His father had been a professional diplomatist, ending his career as British Minister to Rumania, and the son had spent his youth in half-a-dozen European capitals.

The widely-travelled Ward Price, fresh from Hitler and impressed by the might of Germany, came to luncheon with the British Minister. He was full of news of the German aims. The Fuehrer would demand autonomy for the German minority in Czechoslovakia and the withdrawal of the Czechoslovak troops from the German frontier. Slovakia or part of it would go back to Hungary. Bohemia and Moravia would remain independent, but within the orbit of German political influence. The Czechs would have to acquiesce. Small nations must think small. Schuschnigg had nearly caused a European war by trying to outwit Hitler. The Czechs might make history as the race that saved Europe from a catastrophic war. In any case submission was their only hope. If they fought, they would find themselves in the position of Abyssinia.

There were other famous special correspondents in the city. They belonged to every nationality. They filled the hotels. Their cars stood in the great courtyard of the Hradčany while their owners solicited interviews with Dr. Beneš or Dr. Hodža. More than one secret agent was pointed out to me, and, probably, there were many others. I thought of Seton Merriman's diplomatic novels. The vultures were gathering.

If it was easy for me to see all the Czechs whom I wanted to see, I did not neglect the German-Bohemians, among whom I had many friends. During my official career in Prague immediately after the war I had served under a wise chief in Sir George Clerk, who had made it his business to maintain excellent relations with both Czechs and Germans in the Republic in the hopes of promoting a *modus vivendi* between the two races. Even in those days the animosities had been bitter enough. The Czechs were then aggressively anti-German. The German-Bohemians, as they called themselves, spoke contemptuously of the Czechs. The wave of war-hate had not abated.

Then gradually the wiser elements among both races took the upper hand. The Czechs, if not conciliatory enough, saw the wisdom of conciliation. The Germans were offered and accepted three seats in the Cabinet. The three German Parties whom the new Ministers represented became known as the Activists. And but for Czech dilatoriness and the economic slump of 1929, which hit German Bohemia harder than any other area of the Republic, Activism might have succeeded. It had never commanded the support of the whole German minority. It was a movement supported mainly by the German proletariat, the industrialists, and the small landowners. Its foundations already undermined by the economic distress in the German areas, Activism began to lose ground with the advent to power of Herr Hitler. With the annexation of Austria, the movement received its death-blow. The Nazi or Henlein Party in Czechoslovakia became all-powerful.

Its origin and growth provide the drama of one of the most curious episodes in post-war history. To find the roots of the new Party one must go back to small groups of disgruntled Germans who had served in the war, and who found it hard to settle down under new masters whom they had been brought up to regard as traitors. Concurrently with the beginnings of National-Socialism in Germany itself these groups began to organise themselves. They formed an association called the Kameradschaftsbund. They gained control of the German-Bohemian Boy Scouts known as the Wandervoegel.

When Herr Hitler won his first election triumph in 1932, the Kameradschaftsbund began to look for a leader. Its choice fell on Konrad Henlein, a German-Bohemian born in 1898 in Reichenau near Gablonz, which possesses a once-flourishing industry, mainly controlled by Jews, in glass beads and cheap imitation jewellery. In many respects it was a curious choice. Konrad Henlein was then a nonentity. He had served in the war with no particular distinction, and the end of it found him as a prisoner-of-war on the island of Asinara. After his return he became an employee in the branch of a German bank in the place of his birth. From his early youth he had been a member of the local German "Turnverband" or gymnastic society, and in 1925, despairing of promotion in his bank, he accepted a post as gymnastic instructor in Asch.

In its search for a suitable leader the Kameradschaftsbund turned naturally to the "Turnverband", which in German eyes had always been associated with the principle of leadership. In selecting Konrad Henlein the "Kameradschaftsbund" leaders were influenced by several amusing considerations. Henlein's name was two-syllabic and began with H. In Czechoslovakia the greeting "Heil Hitler" was forbidden. But it was easy to say "Heil H." and explain to the police that one meant "Heil Henlein". Undoubtedly, too, the ambitious "Kameradschaftsbund hoped and believed that

Konrad Henlein would prove a pliable and subservient leader. He was no orator. He had never shown any interest in party politics. His chief asset was a pleasing manner which inspired the confidence not only of his supporters, but also of foreigners and even of his opponents. Morally he had a clean slate. He was sober in his habits and modest in his expenditure. He personified the best type of the clean, tidy and industrious lower German-Bohemian bourgeoisie.

But for one disturbing incident Konrad Henlein might have remained in comparative subservience. Early in 1938 the Czechoslovak authorities arrested a group of German-Bohemian Nazis on a charge of homosexual practices. Chief among the prisoners was Heinrich Rutha, one of the leaders of the Kamaradschaftsbund. While he was awaiting trial, Rutha committed suicide, placing a dummy in his bed, which was visible from the tiny observation window of his cell, and hanging himself with his sock suspenders in a corner which was out of sight. After his suicide those who were implicated with him in the homosexual charge were tried, and several Nazis were convicted and sentenced. Like Nazi Germany the Kameradschaftsbund had produced its scandal, and the revelations benefited Konrad Henlein. His stock rose. The influence of the Kameradschaftsbund declined.

Long before Herr Hitler's dramatic coup in Vienna it was easy to follow the snowball growth of the Henlein Party and the corresponding decline in the fortunes of the Activists. At the end of January, 1937, I had a long conversation with Dr. Zajiček, the ablest German Minister in the Czechoslovak Cabinet. He was very fair to the Czechs, or rather to his Czech colleagues, in his comments. He did not doubt their good intentions. He understood their difficulties, especially in regard to their promise to give to the German-Bohemians their full proportional representation in the Civil Service. To implement this promise quickly would mean the displacement of thousands of Czech officials. Yet speed was essential.

"If the Czechs," he said, "do not help us soon with more substantial concessions, we Activists will be wiped out. Henlein
may not be a great man. But he has German-Bohemian
youth behind him."

The Minister spoke calmly, but prophetically. I did not see
him during my 1938 visit, but I met many other Activists.
They were in full retreat, not because they themselves had
been infected by the Nazi virus, not because they longed for
incorporation in the German Reich, but because they realised the hopelessness of their own situation and the dangers
of a now futile co-operation with the Czechs.

There was one prominent German Activist with whom I
had long been on terms of friendship. It is significant of the
change that has taken place, of the menace that hangs over
every German-Bohemian who is not a Nazi, that to-day I
must not give his name. In 1937 he had criticised the Czechs
for their slowness in not solving a problem which might have
been settled long ago. But he had been optimistic. Now he
had abandoned hope.

"It is," he said, "quite useless for the Czechs to do anything for us now. We Activists are dead. Whatever concessions the Czechs may now make, Henlein will say: 'They
do not go far enough', or 'They have been made for me and
through fear of me'."

My friend spoke no more than the truth. Even the Czechs
realised that the Activist game had been played and lost, and
that they now had to deal with Henlein.

I did not see the German-Bohemian leader himself. He
was absent on one of his mystery visits. But I met other
members of his Party. I found their views vague and indefinite. It was impossible to pin them down to a firm expression of their wishes. When I asked them if they desired incorporation with the Reich or if they would be content with a
large measure of autonomy inside the Czechoslovak Republic, they avoided a direct answer. On the whole I gathered
that, given certain far-reaching concessions, they would be

T

satisfied with autonomy within the Republic. But in their general attitude three things were evident. They regarded Herr Hitler as their tribal god. They looked across the frontier to Germany from their own distressed area, and they saw the evidences, if not of prosperity, at least of employment. Although they were polite enough to me, there was a new truculence in their abuse of the Czechs. It was not merely the nature of their complaints—and they quoted many specific instances of Czech misrule. It was the manner in which they were made. In their minds the theory of the Herrenvolk or master-race was dominant.

I must insist on this racial aspect of the German-Bohemian attitude, because it forms the chief obstacle to any permanent settlement of the minority problem in Czechoslovakia. It is an attitude which we British must be chary of criticising too harshly, for in some respects our own attitude towards foreigners is not dissimilar. We ourselves are a Great Power, and we are not free from a Great Power psychology.

To some extent the Americans share these prejudices. I remember how, after the war, the Allied fleets in the Bosphorus had great difficulty in provisioning their ships. The British did most of the work and had a special provision ship, rather black and dirty and called "The Dago". One day the American admiral requested the British admiral to help him with supplies. The British flagship signalled back: "Please apply to 'the Dago' ". The American promptly ordered a cutter and went off to call on the Italian admiral.

I have also been told by a diplomatist that Signor Mussolini's dislike of Mr. Eden has its roots in certain contemptuous remarks alleged to have been made in semi-privacy by the former British Foreign Secretary and reported back to the Italian Embassy and thence, of course, to Rome. Even our internationalists are not free from this taint of racial arrogance. At P.E.N. Club conferences the English delegates ooze a condescending superiority which foreigners find intensely irritating. And, curiously enough, it is our most conscientious internationalists who are unconsciously the most aggressively nationalist.

With us British, racial superiority is a habit. With the Germans it is a cult and, therefore, more dangerous. But it is a factor which must be taken into consideration with regard to every aspect of the Central European problem.

I received little comfort and small hopes of an amicable settlement from my conversations with the German-Bohemian Nazis. To correct my pessimistic tendencies I determined to seek the counsel of that seasoned optimist, Dr. Beneš. A telephone message, late one afternoon, to the Hradčany brought me the answer that the President would receive me at noon the next day. Well before the appointed time I drove up the steep hill past the Schwarzenberg Palace, past the great courtyard where, after the first St. Andrew's Day dinner ever held in Prague, a piper of the Camerons had played before President Masaryk, past the old Cathedral of St. Vitus and the Alchemists' Alley, to the doorway of the President's apartments.

The history of the Hradčany, I reflected, had always been tumultuous. From its windows Czech Protestants had hurled Catholics of the Holy Roman Empire. On its flagstones Catholic executioners had beheaded Protestants. Only in President Masaryk's time had there been peace. He, alone among post-war Central European statesmen, had striven to follow the precept of St. Paul: "Masters, give unto your servants that which is just and equal", and to make of the new Czechoslovakia a state wherein was "neither Greek nor Jew, Barbarian, Scythian, bond nor free". He had been frustrated by the violence of the Opposition and by the obstinacy of his own countrymen. At all other times the clash of contending nationalists had echoed from the walls of Prague's Kremlin.

The sky was heavy and overcast and the atmosphere deathly still. Upstairs, a doorkeeper who had been with Dr. Beneš since my Legation days greeted me in Czech, and showed me into the huge parqueted ante-room. On a large round table were newspapers in half-a-dozen languages and boxes of cigarettes. I strolled over to the tall windows. Below me was the British Legation garden where I had so often practised casting a trout-fly with Sir George Clerk. Stretching far away into the distance was the city with its factory chimneys belching smoke into the stagnant clouds.

While I waited, I noticed a large book bound in vellum and lying open on a small side-table. It was a numbered edition of *Hugh Lane and His Pictures*. On the title page was an inscription signed by Mr. Cosgrave. In all probability the book was the tribute of the representative of one newly-liberated state to the President of another. But to my mind it instantaneously recalled the argument used by every German in Berlin, in Prague, and in London. Britain has taken zealous care to prevent Ulster from being incorporated in a united Ireland. How can she logically oppose the German demand for autonomy for the German-Bohemians in Czechoslovakia? Whenever the British vented their moral indignation over some injustice in Europe, the foreigner always raked up Ireland.

Presently an official announced that the President was ready to receive me. As I entered the room, he came to the door to meet me. He greeted me with the same friendly smile. Was it my imagination that suggested that the smile was more wan than usual? I had spent three hours with him in 1937. Since then he had aged considerably. The iron-grey hair was slightly streaked, like granite that has been lashed by the storms of aeons. He looked tired and for the first time admitted that he was tired. But the spare, wiry figure was as firm and as youthful as ever. Although several years older, he was a far fitter man physically than I was. I thought of our former tennis matches, and reflected rather dismally that to-day he could run me off the court in ten minutes. It is in middle age that the virtues of abstinence and non-smoking reap their reward.

His working day was as long as ever. Although he was now President, he was still the virtual Foreign Minister of his country. He had his grip on everything. His nerves, always like cast-iron, were still unimpaired, and his patience and his persistence were as inexhaustible as they had always been.

In the old days I had nearly always come to him to beg some favour or concession, and rarely had I gone away disappointed. To-day, I came as an outside observer to seek information and to talk politics, and we plunged without preliminaries into the heart of things. As he was not giving an interview, it would be improper for me to repeat all that he said. In his general attitude he was cautiously optimistic and prepared to make the best of things. We talked of Russia and of the unpopularity of the Franco-Czech-Soviet Pact in Yugoslavia and Rumania, of the physical weakness of the League, and of the unlikelihood of any of the small nations committing itself to military action in the name of collective security. He realised all the weaknesses of the situation and took them into consideration. If to believe in the League of Nations, in democracy, and in the blessings of peace is to be an ideologist, then Dr. Beneš is an exponent of ideology. But in diplomacy he is a realist.

About the German-Bohemian problem he was completely frank. The Czechoslovaks would be conciliatory. The Government was doing everything to avoid provocation. Measures had been taken to curb the anti-German activities of newspapers run by German *émigrés* in Czechoslovakia. The Czechoslovak Cabinet would go as far as it could in the way of concessions within the framework of the country's independent status. But there were limits. The problem was no longer an internal one. Its solution depended on the attitude and unknown ambitions of Herr Hitler and the German Reich.

He admitted that the Nazi triumph in Austria had strengthened the Henlein Party. Success always strengthened kindred movements. And in this case the reaction would be influenced by fear. Already many German-Bohemians who had belonged to the Activist Parties were switching over to Henlein in order to ensure for themselves immunity from persecution in the probable event of a Henlein victory. At the same time many members of the Henlein Party might well be a little alarmed by what was happening to the Austrian Nazis, who from the first moment were being superseded by Reich Germans in all the important posts. Within the Czechoslovak Republic the Henleinists could play a rôle and have a large measure of personal importance. If they were incorporated in the Reich, they would be nobodies. He was doubtful if the majority of the Henlein Party really wanted incorporation. On the other hand, he knew that, even if they themselves leaned towards moderation, they would accept and carry out the orders of Berlin.

He did not think that Germany wanted war. But if he was wrong in his supposition, then there were two alternatives. He did not expect any other nation to fight for Czechoslovakia. Nations went to war to defend their own interests. But Czechoslovakia represented a certain cultural standard. In Central Europe she was the outpost of Western democracy. If assured of Western support, she could defend her rights while respecting and honouring the rights of others, and Germany would then refrain from extreme measures. If Czechoslovakia were left to fend for herself, she could do nothing. Into Germany's hands would thus fall the huge Czechoslovak war industry, nearly as big as France's. Germany would then be mistress of Central Europe from the Baltic to the Aegean and would have free access to the raw materials, minerals and foodstuffs, whose lack was certainly one of the factors which deterred Germany from going to war to-day.

He made his exposition with his old-time precision, ticking off his points on the tips of his fingers. But beneath the outward calm I could catch a note of anxiety in his voice when he began to talk of Britain. Occasionally this remark-able little man, who did not learn English until he became Foreign Minister of his country, was at a loss for a word. German diplomacy, he said, had been very successful. It had practised a succession of knocks, and every time the door had been opened. It was a dangerous system, and success was intoxicating. One day there might be a knock to which the door would have to remain closed. That would be a critical moment in the fate of Europe. Britain and France should be firm.

Then he reiterated what, during the past twelve months, Dutchmen, Norwegians, Swedes, Danes, Frenchmen, Hun-garians, Yugoslavs, Rumanians, Bulgarians and even some Italians had said to me: "Britain must be strong."

He asked me my impressions of Czechoslovakia. I told him how much I admired the calm and restraint of the Czech people. I repeated to him what I had said to Prince Paul, King Boris, and King Carol: that, if left alone, the small states could solve all their problems, that they had made remarkable progress, and that the most remarkable progress I had noted was in Slovakia. I told him that every Czech man and woman that I had met was firmly behind their President.

He smiled rather grimly, but he seemed pleased. He has not always had plain sailing in his own country, for, at dif-ferent times, various Czech politicians have been jealous of him. But during my most recent stay in Prague the people had begun to show him a new sympathy and to cheer him in the streets. And, although he never betrays his emotions, I think that these demonstrations touched his heart.

He asked me if I was going to see Dr. Hodža, the Prime Minister. I said that I had had a long talk with him during my previous visit, and that I did not think it kind to bother him with requests for an interview.

"He would see you," said the President, "but he will be glad to save his time. He has his hands full."

It was true. An Anglophil and a Slovak, Milan Hodža is a slow and cautious mover, but he possesses the sense of compromise. In pre-war days he was a Slovak deputy in the Hungarian Parliament. If there is one question which he ought to and does, in fact, understand, it is the rights of minorities. At one time Hodža and Beneš were opposed to one another both politically and personally. Now they were working together smoothly and amicably for the good of their country. They were, I thought, a good team for the solution of the acutest problem in the history of post-war Europe.

My good-bye with the President was of the friendliest. He accompanied me to the door and shook hands firmly. "When you return, come to me. You are always welcome here."

As I left the room, I wondered if I should ever come back to the same Czechoslovakia. I had always admired Dr. Beneš, and never more than at that moment. The Czechs, having been from the first within the orbit of French and, in a lesser degree, of British diplomatic influence, had made the same mistakes during the early post-war years as the French and the British. Concessions should be made to the weak, who may be grateful, and not to the pointed pistol of the strong. For the failure to make these timely concessions Dr. Beneš must share, together with countless other European politicians, his part of the responsibility. But he has always stood and still stands for nearly everything which we British hold dear in culture and in civilisation, and I felt and feel to-day that, if ever his country is overrun by a foreign enemy, he will make his last stand beside the young men in the trenches.

On leaving the President's apartments I went over to St. Vitus's Cathedral before going back to the Legation. Here is the chapel of St. Wenceslaus, the "good king" of our Christmas carol. He was a good Czech. But poor St. Vitus, whose relics repose beneath the cathedral, was no Bohemian, but a

Sicilian who perished as a martyr to the cruelty of the Emperor Diocletian.

For centuries he has been a popular saint with both Czechs and Germans. During the sixteenth and seventeenth centuries it was a popular belief in Germany that good health could be assured for a year by dancing before his image. In this manner St. Vitus's dance became confused with the nervous disorders which it was supposed to cure. Now, because Germans had once danced on the stones of the Hradčany, the Nazis were claiming St. Vitus, his cathedral, and the Hradčany itself as the flesh and blood of Deutschtum!

The Czechs invoke the saint against sudden death and hydrophobia. There were Czechs praying as I left the cathedral.

CHAPTER FIVE

I DO NOT wish to create the impression that Prague was submerged in gloom. That the Czechs felt some apprehension I knew, because some of them unburdened their hearts to me. But a visitor from Mars would hardly have noticed it.

A few months ago I went to Waterloo Station to meet an American friend, a shrewd, widely-travelled observer, who had just arrived in London after a three months' tour of the Continent.

"Gee," he said to me, "I was glad to set foot on English soil this morning. I felt a man amongst men again."

"Why?" I asked innocently.

"Why? Because you British are the only folks in Europe that are not scared."

I would make another exception. During that dark spring of 1938 the Czechs may have felt the earth trembling under their feet. But they were not "scared". The theatres were crowded. It was almost impossible to buy a ticket for the excellent concerts which are the most attractive feature of the Prague season. The representatives of the Sokols, the famous gymnastic society which was the forerunner of all "Health and Beauty" movements and whose exercises, performed in unison, have given a splendid physique to the whole Czechoslovak nation, were busy with their plans for the great summer festival. Football was in full swing. The Czech tennis team, now superior to Britain's, was already in training for the Davis Cup matches.

I went to dinner parties. I received many visits at our Legation. The footman would bring me a card with an unknown Czech name on it. I would ask him to show in the unknown visitor. I would look up to find before me an old Jew friend of fifteen years' standing. Until 1933 he had been rather critical of the Czechs. Now he had Czechified his

name and was proud to call himself a Czech. The Fuehrer
had fulfilled Bismarck's dream by uniting the whole German
race. But in the ruthless process of unification he had united
many incongruous elements against him.

There were other elements who were being drawn into
the Czech orbit by their fear of Germany. Foremost among
these were several prominent families of the old Bohemian
aristocracy.

Proud by nature, Austrian in sympathy, and Legitimist by
allegiance, the Bohemian aristocrats have played an insignificant part in the history of the new Czechoslovak Republic,
although on account of their relations with leading families
abroad their influence is not entirely negligible. In the immediate post-war years, their attitude was one of contemptuous aloofness. They disliked the plebeian masters of the
new state. They resented bitterly the Agrarian Reform Act.
They longed for the day when a Habsburg would again
reign in Prague.

Now the Hitler *coup d'état* had destroyed this dream, and
the aristocrats had to adjust themselves to a new and unpleasant situation. Some, hoping to reap an advantage whatever might happen, were cautiously neutral. One or two
were actively pro-Nazi. But the majority was now for the
integrity of the Czechoslovak state. "Czechoslovakia must be
preserved" was their slogan. As one of the richest princes
said, "What have I to hope from Nazi-ism? Most of my
Legitimist relations in Austria are now in German concentration camps."

I dined out in restaurants, and blond Czech violinists
would bring me a march dedicated to Britain and beg me to
aid them in securing an engagement for London. Waiters,
too, would bring me copies of my books to autograph, for
in Czechoslovakia, even more than in Yugoslavia and Rumania, everyone reads and everyone goes to a university.

I also found a great increase of English culture. When first
I came to Prague at the end of 1919, few people knew any

English. Now English was spoken fluently by all the young
Czechs. The leading Prague bookseller told me that in 1920
English books represented only five per cent. of the total
sale of foreign books. Now more than fifty per cent. of the
foreign books were English.

Here was a remarkable change in a country which until
1929 had been predominantly pro-French and pro-American
in sympathy. French influence was still strong because of the
Franco-Czech alliance, but France's prestige was not so high
as it once had been. American influence had diminished, and
there were two reasons for the decline.

Until 1929 Czechoslovakia, like the other Central European countries, had looked on the United States as the financial giant of the world, a Colossus who could provide un-
limited loans and whose economic methods were to be
followed with slavish imitation. The American slump of
1929 put an end to the loans and destroyed some of Europe's
faith in the infallibility of the American economic system.
At the same time, Americans, realising the appalling state of
Europe and foreseeing the dangers of war, had further developed their natural instinct for neutrality. They lectured
Europe on her follies, but they held aloof. The nation, whose
President had sponsored the birth of the League of Nations,
turned its back on Europe. Under the stress of the pressure
on her frontiers, the Czechs looked nearer home for sympathy and support. American influence receded into the
background.

The Czech attitude towards Great Britain showed the
same divisions as the British attitude towards Czechoslovakia. In Great Britain the pro-League idealists were violently and clamorously on the side of the Czechs, and their
vehement defence of Czech interests was hailed with joy by
a large section of the Czech population. By way of natural
contrast the British pro-Germans and advocates of peace-at-
any-price were equally vehement in their denunciation of
Czech methods, and their partisanship was resented. On the

whole Mr. Eden was a more popular figure than Mr. Chamberlain. But the more responsible Czech officials, who, because they lived nearer to them, understood the grim realities of the situation better than their British supporters, looked to Britain to maintain peace and welcomed Mr. Chamberlain's efforts in this direction.

Like all Slavs the Czechs are a good-natured and easy-going people, and their natural cheerfulness re-asserts itself even in the most trying circumstances. During the spring of 1938 it manifested itself in numerous stories most of which had their basis in the new world-importance which Czecho-slovakia had derived from the crisis. The most popular was one which I seem to remember in a slightly different form from the early days of Bolshevik diplomatic life. It had now been adapted, quite allegorically of course, to the Czech ministers in a Northern capital and in a Latin capital, and during my Prague visit was told everywhere. The two men meet in Prague after a separation of two years.

"Good gracious, Borek," says the Czech Minister in the Northern capital, "you have shrunk to nothing. You must have lost two stone. What's the matter with you?"

"Well, my dear Jiři, it's this way," says Borek. "Czecho-slovakia is now so much in the picture in my capital that I have to lunch and dine out every day and, what with talking to the great ladies next to me, I have no chance to eat."

"Ah!" says Jiři. "That is easily remedied. I have exactly the same difficulties in my capital. I go everywhere, to the Palace, to the Prime Minister's house. But I've invented a formula which lets me take my meals in peace. I turn first to the woman on my right and I say: 'Are you married?' She says 'No.' Then I say: 'Have you any children?' And she doesn't talk to me again. Then I turn to the woman on my left and I say: 'Are you married?' She says 'Yes.' I ask again: 'Have you any children?' She replies 'Four,' and at once I ask 'Whose are they?' And she doesn't talk to me any more. After that, I address the woman opposite me: 'Are you married?' She says 'Yes.' 'Have you any children?' She says 'No,' and then I ask: 'How do you do it?' And she doesn't talk to me any more, and I enjoy my meal."

Borek's face beams. "Splendid," he says. "I'll try your formula in my capital."

The two men meet six months later. Borek's clothes hang more limply on him than ever. "Heavens, man," says Jiři. "You've lost another stone. What's wrong with you?"

"Well, you see," says Borek, "it's these infernal luncheon and dinner parties . . ."

"I know," says Jiři, "but didn't you try my plan?"

"Yes," says Borek, "but it doesn't work in my capital."

"How do you mean it doesn't work?"

"Well, you see, I did everything you told me to do. I turned first to the lady on my right and asked 'Are you married?' She said 'No.' I followed the formula: 'Have you any children?' 'Do I look a complete fool?' she said. And then she went on talking. Then I addressed the woman on my left. 'Are you married?' 'Yes.' 'Have you any children?' 'Four.' And then, just as you told me, I asked 'Whose are they?' 'Well,' she said, 'if you want to know the truth, I'm not quite sure myself.' And she went on talking. Finally, I turned to the woman opposite me and went through the formula again. 'Are you married?' 'Yes.' 'Have you any children?' 'No.' 'How do you do it?' All she did was to smile and say: 'Well, Your Excellency, if you'd really like to know, you'd better come round at five this afternoon.' And she went on talking."

There were other gaieties in Prague. If the Legation worked long hours, there was some relaxation in the evenings. I enjoyed the comfort of the Legation, transformed and greatly improved since my time and exotically furnished with Basil Newton's Chinese treasures brought back from his long sojourn in Peking. I found, too, on the Legation staff an old friend in Harold Gibson who had been with me in Russia and who had accompanied me on the dreary train journey from Moscow to the Finnish frontier after I was expelled by the Bolsheviks in the late autumn of 1918.

In 1937 Gibson had given a gay party for me with Russian gipsies to sing to us and Nikolskaia, the Russian prima ballerina, as the chief guest of the evening. Most of the members of the Legation had been present. We had laughed, danced, sung and made merry. At that time Prague had seemed one of the most peaceful centres in Europe.

Now, only a short year later, the pendulum had swung from peace to the threat of war, and the new situation was reflected in the more sober attitude of the local British. On this occasion Gibson gave a small dinner-party at which, by a natural instinct, we avoided the one subject which occupied all our thoughts by day. We talked instead of old times. Although in 1918 the Ogpu or Cheka as it then was called had played havoc with most of my personal belongings, Gibson who lacks neither courage nor phlegm had managed to bring out of Russia with him a camera and to use it during our train journey. He now produced for my amusement and edification photographs of our prison-days and of our undignified exit from Russia: pictures of the British Mission playing football while under house arrest and a grim snapshot of me and my colleagues engaged in a strenuous battle of pitch and toss with silver roubles against the French General Lavergne and his Mission on the platform of Bielostroff, the frontier station, while our Lettish guards looked on with dignified amazement.

I enjoyed these evenings. But my natural liveliness was restrained, and my last party in Prague rekindled in my breast the feelings of apprehension and pity which I had felt from the morning of my arrival. I went with my Czech publisher to see Karel Čapek for whom I have a great admiration. Karel, short, slightly built and clean-shaven, is now in the "forties", but he looks much younger, and when he smiles his face is almost boyish. He is one of the great men of Europe and, like most modern writers, he is a democrat and a progressive. He has a beautiful and attractive wife who under the name of Scheinpflugova is a well-known Czech poetess and Prague's leading actress. His villa, decorated with the paintings of his brother Josef, has more atmosphere than any author's house that I have ever visited, and he is a liberal host to a whole band of writers, painters and intellectuals. The villa was one of the very few houses to which the late President Masaryk used to go regularly, and to-day Dr. Beneš follows the precedent set by his illustrious predecessor. When I say that Karel is the devoted admirer and disciple of Masaryk, you have his political make-up and his outlook on life.

My visit was to be a surprise. But the surprise was mostly mine. When I came unannounced into the pillared main-room, it was full. Twenty-five of Karel's friends, politicians, journalists and writers, were seated on the long divan seat which ran round all the walls. Some I knew; others I had never seen.

Twelve months ago we had had a very gay party here after the performance of Karel's anti-dictator play *The White Sickness* which was given in London in the spring of 1938 under the rather stupid title of *Power and Glory*. The party had been a complete success. Scheinpflugova had seen a facial resemblance, scarcely flattering to Čapek, between her husband and myself. The tables had been laden with every kind of Czech dainty. There had been delicious Pilsener beer and French cognac. At the end of the evening Karel had in-sisted on producing a bottle of Scotch whisky, a rare and to me unknown mark which had been given to him during one of his visits to England. We had drunk each other's health, and he had sworn that the next scene of his travels and of his next travel book would be Scotland. Everyone had been happy. Everyone had talked at once.

Now I saw before me a sea of solemn, earnest faces. Ob-viously Karel and his friends had been discussing the situa-tion and had been asking one another what these infernal, enigmatic British were going to do. My entry produced a sudden silence.

I felt a momentary embarrassment which was not entirely relieved by Karel's friendly greeting. But I took a seat, and, having so recently come from Vienna, was soon being bombarded with questions. I could tell these Czech democrats about Vienna. But when they began to ask me what Britain would do in this or that eventuality, I was again confused and ill-at-ease.

Karel, however, came to my rescue and carried me off to another room to feed me on "horky parki" (Frankfurter sausages) and Pilsener beer and to have a private talk. Čapek is a profound and convinced humanitarian who feels intensely the inhumanity of Europe. His recent writings and his recent plays have been devoted to a humanitarian crusade. He did not deny that the Czechs had made mistakes which should be rectified. But he resented the violence and the deliberate lies of German propaganda. He doubted the sincerity of German promises. Yet I think that his political purview took in a wider field than the interests of his own country. He felt as a personal shame the breakdown of democracy, which in his eyes was synonymous with civilisation, and of the failure of the democratic countries to make a stand against aggressive bullying.

I chaffed him gently about his promised visit to me in Scotland. He told me that he had been invited to attend the first night of his play in London and that he would like to accept. The times, however, were too critical. Besides, he would now have to travel through or over German territory. That was one result of the new situation created by the annexation of Austria. In one sentence it told the whole story of the encirclement of Czechoslovakia.

Gradually the others drifted into the room, and I had long talks with a middle-aged deputy of the Czechoslovak Parliament, who was also a professor of philosophy, with the editor of a Prague newspaper, and with an official of the

u

Czech Foreign Office. They spoke calmly and without bitterness. They showed no fear. But I felt and they felt that they were standing on the edge of an abyss.

A little later a man announced that Herr Hitler was just going to start his broadcast speech on his Vienna triumph. The guests trooped back into the big room where the wireless set stood by the wall. Karel pressed me to stay. But I felt that my presence might cramp the comments of my Czech friends. I had heard the Fuehrer in the flesh and on the air several times. I could read his speech in the morning newspapers.

Pleading the excuse of a supper engagement, I said my good-byes. Once again I had the impression of finality. These men, kind, sensible, compassionate, might live, but their world perhaps was dying. In the last 25,000 years there had been no improvement in the anatomical status of man. If anything, his brain had grown smaller. Had there been progress in other directions? Man's written history was the record of the rise and fall of succeeding civilisations. There had been a great advance in mechanical invention, but in everything that concerned the mind, in those higher spheres of thought which distinguished civilised man from the savage, man had stood still or had advanced only to ebb like the tide. Was the civilisation of A.D. 1938 superior to the civilisation of 438 B.C.?

My mind went back to a summer evening a few years ago at Oxford when I was lecturing on "Idealism and Realism in Foreign Affairs". In those days the realities of the European situation were not readily realised in Britain, and, while not trying to curb idealism, I did suggest that in foreign affairs we had to face day-to-day facts. During question time a young man rose to rebuke me. Could I deny that for the first time in history man had now proclaimed his belief in a League of Nations and in the sanctity of international peace? I could. Zeno and the Stoics had taught the doctrine of the universal brotherhood of man, without distinction between Greek and barbarian, between freeman and slave, and had preached the duty of universal benevolence and justice. But the race had been to the strong, and the barbarians had destroyed Greece.

Would it be different to-day? The strength was with the Germans. Yet which was the higher civilisation? The civilisation of guns or of butter? The culture of Masaryk or the Kampfkultur of Hitler? Prague was a home and a haven for all men. But Germans who professed a different civilisation from Nazi-ism—not merely German Jews but Aryans like Thomas Mann—were in exile from their own country.

CHAPTER SIX

IN THE SPRING of 1938 many exiles from Germany were living in Prague. Their anti-Nazi activities had been curbed, but they themselves were well treated. So long as they did not interfere in politics, their freedom of movement was not curtailed. The only danger to which they were exposed was at the hands of their own countrymen, who more than once had crossed the frontier like thieves in the night to wreak a bloody vengeance. In this manner the erudite Dr. Lessing had been brutally murdered.

Some, but by no means all, of these exiles were Jews. Several had been well-known public figures in the days of the German Republic. A long experience has taught me to mistrust news gathered from *émigré* sources, not because the purveyors of such news are necessarily dishonest, but because their views are biased and their sources of information second-hand and, for this reason, unreliable. I therefore avoided *émigrés* as far as was possible without committing a breach of good manners. But on the suggestion of an English friend I did see a prominent German exile in Prague. He had filled a position of great responsibility under the Bruening Government. He was a Jew who had won the Iron Cross during the war. In every respect he was an outstanding man, remarkable in his freedom from prejudice and in the love which he still bore for his country.

He gave me a masterly analysis of the reasons for the decline of the Republic and for the triumph of Nazi-ism, blaming, less than I have heard some British ambassadors blame, the failure of France and Britain to give timely support to Stresemann and, later but not even then too late, to Dr. Bruening. Then I plied him with questions. Knowing that he was in touch with anti-Nazi friends in Germany, I asked him if there was much internal discontent under the Nazi régime.

"If you had asked me that question six months ago," he said, "I should have told you 'yes'. To-day, I am not so sure. I know my people. You must not underrate the effect of events like the annexation of Austria on all Germans, including even the proletariat. Success goes to the head of the German people more quickly than any wine."

Then I asked him if he thought that Germany was unable to go to war just now because of her shortage of foodstuffs. I quoted General von Fritzch's remark: "You cannot begin a war with bread-cards." Once again he told me to discard any optimism on that score. For months now Germany had been building up large food-reserves. If the German population were kept short of butter or any other commodity, the restriction was the result of a policy adopted deliberately as part of the disciplinary training for a possible war.

He also warned me against the comfortable belief that dictatorships do not last. It was true that dictators rarely left personal successors. But military dictatorships were in a different category. No empire had lasted so long as Rome, and the Roman Empire was in its essence a military dictatorship.

His views seemed to me to be sound. Throughout the past twelve months during which I had been travelling in Europe I had asked everyone I met, from Dr. Colijn to the most junior British Minister, what would happen if Hitler, Mussolini and Stalin were to die suddenly on the same day. In which country would there be the greatest political change? I heard various conflicting views about Italy and Russia. Most people thought that the greatest transformation would take place in Russia. Some even said that Russia would go Fascist. Others predicted grave internal troubles in Italy. But everyone without exception was unanimous that Germany would remain strong.

The Duce and Stalin told their peoples that they were strong, and by dint of frequent repetition some of them believed what they were told. The Germans were conscious of their new strength, and of that consciousness I saw an illuminating example in Prague.

As my stay there drew near its end, I called at the German Legation, partly to see an old friend in von Halem, whom I had known in London and, partly, to obtain such facilities as I could for my journey to Berlin. The German Legation abuts on our own. Its back windows look on to the Legation garden. In pre-Hitler days we had been good neighbours. But the Germans had been diffident and unassertive. Now all was changed, and the greatest change was in von Halem himself. In his London days he had been a shy young man with a gentle disposition and charming manners. Here in Prague he was as friendly, as charming and as kind as ever. But there was a note in his voice which revealed the new confidence born of a regained self-respect. He pooh-poohed the idea of trouble over the German-Czech dispute. His whole manner seemed to indicate the impossibility of anyone seriously thinking that the Czechs could reject the German demands. He handled my personal problem with lightning rapidity. He picked up a telephone receiver and spoke a few authoritative words to the commandant at the German frontier station. A couple of "Heil Hitlers!" and the matter was settled.

Ten years ago I should have laughed if von Halem had greeted me with heil anything in London. But now I was impressed. He did not say, as King Boris had said, "We no longer feel ourselves like Abyssinians," but his whole bearing showed that as a German he acknowledged no superior race in Europe.

On my last day in Prague I made a long excursion into German Bohemia. I must confess that the object of my journey was not political. During my long residence in Czechoslovakia I had known German Bohemia better than any other part of the countryside, mainly because it lies towards the mountains from which flow the swift-running trout streams. In the Eger district on the western frontier the local

German population had been sullenly and sometimes trucu-lently anti-Czech from the first days of the Republic.

Curiously enough, it was Dr Beneš himself who told me that at the Peace Conference both he and President Masaryk wished to leave at least a part of this district to Germany. The Allied Powers, however, had insisted on including it in the new Republic, and from that day the Czechs had been faced with trouble.

But the real Deutsch-Boehmen, who lived to the north, were pleasant people, honest, clean, thrifty, hard-working and peace-loving. Already in 1920 I had seen the efforts of certain local politicians to fan the slowly dying embers of hate. These efforts had no marked success until 1933, when young Nazi speakers, conducting a systematic and intensive campaign, roused the population with speeches about Ger-man honour and German prestige. I mistrust the honour of politicians. It comes too readily to their lips. It accords too well with Bailie Nicol Jarvie's definition in *Rob Roy*: "Hon-our is a homicide and a blood-spiller that gangs about mak-ing frays in the street."

In Prague I had heard and seen enough and too much of the German-Czech dispute. On my last day I wanted to go back into the pleasant past and to take away with me a happy memory of the beautiful Bohemian countryside. In my mind ran the idea of a last pilgrimage. For many years I have taken an almost macabre interest in the Sarajevo murder which started the world conflagration in 1914. I had frequently visited Sarajevo and Konopišt, the Bohemian country-seat of the ill-fated Archduke Franz Ferdinand. Now I would complete my topographical knowledge of the murder by a personal inspection of Terezin, the former Aus-trian military prison in North Bohemia in which Prinčip, Gabrinović and Grabež, the three youthful assassins of the Archduke, were imprisoned.

To-day, Terezin is the chief military prison of Czecho-slovakia. But it is something more than a prison. It is an important military centre occupying a central position between the Czech Maginot lines. In order to visit it, I had to obtain a special permit from the Czechoslovak Ministry of War.

Armed with my pass, which was readily granted, I set out in a high-powered car with Mr. and Mrs. Bubela and a Czech professor, who was to explain to me the mysteries of the châteaux and Barok churches which dot the Bohemian countryside. I do not remember so glorious a March as that March of 1938 in Central Europe, and of a miraculous month of days my last day in Prague was the most miraculous. No breath of wind disturbed the upward ascent of the smoke from the chimneys of the cottages. There was no cloud in the skies, and the sun beat down on the rich fields and warmed the young grass until it seemed to grow before my eyes.

For the first twenty miles we passed through fields of arable land, and once again I could admire the everlasting wonder of a sturdy peasantry which knows how to turn every inch of the soil to profit. Even the road was lined with fruit-trees, which in summer would yield a rich harvest of cherries. The scenery, however, was flat, and it was not until we had left Melnik behind us on our right that my heart leapt to the sight of the mountains. There before us were the green hills of the Mittelgebirge, their lower slopes covered with vineyards. Away to the right loomed the Riesengebirge, the Giant Mountains, which take their name less from their height than from the queer shapes into which Vulcan has wrought their summits.

In past aeons volcanic eruptions had thrown up these mountain bulwarks to create a natural frontier to a land blessed beyond most others by the richness of its soil. There was no barrenness, such as characterises the Scottish Highlands, about this Hochland. The fertile plain led to the very foot of the hills. Sleek cattle, unattended and undisturbed, browsed in the lush meadows. Here, if anywhere in Europe, was a land which Nature had fashioned for the peace and contentment of man's soul.

Yet the peace was only on the surface. As we drew nearer to the hills, Bubela pointed out to me a series of grass-covered mounds, so low as to be scarcely noticeable, which spread themselves at a distance of a hundred yards across the fields. They were the entrances to the famous subterranean Czech defence lines. Man had learnt to fly only to destroy, and in self-defence the same man had been driven back to his primeval cave existence. Everywhere were notices stating that photography was forbidden and every camera liable to instant confiscation. For all the outward peacefulness of the countryside we were in the most carefully guarded military district of Europe.

We drove down a long avenue of poplars and, at the end of it, came suddenly into the little fortress town of Theresienstadt or Terezin, as the Czechs call it. Czechoslovak staff officers were waiting at the barracks door to receive me, and we went at once to the prison—a series of low, dull-red brick buildings, surrounded by grass-covered ramparts, a moat, and dams for inundating the fields. A small river called the Ohře runs close by. It looks like a trout-stream, and I saw several people fishing. But the river contains only coarse fish. In the streets I saw few signs of life. In the heat of the sun the little town seemed to be asleep. It was built by the Emperor Josef II in 1780 as a stronghold. When the fortress became antiquated, the Austro-Hungarian authorities converted it into a military prison.

At the prison gates I met the Governor. He was, of course, a soldier, and had served during the Great War in the Czech legion in Russia. A great reader and a humanitarian, he impressed me by his gentle manner and by the keen interest and pride which he took in his work. He was essentially a reformer and not a gaoler.

We went straight to Gavrilo Prinčip's cell. It has been reconstructed, but there has been no great change. Its vaulted roof distinguishes it from the ordinary prison cell, but in every other respect it is a grim hole. A plank bed stands against the wall. There is a wooden chair and a small wooden table with a metal jug of water and a metal cup on it. There is no other furniture or fitting except an iron ring, to which in the past unruly prisoners were chained. No light enters into this den. There is no window, but only a small spy hole in the door for the warders to see through. The cells of Nedelko Gabrinović and Trifko Grabež, Prinčip's colleagues in misery, were in the same row and were similar in appearance. They made a shattering impression on me. Prinčip, Gabrinović and Grabež had been fanatics. If fanatics were dangerous, was it not better to shoot or hang them than to expose them to this living death? But at the time when they blew the Archduke Franz Ferdinand into space the three Yugoslav assassins were under twenty. Under the old Austrian code they were too young to suffer capital punishment, and, with a respect for the law not observed to-day, they were given life-sentences and sent to Terezin. All three young men died of tuberculosis within four years. The last to expire was Gavrilo Prinčip, a fanatical idealist and the chief organiser of the assassination. He died on April 28, 1918, six months to a day before the collapse of Austria.

I remembered vividly the terrible stories that I had often heard from Serbians of his maltreatment at the hands of his Austrian gaolers. He had endured the sufferings of a martyr. His sores had been wilfully neglected by the prison doctor. He had been starved to death.

I asked the Czech Governor if these stories had been exaggerated. I was glad to hear from so reliable a source that they were wholly untrue. Neither Prinčip nor his colleagues had been badly treated. Their Austrian gaolers had shown no personal cruelty. It was true that the prisoners had been under-nourished. But Austria herself was starving. Undoubtedly, lack of light and of proper foodstuffs had told on their health. But the main cause of their death was homesickness and the inevitable depression caused by their life-sentence.

I was also relieved to learn that the three cells are now, more or less, relics of the past. They are used only very rarely as a disciplinary punishment for refractory prisoners, and then only for a maximum of twenty-four hours.

I made an inspection of the whole prison. Although it is the chief military penal establishment of Czechoslovakia, there were not more than a hundred prisoners. Most of them were serving short sentences. The treatment was more educational than punitive. Every prisoner was taught a trade: book-binding, carpet-weaving and brush-making. The carpets of Terezin fetch a high price, and in the tailoring department I saw a lady's tailor-made, turned out with a cut and finish which would have made the eyes of Mr. Montague Burton sparkle. With immodest curiosity I looked furtively to see if any of my books were among the English translations. But the most modern work that I could find was a bound copy of *The Pickwick Papers*.

I have visited prisons in many countries. Terezin compared more than favourably with the best. I was not to leave it without seeing a tragedy which belonged, not to the past of Prinčip, but to the living present. In one cell was a Czechoslovak officer, or rather a former officer, for he had lost his honour. He was a Czech and not a German-Bohemian. He had been convicted of an officer's worst crime. He had sold military secrets to Germany. Ministers and soldiers talked much of honour, but in all countries governments used money to induce men to commit treason. Here in Terezin it seemed as dishonourable as the dishonour of the degraded traitor.

Before saying good-bye to the Governor, I asked if I might see the cemetery. I was taken to a large enclosure near by. To the right of the gate there is a little chapel. Facing the main entrance is a large gilt Christ on a black cross. The cemetery is divided into three sections, for Terezin is in the centre of a mixed district, and there are Czech, German and Jewish names on the gravestones. The military section is on the right. Near the south wall, by the side of a path, stand three grey wooden crosses in front of a stone pillar, plain except for the laurel wreath design near the top of the column. In front of the pillar there is a little stone enclosure with a gravel of small coloured glass crystals. On the crosses there are three small plaques with the names Gavrilo Prinčip, Nedelko Gabrilović, Trifko Grabež, and the dates of their deaths. Underneath each name are the words: Srpski trpitel —Serbian martyr. The earthly remains of the three are no longer beneath the crosses. After the war the Yugoslav Government brought them home, and they are now interred in a national grave in Sarajevo.

To the Yugoslavs, and, indeed, to all Slavs, they are martyrs; to the Germans and Austrians they are traitors and murderers. Neither the war nor the post-war peace had killed these distinctions. Already in Austria the Germans were preparing to make martyrs of Otto Planetta and the other murderers of Dollfuss, and to honour their memory by re-interring them in a heroes' grave. Here in this Terezin district Konrad Henlein was a hero to the Germans, but to the Czechs he was little better than a traitor. As Tolstoy wrote, what is terrible in life is not the incoherent, stupid, personal folly of individuals, but the general, organised, public, intellectual folly of our world.

I turned away, and the Governor led me to the other end of the cemetery. I crossed the low wall and in a sloping field, lined by a row of trees, I saw thousands of little tin plaques like those which well-to-do British people use to mark the names of the flowers in their garden. Here they marked the names of human beings—the thousands of prisoners-of-war who died in captivity in Terezin. The graves were well tended and neatly arranged. I found the names of thousands of Russians. But many nationalities were represented in this buried League of Nations—Italians, Poles, Finns and Serbs.

Between the lines of tin plaques was a row of ornamented stones. They marked the graves of the Jews, who now lay apart in death as they had lived apart in life. This differentiation, I was told, was not made by the Austrian authorities. The living Jewish prisoners had wished to honour their dead comrades in this manner, and had spent their spare time in making the stones and in carving the designs.

In place of a name several plaques bore the two words: origin unknown.

This was no heroes' cemetery honoured by a whole nation and tended with loving care by the relatives and descendants of the dead. These men had been brought here to languish in captivity, to starve and to despair, and to die far from their homeland.

I should like to be a dictator for twenty-four hours in order to reform the teaching of history in the schools of the world. The text-books for British schools should be written by Frenchmen, those for French schools by Germans, and those for German schools by Englishmen. Or, better still, the histories taught in the schools of the Great Powers should be written by neutrals. I should abolish the pictures of battle-fields. I should replace them by photographs of these war-prisoners' cemeteries, where the innocent victims of the contending nations lie buried side by side.

I took my leave of the kindly Governor, and we drove on to Litoměřice or Leitmeritz, an old Czech city which during the course of centuries has been strongly Germanised. On our way we passed a field in which a group of Czech soldiers were playing football. It was from this field that in October, 1918, after the collapse of Austria, the Czech troops marched, with bands playing, to Leitmeritz to take possession of the town. The band played the march *Up the Habsburgs!* It was the only tune that it knew or had practised.

Leitmeritz was very clean and very peaceful. As it was Saturday afternoon, there were many people in the streets. Most of them were speaking German. Bubela wished to take me to a small wine-garden in the hills in order to show me the view. Being hazy of the local geography, he stopped the car and asked the way. He put his question in German and received a very civil answer. Not for the first time I noted that there is little hate between peoples when the politicians are not present.

The German-Bohemian who gave Bubela his bearings was a working man. Perhaps he was a Socialist. There were many Socialists in this German-Bohemian industrial area. This was another aspect of the crisis. In some respects it was the most serious. Were we, the British, to use our good offices to persuade the Czechs to give to the German minority in Czechoslovakia a measure of autonomy so large that it would enable the Nazis to trample on their fellow-countrymen who disagreed with them? The Nazis would not be satisfied without this concession. Already they were saying that no Socialist could be recognised as a German. And even if German were to be allowed to deal with German as the majority decided, what of the eight hundred thousand Czechs who would then become a minority in the German area? The Germans who raged so furiously over the treatment of German minorities in other countries did not tolerate minorities within their own confines.

After a roundabout climb we reached the wine-garden with its little inn and roof-terrace. As it was so early in the year, there were no other visitors. The Wirth was a German. Pleased by the arrival of unexpected customers, he was all smiles and friendliness, making us taste all his wines, both new and old, and producing a fearsome concoction called raspberry wine, which Mrs. Bubela liked. He was an expert on wines and talked of them with loving knowledge. Never before, he said, had he collected so many beautiful wines. He was full of optimism and confident that he would have a record season. In the past, times had been hard, for he had to rely on local custom. But now the fame of his inn was spreading. Motor-cars, increasing in number yearly, would bring visitors from Prague and from Dresden. The possibility of political complications did not seem to enter into his mind.

From the terrace there was an enchanting view over the rolling ranges of mountains and valleys. The whole scene reminded me of an Italian landscape. The olive-green hills, the vineyards, were Italian, and in the sky there was a riot of colour which would have defied the imagination of a Turner.

We stood in silence while we watched the sun, like a vast blood-red globe, sink behind the valley of the Elbe. Doubtless, the Bubelas were wondering if in the summer they could come back to drink a glass of wine on this quiet terrace roof, if the Wirth would welcome them as he had welcomed us to-day, or if by then the keepers of his political soul would have poisoned his mind with the toxin of racial hatred. There was a questioning look in Mrs. Bubela's eyes more eloquent than words of apprehension.

My own thoughts were not very optimistic. My memory went back to Rainer Maria Rilke, the gentle poet who, loathing the war in which he was forced to serve, refused the military decoration which the Austrian Government wished to confer on him. Rilke was a German-Bohemian, but he was no nationalist. His fatherland was the whole world. He died in 1926. Had he lived, his voice would have been raised against the madness of infuriated nationalism. Yet now that he was dead the Nazis were trying to claim him as one of their own, and the Fuehrer had bought a bust of the poet. In a saner world, I was confident, Germans and Czechs could live together. But the world was not sane, and the Germans did not want to live with anyone except on their own dictated terms.

Then I remembered that in this German-speaking district nearly every Czech that I had seen had been in uniform. Nor did I know how many of these Czech soldiers were Czech citizens only in name and not in blood. That was the weakness of the Czech position. If Czechoslovakia were to go to war, or to be forced into a war with Germany because of the German-Bohemian minority, how could she expect the Germans in her own ranks to fight against their fellow-Germans?

In any case the Czechs could not fight alone. Internal aggression, Herr Hitler's new weapon, might be as aggressive as an invasion from outside, but he had the strength. And this strength the Czechs could not afford to ignore. "What king, going to make war against another king, sitteth not down first and consulteth whether he will be able with ten thousand to meet him that cometh against him with twenty thousand?" The balance in favour of the Nazi king was not two to one, but seven to one.

Was this a quarrel in which we should take sides or for which we should go to war? Not until we had exhausted every effort to find a peaceful solution. Not unless Germany's ambitions were more sinister than her professed desire to obtain equal rights for the German minority in Czechoslovakia. Minorities were a curse and a nuisance in the world, and the lot of a small state with a large minority was doubly hard.

On our way home we stopped at Doksany, once an ancient convent of the Norbertines and later transformed into a castle. To-day it is one of the country seats of the Counts Aehrental. Its chief attraction is its Barok church, which is the finest in Czechoslovakia, and the Czech professor who accompanied us expatiated at considerable length on its architectural and mural glories. But Bubela had told me that beneath its floors was the burial vault of the Aehrentals, and I wanted to see it. Down we went into the Roman crypt, clammy with the sunless air of ten centuries. Several coffins, covered with rather dusty black memorial bands with gilt lettering, stood on stone blocks. The swords of the dead Counts lay beside them. On one coffin I read the name: Alois Aehrental, Foreign Minister of His Imperial Majesty, the Emperor Franz Josef.

Count Alois Aehrental was the Austrian Minister responsible for the annexation of Bosnia and Herzegovina. That annexation had put several million Slavs under Austro-Hungarian rule. It had been the primary cause of the Sarajevo assassination, and the murder of an Archduke had cost the lives of millions of men and had altered the map of Europe. Yes. Minorities were a curse. Herr Hitler himself had always said so. Would he stand by what he had said, or would he change his mind as he had changed it after the re-occupation of the Rhineland when he promised to launch "no more diplomatic surprises" on a startled world? The riddle would be answered long before the book which I was writing would see the light of day.

x

CHAPTER SEVEN

IT WAS ON a Sunday morning that I arrived at the Anhalter Bahnhof in Berlin. The station stands in the part of Berlin which I have known longest. From the neighbouring Potsdamer station I used daily to take the little suburban train to Gross-Lichterfelde during my student days in 1905 and 1906.

The hour of my arrival was unduly early, and the station was almost empty. I went to the official money bureau to change a pound, and, while I waited, my eye caught a large poster. It showed a map of Africa. Below Cape Town were the words: "German Colonial League"; above the Sahara stretching from Oran to Port Said ran the plaintive propaganda cry: "How Long Without Colonies?"

At my hotel I found numerous messages and invitations from German friends. I should answer them to-morrow. I was determined to keep my first day to myself. I had a long connection with Germany. It was the first foreign country in which I had ever lived. Except during the war years I had visited it regularly ever since. Although my student years had been spent in Berlin, I preferred South Germany to the North. In recent years, owing to restrictions on my time, I had been more frequently in Munich than in the German capital. Nazi Berlin was therefore almost unknown territory to me.

During the first post-war decade my sympathies had been with men like the late Gustav Stresemann and Dr. Bruening, and there were many features of Nazi-ism which I disliked and still dislike. I had, however, met a considerable number of prominent Nazis long before they came into power. I had heard Herr Hitler speak in his beloved Munich. I had been shown over the famous Nazi "Brown House" in that city by that earnest, ascetic philosopher, Alfred Rosenberg, and under his guidance had inspected the printing presses of that child of his creation, the now all-powerful *Voelkischer Beob-*

achter. By way of returning courtesy I had piloted him during his first visit to London—not his official visit in 1933
when he was severely "heckled", but a previous visit made
two years earlier, when he was incognito in London for a
week.

Our first meeting, arranged by a friend in Munich, had
been curious. A Balt by origin, Alfred Rosenberg had been
in Russia during the Bolshevik revolution and knew me by
name and notoriety, if not in the flesh. After taking his
degree as an architect in Riga, he had come to Munich in
1919. There he had come under the influence of Eckhardt,
the Nazi poet, and had begun to speak in the streets against
Marxism. Adolf Hitler was already engaged on a similar task
with a small group of his own. The two men met and became
firm friends.

In those days Herr Hitler's chief amusement was motor-
racing. He did not race himself, but he studied the life-story
and speeds of the great drivers in much the same way as a
British schoolboy pores over the batting and bowling aver-
ages of the professional cricketers. The cares of office have
curbed the Fuehrer's early passion, but its traces are visible in
the superb motor-roads which he has had constructed from
one end of Germany to the other.

I remembered very vividly my conversations with Rosenberg in London in 1931. He had told me with supreme confidence that the Nazis would never attempt a *coup d'état*.
There was no necessity. They would reach their goal by constitutional methods and they would achieve power within
six months. He was only seven months out in his prognostica-
tion, but I was not prescient enough to realise that he spoke
with prophetic assurance. Nor were the lions of Fleet Street
better informed. When three months later Rosenberg telegraphed to me from Munich asking me to come at once because he had arranged for me to see Herr Hitler, my editor
refused to let me go. To the British Press the future Fuehrer
was still a demagogic mountebank whose oratory was a

nuisance to Europe, but not a serious challenge to the exist-
ing régime in Germany.

Now the Nazis had ruled in Berlin for five years. I was
interested to see how the ardent young men of Munich had
carried out their mandate.

I took a taxi and drove round the town. The streets were
still beflagged for the Vienna rejoicings. Nowhere in the
world have I seen such a profusion of long banners. They
hung blood-red from the top windows of the houses almost
to the heads of the pavement walkers. In Unter den Linden
and the Wilhelmstrasse the only buildings which were not
draped with swastikas were the French and British Embassies.
I drove past the German Foreign Office and saw again the
yellow, sweating face of Gustav Stresemann. I had talked to
him there for more than an hour shortly before his death.
He had criticised Franco-British policy for its failure to support the German Republic during the immediate post-war
years. Between Hitler and Stresemann there had been only
one cardinal difference. Their ambition and their goal had
been the same—a strong and united Germany. But Stresemann was prepared to create his strong Germany in the
spirit of the new Europe. He had failed, and the French and
we had been largely responsible for his discomfiture. Now
he was forgotten, and the Nazis, thorough in all their
methods, had taken care that he should remain forgotten.
Near my hotel was the old Stresemannstrasse. The name had
been changed.

I remembered the dying statesman's last words to me:
"Now nothing remains except brute force. The future is in
the hands of the new generation. And the youth of Germany,
which we might have won for peace and the new Europe,
we have lost."

The streets were full of young men now. All were in uniform. The majority wore Air Force badges. What struck me
most was their extreme youthfulness.

I noticed many changes since my last visit in 1934; vast,

tremendous changes since my first long stay in 1905. Many
old landmarks had disappeared. Others were going as fast as
the Fuehrer could remove them. Berlin was being rebuilt.
That was his dream, as he pored in Berchtesgaden over his
architects' plans. To perpetuate his name in roads and buildings, to incorporate within one Reich the whole German
race; these were his ambitions and the heritage which he
wished to hand down to history. And to achieve both aims
he was working with feverish haste. For the Fuehrer is a
fatalist. He believes that Fate has given him only a limited
time in which to fulfil his mission.

Gone was the old, spotless, tidy Berlin. Hoardings and
scaffoldings were everywhere. The Tiergarten was in a mess.
The Tiergartenstrasse itself was condemned. Its houses were
to make way for the new quarter in which the totalitarian
state intended to concentrate the foreign embassies and legations. Already the anti-Nazi wits—and there are some still—
had christened it "The Diplomatic Ghetto". And wherever
you walked, the dust, a rich, white dust, covered your shoes
in five minutes.

The Berlin wits have another story about this feverish
building campaign. "Berlin," they tell you, "is free from all
dangers of air-attacks." You ask why, wondering in your
innocence if the German anti-air-raid precautions, very visible with their conic-shaped, concrete air-shelters and first-
aid stations, are so perfect. Then you are given the explana-
tion: "A week ago Stalin sent over secretly a couple of
Russian aeroplanes, camouflaged as German, in order to
make a reconnaissance. The observers reported that there
was nothing in Berlin to bomb. The city had been destroyed
already."

Presently I paid off my taxi. I had made a sudden resolution to spend my day in the same manner as I had spent my
Berlin Sundays in the serious, penniless days of my youth. I
walked along Unter den Linden to the Kaiser Friedrich
Museum, where under the forceful guidance of Professor

Tilley I had first learnt to take an interest in pictures. The gallery, one of the finest in the world, was almost empty. In pre-war days it had always been crowded on Sundays, and I was at a loss to understand the change. Did it signify a declining interest in the old Kultur? Perhaps Berlin now lived in the streets. Perhaps everyone was at the Exhibition of Degenerate Art, sponsored by the Fuehrer himself in order to convince his people of the evil tendencies of the Jewish influence on German art.

The second reflection was more or less true. I went later to the Exhibition of Degenerate Art. It was crowded. On the whole, it justified Herr Hitler's object. The pictures were unwholesome and decadent. But the new Nazi art, shown by way of contrast, was unimpressive and lacked originality.

On my way back I saw a small well-behaved crowd outside the old guard-house in Unter den Linden. I joined the queue and went in. This little Greek temple now houses Berlin's shrine to the "Unknown Warrior". But Germany's remembrance day is not "Armistice Day", which is a day of shame, but the first Sunday which falls closest to the date of the founding of the Iron Cross. The date falls in March, and remembrance day had been observed on the Sunday previous to my arrival. As I walked round in the circle, as slow-moving and as dignified as the circle which walked round the coffin of King George V in Westminster Hall, the scores of wreaths, from regiments, from Nazis, from ex-servicemen's organisations, were still fresh.

Near the Potsdamerplatz I lunched alone in an Aschinger restaurant, which is the Berlin equivalent of our London Lyons. The food was wholesome and fairly well-cooked. I noticed no restrictions. I had all the butter that I wanted. The place, too, was full. But there were no uniforms and no Brown Shirts. The public was composed entirely of stolid bourgeois of the lower middle class. There were several family groups of husband and wife with one or two children. The women were dowdily and rather shabbily dressed. Their time was divided between filling their own mouths and those of their offspring. The husbands plied a diligent knife and fork. Then, when their hunger was satisfied, they took out a cigar, lit it deliberately, and smoked and read the newspaper. What struck me most was the unwonted silence. There was none of the loud hum of conversation which never ceases in a Prague or Bucharest restaurant of the same class, none of the noisy laughter which I used to hear in the Berlin of seven years ago. The German lower middle class has always been disciplined and well-behaved. But now these men and women said nothing, or talked in quiet whispers as if an unseen restraint sat on their lips. Their faces, serious and care-worn, were a reflection of the general picture that I had observed that morning in the streets.

There has always been something aggressive in the physiognomy of Berlin. But to-day you notice three distinct types among the population.

First, there are the active Nazis as personified by the Brown Shirts and the Black Shirts. They look hard. They cultivate a tough efficiency, and not infrequently they confound efficiency with brutality.

Then there is the military, which to-day embraces almost the whole youth of the country. It is a healthy and not unpleasant youth, disciplined, athletic, serious in purpose and, on the whole, good-natured. In its bearing it shows its pride of race, but not so aggressively as do the organised members of the Nazi Party.

Finally, there are the over-forty civilians: the clerks, the minor officials, the tradesmen, the small people who compose the bulk of every nation. Their faces look pinched. There is a strained look in their eyes, as though the burden of supporting a nation in arms were too heavy for them. They carry their money in a purse and count every pfennig. They work because they have always worked and because to-day, in a totalitarian state, saving has lost its sense. They are the stragglers in a sprint in which the whole population is bound to take part and, because the race is to the young and to the strong, they seem to lag behind. Nazi-ism is a movement of and for youth, to whom life is still a realisable expectation. To the "over-forties", who have lost their illusions, it offers neither comfort nor security. In England middle age is in the saddle. It holds the high offices; it has the money; it has the best time. In Germany it belongs already to a despised past. And this is the fundamental difference between the new Germany and the old England.

When I had finished my luncheon, I strolled over to the Potsdamer station and took a third-class ticket to Gross-Lichterfelde-West. On my arrival I had some difficulty in finding my way to Ringstrasse 40, where as a youth I had lived for a year and studied German and the then new science of phonetics under that great man, William Tilley. Then the town had been in the country; now it was an integral part of Greater Berlin. The house was still there, but its bricks and stucco were all that remained of the past. Tilley was dead, and the surviving members of his family were teaching phonetics in half-a-dozen different countries. Gone was the little shop where I used to buy penny cigars and exercise books and cheap prints of Rembrandt and Vermeer. Gone, too, was the field in which I tried to teach rugby football to the German students, who gave me conversation lessons.

Rather sadly I looked up at the balcony window of my old room and thought of the changes in the place and in myself. Those months in the Ringstrasse had been the most serious in my life. Except for a juvenile and very romantic affair with a young German girl who lived next-door my conduct had been exemplary. Here I had first learnt how to work, to appreciate Germans, and to love Germany. To-day I should like to have been able to write that I still loved Germany, although I disliked many features of Nazi-ism. But such a phrase was anathema to every German, an insult to the German nation.

Even old acquaintances like Freiherr von Rheinbaben, once the disciple and devoted admirer of Stresemann, now said: "We cannot and will not listen to phrases like that. Germany and Nazi-ism are identical."

If that were true, I was a misfit in the new Germany.

I walked over to the Kadettenanstalt, Germany's great military college, where hundreds of famous German officers had received their first training. I remembered very vividly meeting the cadets on Sundays on the way to the station to spend the afternoon with their parents. They looked very serious and very smart in their neat blue uniforms and cream-coloured gloves.

Perhaps I had seen Goering among them, for at school he had gone on a hunger-strike and had feigned illness until his diplomatist-father promised to send him to the Kadettenanstalt and to allow him to become an officer. It was true that I was several years older, but in those days some of the cadets were little more than babies, and in this manner our times in Gross-Lichterfelde may have coincided. I tried to picture Goering as a cadet. He had been slim and agile then. During the holidays, when he was staying with his parents at an old castle, he had startled the whole household by swinging himself down from the high tower on a rope. He is still an ardent Alpinist. But even this dizzy feat suggested nothing concrete to my mind. There are people whose face and figure scarcely change with the passing of the years. There are others who are unrecognisable after an interval of ten years. Trying to picture Goering as a boy officer was like trying to imagine Falstaff as a tight-rope walker or Lord Castlerosse as a naval cadet.

In those days the Kadettenanstalt represented everything that was most honourable and gentlemanly in German military life. At least once a year the Kaiser or one of his sons came down to inspect the future *élite* of his corps of officers. Famous generals accompanied him, and the good citizens of Gross-Lichterfelde assembled in the road in their hundreds and peered through the railings as the boys formed fours and marched to the goose-step.

To-day, the Kadettenanstalt has a more sinister attraction to the modern sightseer. After the ill-fated coup of June 30, 1934, when General Schleicher and the notorious Colonel Roehm tried to overthrow the Fuehrer, some of the mutineers were brought to Gross-Lichterfelde and shot within the precincts of the military school.

Yielding to another impulse, I hired a car and drove out to Schlachtensee, the little lake halfway between Berlin and Potsdam, where in romantic scenery of the Grunewald I used to row my girl and give her coffee and cakes on the café-terrace. Now it was as crowded as the Serpentine. Since the war every German has become a sun-worshipper, and, although we were still in March, hundreds of Berliners were enjoying the warmth of a wholly exceptional spring. Here there was little or none of the restraint that I had noticed in the streets of Berlin. In the open air the public had thrown off its cares and had left its politics and propaganda at home.

Only one feature of the scene reminded me that in this new Germany freedom was circumscribed or, at best, confined to units of one race and of one political colour. Since the war I had often re-visited the lakes near Berlin. In pre-Hitler days Jews had predominated among the throng of holiday-makers, especially at Wannsee, where they had yachts and motor-boats and fine villas by the lake-side. Here at Schlachtensee, although I scanned many faces, I did not see one non-Aryan.

Berlin's countless lakes have not lost their popularity. One, the Lietzensee, is now a main residential centre for Nazi officials. It is an old and frequently flaunted accusation by Nazi orators that, under the Republic, official jobbery flourished and bureaucracy battened on the state. When a people is starving and impoverished, it is easy for agitators to rouse its hatred against the bureaucracy. Both during the struggle for power and after the Fuehrer's triumph the

Nazis played this card for all it was worth in their efforts to besmirch the Socialist and Liberal régime. They invented a name for the superfluous bureaucrats and it became a household word in every German home. They called them "Bonzen", for which the best English equivalent is "tin gods".

It is, I think, undeniable that the Nazis had some grounds for their accusations. The German bureaucracy, once as honest as our own, has never recovered from the corrupting effects of the war. It has not recovered yet. Under the Nazi régime nepotism and jobbery have not been suppressed, and there are many critics even in pro-Nazi circles who maintain that for every "Bonze" who lived on the state under the Republic there are now four.

This prevalence of uniforms and badges has provided the wits with another joke. When Signor Mussolini paid his state visit to Berlin in 1937, the wags suggested that the Lietzensee should be rechristened "Il Lago di Bonzi".

From Schlachtensee I drove on to Wannsee, but I came too late to see more than the sunset. The waters of the great lake were unruffled. The boats were already moored and the terraces of the lake-side restaurants almost deserted. The crowd of Sunday sunshine seekers was on its way to the station. I paid off my driver and followed them on to the platform to wait for a train which would take me back to Berlin. The platform was packed. But there was no jostling and pushing. Mothers straightened out the frocks of their little girls and pulled the arms of fractious sons who strayed too near the railway-line. Muscular youths extracted bars of chocolate from the automatic machines and shared them with their friends. Sturdy girls, their faces free from lipstick and make-up, scribbled picture-postcards and posted them in the neat, blue, station post-box. It was a good-natured and orderly crowd.

This time I travelled first-class, for, if at fifty the spirit was still willing, the flesh was not so strong. I was tired and a little lonely. But it had been a peaceful outing. I had recaptured some of the past. I had compared the pre-war yesterday with to-day, and had found the present less different from 1906 than it was from 1926. True, there had been uniforms everywhere, but the militarism had not yet obtruded itself objectionably. Germans seemed to be spending their Sundays in much the same manner as they had always done. That first Sunday was to prove itself my pleasantest and most care-free day in Berlin.

CHAPTER EIGHT

MONDAY BROUGHT ME out of my day-dreams into the grimmer realities of the working week. My first duty was to pay a few obligatory official calls, and, having arranged an appointment by telephone, I set out on foot for our Embassy. On my way to the Wilhelmstrasse I was held up for over half-an-hour by a vast concourse of people on the Pariserplatz.

Half Berlin had taken the morning off to cheer the march past of the Fifteenth Vienna Infantry Regiment. If the leading German Nazis had gone to Vienna, the Austrians were now being brought to Berlin. Officers and men were still in Austrian uniform. Their physique and their martial bearing were impressive. They had surrendered voluntarily to a brother race, but they marched as conquerors. The enthusiasm of the crowd was tumultuous. If Germany had won the war, the victorious Prussian troops returning to Berlin could not have received a warmer welcome.

Close to me a burly bourgeois in a bowler hat started *Deutschland, Deutschland, ueber Alles*, and with full-throated energy the crowd took up the refrain. As the words "Von der Maas bis an die Memel" rang out across the square, I felt a momentary trepidation. Memel would be the next crisis in the agitated affairs of Europe.

The emotional fervour of the crowd was dangerously inspiring and infectious even to a foreigner. I looked at the Austrian officers. Their chests were puffed out, their faces set in a vacant military expression. Were there no Habsburg sentiments beneath these stiff tunics? Even *Deutschland ueber Alles* was an Austrian hymn composed by the Austrian Haydn for an Austrian Emperor. I could not help thinking of the stage-set triumphs of the ancient Romans.

Nor were the troops the only Austrians who were brought to Berlin to swell the Nazi joy-ride. On the next day two thousand Viennese workmen streamed out of the Anhalter station to receive a similar welcome and to parade before an equally enthusiastic crowd. Not the least important feature of the Nazi movement is the official eagerness to capture and retain the affections and allegiance of the working-classes.

At the Embassy I found Sir George Ogilvie Forbes, whom I had known twelve years ago in Belgrade. Since then he has been in many difficult posts: Mexico and Madrid, where he did splendid work during the worst part of the Spanish Civil War. To-day, he is Counsellor of Embassy in Berlin. But he will go much farther. He is big in bulk, big in mind, and quite imperturbable in manner. He stands over six feet high in his stocking-soles and scales over fourteen stone. He is always good-tempered. He does not talk much; he does not take sides. He plays the bagpipes.

Soon after the war Kemal Pasha was asked who was the best diplomatist that he had ever met. He said without hesitation: Sir Horace Rumbold. He gave his reasons for his choice. Sir Horace, he stated, never said more than he needed to say, but when he said anything you knew that it represented to a hundred per cent. the view of his own Government. George Ogilvie Forbes is of the same type. If I were dictator of Britain, I should make him an ambassador at once and give him the toughest post that is going.

He took me off to luncheon at his house in West Berlin. His bookshelves were lined with Scottish books. His other guest was Professor Meyer, the world's leading authority on the history of Catholic Scotland. We discussed Scottish affairs, and then he walked me back a long two miles to the Embassy where, after wiping the dust from my shoes and trousers, I had an hour-and-a-half's conversation with Sir Nevile Henderson, our Ambassador.

When I saw him first in St. Petersburg twenty-six years ago, Sir Nevile was a powerfully-built man in the prime of his vigour. To-day his figure has shrunk a little. Although the sun was blazing and the thermometer at midsummer level, the central heating in his room was at full blast and a

huge fire was burning in the grate. He wore two waistcoats
and shivered in them. He was just recovering from an attack
of influenza.

He is a man of strong views and is not afraid to express
them. He understands the twists and turns of the Nazi movement. He knows its virtues and its faults. If he does not ignore
its dangers, he prefers the commonsense of peaceful diplomacy to the violence of the ideologists. Wherever he has
been *en poste*, he has always succeeded in establishing exceptionally close relations with the leading personality of the
country to which he has been accredited. He is a keen game
shot.

When he was Minister in Belgrade, he went shooting
with the late King Alexander and became his best friend.
To-day, he shoots with General Goering and is on good
terms with him. As Mr. Balfour once wrote to me when he
was Secretary of State for Foreign Affairs, one of the three
chief duties of a diplomatist is to make himself agreeable to
the Government of the country to which he is accredited.
In this respect Sir Nevile has been remarkably successful.

Incidentally, the British public, who regard or used to regard General Goering as a cross between a uniformed buf-
foon and a tyrant, are mistaken. Old régime Germans fall
into another error. They prefer him to all other Nazis because he is of good birth, and because they think, like Caesar,
that fat men are not dangerous. General Goering has his
faults. He likes extravagance and exotic display. On one
occasion, when an English diplomatic friend of mine went
to see him, his pet lion cub forgot itself, and the General had
to break off the conversation in order to go and change his
trousers. But for all his minor weaknesses the ex-air ace is
essentially a man of action, and his greatest characteristic is
his stupendous energy. It is true that without Herr Hitler he
might never have emerged from his post-war obscurity. It is
equally true to say that since 1932 he has been the chief instrument of the Fuehrer's triumph. He is the real organiser

of Germany's armed might and the creator of Germany's air-force, and his achievement stands out as a miracle of hard work and tireless industry.

In character he is a curious combination of contradictions. A passionate hunter, he has gained many admirers, not confined to his own countrymen, by abolishing vivisection in Germany. He can be tolerant towards non-Aryans whose activities are useful to the state. He has protected General Milch, who is his chief adviser on air matters and the purity of whose Aryan ancestry is open to doubt. But for all his bulk he is by no means easy-going. He can be ruthless towards political opponents. He might be a good friend to Britain. He could also be a relentless enemy. And if there were a European war to-morrow, he would be the most important and the most dangerous man in Germany. Already to the younger generation of Germans he is a greater figure than Ludendorff, Hindenburg, or any of the German commanders of the Great War.

On my return to my hotel I found a message from Prince Louis Ferdinand, the Kaiser's grandson and the first Hohenzollern to visit England after the war. We were old friends. Since 1928 I had been in intermittent correspondence with the Kaiser and had been three times to Doorn to see him. When he sent his grandson to London, I acted in some sort as the young Prince's cicerone, and took him to visit the Duke of Windsor, who was then Prince of Wales. Since then I had seen much of him. Tall, good-looking, and Byronic in appearance, he has travelled widely. For some years he lived in the United States, working as a mechanic in the Ford factory in Detroit. He knows American life thoroughly, and has met most of the leading Americans from Henry Ford to Franklin Roosevelt. He has absorbed much of the mental outlook of the New World. Some of his best American friends are among the workmen of the Ford factory. He still corresponds with them. His fluent English is generously larded with American idioms.

In the sense that he is a "good mixer", talks half-a-dozen languages, does not care whether he sleeps in a shack or a palace, and accepts a man at his face, and not his Debrett, value, Prince Louis is an internationalist. He is now an employee of the German Luft-Hansa in Berlin, takes his duties seriously, and is at his happiest when his firm sends him abroad as a commercial ambassador to push German air products in foreign countries. He has done his military service as an airman and is fully qualified as a military pilot. There is, however, nothing military about his appearance. He looks more like an aristocratic poet than a platoon commander. Since his elder brother's marriage, which was not approved by the Kaiser, he is in the direct line to the throne and is the hope of the German Monarchists. He would make a very modern Kaiser, for he is essentially a child of the modern age. His toys are the toys of mechanical invention. If he does not lack dignity, he has little use for frills or stiff shirt-fronts.

His message to me was an invitation to lunch at Cecilienhof, the Potsdam home of his mother, the Crown Princess. He wanted me to meet his bride, the Grand Duchess Kyra, who as a daughter of the Grand Duke Cyril, the nearest living relative of the late Tsar of Russia, is almost as near a lost throne as Prince Louis Ferdinand himself. I met him and his bride the next morning at the old Hohenzollern house in Unter den Linden, and all three of us drove down to Potsdam in a high-powered open car. As the Grand Duchess Kyra, Russian in everything, was late, we had to make speed. The Avus, Berlin's Great West Road—incidentally built long before the Fuehrer's advent to power—was in splendid order, but Prince Louis Ferdinand's eighty miles an hour was too much for me, and I ended the journey hatless and breathless.

Cecilienhof, which stands close to the romantic Virgins' Lake, is a rambling building, constructed haphazard, but full of the homely atmosphere of an English country house. The

Crown Princess Cecilie, half-Russian by birth, gentle in manner, and generous in her tolerance, is, I imagine, mainly responsible for this pleasant atmosphere. Her large family worship her. She has brought them up admirably, and her daughter, the young Princess Cecilie, is the most attractive princess in Europe.

There was nothing ornate in the internal decoration of the rooms, no collection of medals and snuff-boxes, no gallery of family photographs. The only trappings of royalty that I saw was a large new portrait of the Crown Prince staring at me very vividly from an easel in the main sitting-room. It had to do duty for his presence, for, still strenuous at fifty-six, this energetic sportsman was away playing golf.

Luncheon was a family meal. The only other guest besides myself was a pre-war German diplomatist. The conversation, conducted in a mixture of German and English, never went below the surface of things. I could feel that, as Germans, these functionless royalties were proud that Germany had regained her place among the greatest nations of the world. But I did not know, nor could I ask, what they thought of the new régime. I had met royal exiles living in foreign countries. They, at least, could speak freely. But these were exiles in their own country, and the joy of living at home was tempered by the necessity of an unceasing vigilance over all their utterances.

On my way back to Berlin I had a fleeting glimpse of Potsdam. In my student days in Berlin it had been the chief scene of my Sunday outings. I liked the pomp and circumstance of the place, the white uniforms and black horses of the Kaiser's bodyguard, and the music of the Pomeranian Grenadiers. It amused me to visualise Voltaire in Sans-Souci.

Now the place seemed deserted and in need of a new coat of paint. Outwardly it has changed less than any other town in Germany. But the Kaiser has gone, and with him have disappeared the bright uniforms and the glittering swords.

I was not the only visitor to Potsdam on that day. The Fifteenth Viennese Infantry Regiment, into whom I always seemed to be running, was also here, standing at the vault of the grave of Frederick the Great in the famous Garrison Church. As long as the Fuehrer lives, there will, I think, be no other Kaiser in Germany. But if the living generations of the Hohenzollerns are kept rigorously in the background, the names of the great German royalties of the past are still honoured, and to every Nazi Frederick the Great, who by seizing Silesia made the greatest rape in history, is the chief national hero after Hitler.

On the next day Prince Louis Ferdinand and his bride came to luncheon with me in Berlin. It was an amusing meal enlivened by a frank discussion on marriage. Both the young persons were modernists, knowing the pitfalls of married life, excited yet pretending to be bored by the details of a wedding which, owing to the difference in their religions, required three separate marriage services, but chiefly interested in their honeymoon and whether they would receive the Kaiser's permission to make the world tour which they had planned. The affairs of the Hohenzollern family are still managed on a patriarchal basis. Not only the Kaiser's sons, but his grandchildren receive their allowance direct from him, and receipt of the patriarchal favour depends on submissive obedience to the patriarchal fountain-head.

Mindful of my recent experiences in Yugoslavia, I told Prince Louis Ferdinand that if I were a young man I should choose a wife from the new generation of Russian *émigrés*. They had seen the underside of life. Hardship had taught them how to work, and had knocked the social nonsense out of them. The Grand Duchess seemed pleased. She struck me as a vivacious, attractive young woman, plentifully endowed with intelligence, commonsense and her proper share of Russian charm. Although men with artistic temperaments are, more often than not, difficult husbands, I thought that she would make Prince Louis an excellent wife. There is a remote possibility of their marriage affecting the course of European history at some future date. It represents the closest union between the Hohenzollern and Romanoff families in our times. Neither family has been too well treated in Britain. Neither is likely to forget entirely the disappointments and humiliations of dethroned monarchy.

My meeting with Prince Louis Ferdinand was merely a pleasant interlude in my busy round, and, naturally, I was more concerned with Germans who were nearer to the political heart of things. Admittedly, most of my old German friends were definitely anti-Nazi or, at best, lukewarm in their support of the new régime. The anti-Nazis, and they are still numerous, live in constant dread of Gestapo visitations. Although outwardly Berlin is orderly and quiet, the atmosphere is not wholly unlike that of Moscow. The secret police go everywhere. Telephones of suspects, of those whom the Nazis say have guilty consciences, are tapped. What my anti-Nazi friends complained of most was the denunciations of innocent people and the private vendettas carried out by Gestapo agents.

I found my anti-Nazi friends depressed and depressing. There were few who were not convinced that the Fuehrer was suffering from dementia. They warned me against the dangers of a European war, which they said was inevitable. They told me that there was no limit to Herr Hitler's ambitions and that, even if there were a limit, the movement he had launched could not now be stopped. The machine was running away with the "Fuehrer", which is the German word for chauffeur. His followers could not be content with any peaceful solution of the German-Bohemian question. Already they were writing and talking of Prague as a German city, architecturally too beautiful to be left in the control of "Schweinehunde" like the Czechs.

I heard many other stories from these sources: tales of disappearances and of brutal maltreatment in the concentration camps. My informants were not Jews. What was difficult was to discover how large a section of the community these measures affected, and this neither I nor anyone else could check with any certainty.

What I call my lukewarm Nazi friends were in another category. Most of them belonged to the civil service or the army. Many were still in the service of their country. Nearly all were nominal supporters of the régime, although few or none had actually joined the Nazi party. Their conversation was guarded. They certainly did not want a European war, although I could see that they were afraid that it might come. Nor did they approve of the Fuehrer's diplomatic methods. Like several Italian diplomatists that I have met in recent years, they regretted the fact that in the totalitarian states the reins of diplomacy were in the hands of men who had never travelled and who had no personal knowledge of foreign countries. At the same time they showed some admiration for Herr Hitler personally. Most of them drew a marked line between the Fuehrer and the rank and file of his party. This was especially true in the case of an army officer friend, who was grateful to Herr Hitler for what he had done to restore the prestige of the German officer and of the German soldier. There were few who did not support the Fuehrer's demands for colonies. There were fewer still who did not blame Franco-British policy for the part that it had played in facilitating the overthrow of the Republic. As Germans, all of them were proud of Germany's new strength.

On some of them the annexation of Austria had had an intoxicating effect. There was one old friend who was as delighted as a child with a new toy. He was a South German and an anti-Prussian. Out of the annexation he had woven a new dream of a Greater Germany, which would be a permanent check to Prussian domination, and in which Herr Hitler, an Austrian, would rule his Reich from Munich. This was romanticism run mad. Yet no Englishman will ever understand Germans until he realises that, in spite of their thoroughness, their immense theoretical knowledge, and their passion for compiling dictionaries, every German born into this world has in his bones the marrow of an incurable romanticism. This dream of an Austrian-ruled Reich might be absurd. But was it more absurd than the passionate enthusiasm of the Fuehrer, a little dark man of Alpine stock, for the tall, blue-eyed, dolichocephalic Teuton blond?

Nationalism, like revolutions, has a habit of devouring its children. I remember some years ago receiving a visit in London from M. Chenkeli, a Georgian compatriot of Stalin and a mild Menshevik whom I had met in Russia during the Kerensky régime. He was then in exile, and was bitterly opposed to the Bolsheviks. He came to consult me about the possibility of obtaining financial aid for the supporters of Georgian independence. I told him that I considered his mission to be futile. I suggested to him that he should approach some of the rich Russian *émigrés* in Paris.

"I have been to them already," he said.

"Well, what did they say to you?" I asked.

He smiled. "They said to me: 'What! You come here to ask us for money to help you to drive the Russians out of Georgia! We want all the money and means we can raise in order to drive the Georgians out of Moscow!'"

One day perhaps a fanatical Prussian Nordic would arise who would demand the expulsion of the Austrians from Germany!

I was perplexed by the conversation of my Berlin friends. They themselves seemed lost in a situation which had reduced them to minor cogs in an all-powerful machine. They were good Germans. They would stand by Germany whatever happened. Yet they looked to Britain to maintain the peace of Europe. They favoured an Anglo-German understanding, but they wanted Britain to be strong in order that a check might be put on dangerous ambitions and the risks of war minimised.

Although these conversations, nearly always accompanied by generous German hospitality, filled most of my days and nights, there is something in the climate of Berlin which enables one to do with very little sleep. Frequently on my way home from a dinner-party I would go off on a long walk by myself.

How well I remembered the old Berlin by night. Then vice had flaunted itself unashamed. How often had I done the round of the *Nachtlokals*, more commercial in their rapacity than those of Paris, more viciously sordid than the lowest haunts of Belgrade and Bucharest. In the Friedrichstrasse painted youths carrying cigarette cases in their left hand had accosted me with unchecked effrontery. Carmine-lipped daughters of joy had plied their trade openly by night and day. Houses of assignation were numerous. There had been other "dives", more difficult to enter, where all the women were dressed as men; others again where apologies for men masqueraded in women's clothes.

Now the pavements were almost deserted. Passers-by were few. There were no street-walkers. Such women as there were walked with male companions. Others hurried home with confident strides. The lazy, leering procession of lascivious pleasure-seekers was a thing of the past. Doubtless, in a city of Berlin's size vice still existed. But it had gone underground. Berlin by night had been cleaned.

This much might be set to the Fuehrer's credit. This, and the provision of work for the whole German population! Until six years ago it was almost impossible to walk a hundred yards along a main thoroughfare of any German city without being plagued by suppliants requesting alms. During my present visit I did not see an idle man in Berlin. No beggar accosted me. It is true that most of the young men were conscripts either of the armed forces or of the Labour battalions. But the demoralisation of unemployment had been banished, and the physical benefits to the whole nation were manifest to anyone who cared to see. In Berlin I saw no hollow-chested youths standing, cigarette in mouth, at the corners of the streets.

As for the German women, they, too, had changed. Under the post-war Republic there had been unpleasant contrasts between poverty and wealth. The rich women had been flamboyant, expensively dressed, and magnificently made-up. They had pulled many strings behind the curtain of the political puppet-stage. Now the contrasts had disappeared or, at any rate, had been narrowed. If you saw lipstick or rouge, it was on the face of some foreigner, the wife or daughter of some member of the diplomatic corps. In one respect all German women were now alike. They took part in the "Strength through Joy" movement. They paraded their muscular limbs on the great stadia of Germany. They were not unattractive, but they looked hard—hard in face and hard in physique.

There was an earnestness about them which was new to me. Again, it was not confined to one section of the community. It was as evident in the Berlin society woman as it was in the most rabid Nazi woman worker. The contrast with the London society women of 1938 was startling. In London débutantes were dancing "The Big Apple", "The Palais Glide" and the "Lambeth Walk", and a rich American hostess was arranging dancing lessons for the middle-aged at her house so that the dowagers might not criticise. In the Bond Street photographers' shops you saw photographs of pretty girls in Court dresses and of good-looking young men. The windows of the big photographers in Unter den Linden were filled with huge portraits of the Nazi leaders. In London man was a suppliant at woman's feet. The Berlin woman stood behind, and waited on man. She played a secondary part. Her place in the body politic of the nation had been relegated to the kitchen and the marriage-bed.

In his attitude towards woman's function in the national life the Fuehrer obviously shared Napoleon's views as expressed in the Emperor's famous answer to Madame de Stael's question: "Whom do you regard as the first among women?"

"The one who has the most children."

Perhaps the motive of both men was the same. It was the constant complaint of the Nazis that Germany needed open spaces for her vast population. When I was in Berlin, the most popular book among a nation that has ceased to read literature was a work called *People without Room*. Its sale had already run into hundreds of thousands of copies. Yet, without the requisite open spaces, the Fuehrer was striving his utmost to popularise the increase of children. By the magnetic combination of his own persuasive oratory and of liberal marriage premiums he was now able to boast that within five years he had raised the birth-rate of Germany by over 300,000.

It was stupendously impressive and stupendously disturbing. A Freudian, I think, could write an interesting analysis of the importance of sex in the development of the Nazi movement, not in the narrow sense in which the layman understands sex, but in the broader aspect of the influence of the general relationship between men and women on the character of a nation.

My own view is that the war psychosis in Germany is closely connected with the relationship of the sexes and with the position of woman in the state. There is some hope of preventing wars if you make woman the companion and intellectual equal of man. War becomes inevitable when you reduce the status of woman to that of a brood-mare. Apart from what may be a deliberate desire to produce cannon-fodder, this relegation is nothing less than a return to the primitive state in which the main functions of man are those of the warrior and the lover.

There is, I admit, one flaw in this argument. Not all women are pacifists, and to many the warrior-lover is still the most attractive of all males.

CHAPTER NINE

OF THE MANY conversations which I had with Germans in Berlin I think that the most interesting was my talk with Karl Silex. It was, at any rate, the frankest.

Silex had been a naval officer in the war. After the Armistice and the suppression of the German Navy he had found himself penniless and without a job. With typical German energy he had set himself to earn his living in whatever manner he could. One day a friend asked him to write a Stock Exchange article for a Berlin newspaper. The article was good enough to gain for him a post as a financial reporter. From these small beginnings he became a first-class journalist.

I had known him in London where for several years he was the correspondent of a German newspaper. He was a man of culture, a shrewd observer, and, I think, a sincere admirer of Britain. He had written an excellent book on the English. To-day, he is the editor-in-chief of the *Deutsche Allgemeine Zeitung* and the most widely-read publicist in Nazi Germany.

I went to see him at his flat and found him surrounded by newspapers and smoking a pipe in bed. He had broken a leg in a ski-ing accident and was conducting his paper by telephone from his couch. He was as friendly and as charming as ever. He wore no swastika on his pyjama jacket. Indeed, I believe that he has never joined the Nazi Party. But he had changed since his London days. To him, as to Herr von Reinbaben, Germany and Nazi-ism were now identical.

We discussed every aspect of the European situation, and, first and foremost, the question of Anglo-German relations. He told me that the Fuehrer was a pacifist in the sense that he understood, better than most people, the danger and folly of a European war. He said that from the first Herr Hitler had always desired an amicable understanding with Britain.

Germany still sought this understanding, but between equal nations there must be equality of treatment.

The Nazis were fully prepared to recognise Britain as the chief naval Power and, therefore, as the leading Overseas Power.

Germany was the leading Continental Power. Her legitimate interests on the Continent would have to be recognised by Britain.

He told me frankly that German feeling towards Britain was not as friendly as it had been. Germans had three grievances against the British. Every time Germany took a step in defence of her legitimate interests she found her path blocked by Britain.

All Germans, irrespective of their political views, disliked the mania of certain British ministers for delivering moral lectures to other countries. Germany did not interfere in the internal affairs of Britain. She had a right to expect that the British should not interfere in hers.

Above all, Germans were disgusted by the anti-German campaign conducted by a large section of the British Press.

When I suggested tactfully that it might be difficult to come to an understanding owing to the German penchant for "diplomatic surprises", he met my implied criticism with a counter-attack. Out came the Treaty of Versailles, the horrors of the immediate post-war years, the mockery of a League of Nations from which Germany had at first been excluded, and the peroration: "When we were weak, you held us down. What we have achieved, we have done solely by our own strength. To-day, there is a new situation—and a new Germany."

Although he did not say the actual words, his attitude implied: "if you don't like it, you must lump it."

Again I suggested that Germany's legitimate interests might clash with the legitimate interest of other countries. I mentioned Czechoslovakia. I told him that I had just come from that country and that I had lived there for years. I said that I considered it one of the most progressive and best-governed countries in Europe.

He smiled rather pityingly. It was, he said, unthinkable that three-and-a-quarter millions of Germans should be treated as a subject race, and that was how the Czechs had treated them since the first days of the new Republic. The situation would have to be remedied. He was confident that the remedy would not involve a European war.

My argument that the British Press was free was met with another smile. This time it was a knowing smile which seemed to imply: "Come now, Lockhart, you can't pull that particular piece of wool over my eyes." He countered the argument with a question and an assertion. "Which do you think is preferable: a Press that is controlled to the extent that it may publish only verified news or a Press that is allowed to publish deliberate untruths? With a few exceptions no British editor has as free a hand as the editor of a German newspaper."

I did not argue the point further. I might have pointed out that the German Press, which was so sensitive to criticism of Germany, attacked other nations like Czechoslovakia in a language unparalleled in the history of journalism. But I was here to gather information, not to engage in polemics. I went on with my questions. "What about the Jews?"

On this subject Herr Silex was not so communicative. I should like to think that he is not a violent anti-Semite, for he is a kind and pleasant man. Nevertheless, he did not criticise the official attitude. German Jews, he said, were Germany's concern. We British did not understand them. We had no Jewish question in the sense that Germany had. When we had a Jewish problem, our own attitude would be different.

I left Karl Silex with a nostalgic feeling of regret. I had liked him in the past. I still liked him. But since 1933 we had travelled in opposite directions.

I found, nevertheless, that the sentiments which he had

expressed quite dispassionately were shared in accentuated form by every supporter of the Nazi régime that I met. Germany wanted peace, but she wanted it on her own terms. And the experience of the post-war period had taught her to believe that her new armed strength was her best diplomatic weapon. There are few Germans under forty who do not accept the Fuehrer's axiom: "all the wisdom of this earth is as nothing unless served, covered and protected by force."

In Berlin the signs of force were manifest everywhere. In my hotel I was awakened every morning at six by the sound of fife and drum, by the tramp of marching feet, and by the whirr of flying aeroplanes. Above all, by the aeroplanes. A few months before my arrival in Berlin, America's most famous airman had visited the German capital. He had been shown something of Germany's air strength, for General Goering is proud of his achievement. On his return the American told his impressions to an English friend of mine in the one sentence:

"If I were an Englishman, I should feel uneasy."

Americans may feel safe, but every European who knows the new Germany cannot be wholly free from apprehension.

The attitude of the average German Nazi towards the Czechs was even firmer and more uncompromising than that of Herr Silex. It was not confined to a sense of injustice. Most impartial observers would admit, I think, that the large German minority in Czechoslovakia has suffered some injustice, even if the German grievances have been artificially fomented. But in Berlin the German attitude had its roots in that racial superiority which the British claim or used to claim for themselves in Eastern countries and on which the foundations of their colonial empire were built. In pre-war days I was old enough to remember the anger caused among the Poles by Prince Buelow's official reference to them as "prolific rabbits who were a nuisance to Prussian landowners." In their abusive references to the Czechs the Nazis descended to a lower scale in the animal world.

As for the Jewish question no Nazi and few Germans except the violent anti-Nazis were sane on the subject. Their hate of the Jews was like a rabies that had infected a whole nation. Yet, if there is to be appeasement in Europe and some measure of understanding with Germany, the German attitude towards Jewry cannot be ignored. Hate is always unreasonable, but it is rarely groundless, even if the grounds themselves are mean and despicable.

Most Nazis, when they can be persuaded to refrain from abuse, give the same excuse for the violence of the anti-Semitic campaign in Germany. The Jews, they say, are parasites. Their genius is unproductive. They batten on and exploit the poorer German majority. Their parasitical qualities were always detrimental, but, owing to the weakness of the Socialist administration, they became disastrous to the state during the difficult post-war years. At a time when the mark was tumbling the financial cunning of the Jews enabled them to prosper while Germans were being ruined. They used their prosperity to extend their grip on the public services, the liberal professions, and the Press, until their representation far exceeded their proper proportion.

There is nothing new in this theory. Although it is unsound economically and only true to the extent that the Jews are more intelligent, work harder, and drink less than many Aryans, it is the chief basis of anti-Semitism in most countries. For the movement is not, and never has been, confined to Germany. I can still remember the unreasoning fury of the anti-Semitic outburst in France during the long years of the Dreyfus case, when anti-Semitic families went to church and left ostentatiously before the sermon because the priest or minister was pro-Dreyfus. In pre-war Russia I have seen dissolute hooligans beat up Jews while the police looked on and smiled. Since the war I have met Hungarians and Poles who could not speak two sentences without cursing a Jew, and in more recent times I have heard a Rumanian minister discuss with dispassionate calm the necessity of introducing restrictive measures of a far-reaching nature against the Jews in Rumania.

But the chief reason for the persecution of the Jews in Germany is never mentioned by any Nazi. Anti-Semitism is a deliberate part of Nazi policy fomented more for Nazi political purposes than because of any deep-rooted racial antipathy to the Jews.

Every revolutionary party, and the Nazis are essentially a revolutionary party, uses hate as its chief instrument for acquiring support. In Russia the Bolshevik minority stirred mass hatred of the war into a tidal wave, and on that wave they rode to supreme power. In Germany the Nazis had an even easier task. Where poverty and unemployment are widespread, hatred is easily roused. It was not enough for the Nazis to lay the whole blame on the Allies. All German parties did this. In order to win votes and gain supporters, the Nazis had to find an object of hatred nearer home. The Jews were ready to hand. Under the Republic some of the richer Jews, at any rate, had made an ostentatious display of their wealth. It was easy to persuade the German people that their economic sufferings were caused by parasites who had fattened on the poverty of others and ruined the good German currency. As far back as 1924, hatred of the Jews became a foremost plank in the Nazi programme. It has remained there ever since.

There is, I think, another reason for Nazi anti-Semitism, and this is connected with Russia. Although most British people regard Germany's mistrust of Russia as a sham mistrust and as a convenient cloak for re-armament and sinister ambitions, I believe that this view is based on false premises. Just as the smaller Slav nations fear German aggression, so, too, Germany has a genuine dread of the greater Slav danger to herself. This dread is partly racial. To every German the Central European problem presents itself as a struggle between Slav and Teuton. But the German dread of Russia is also actuated by the fear of Communism. Like every country which has had the Communist terror on its doorstep, Germany is violently and rabidly anti-Communist. In China today the Chinese make a distinction between white races, yellow races, and Russians. The German Nazi does not recognise a Bolshevik as a human being.

I have met no German Nazi to whom Bolshevism is not synonymous with Jewry. It is useless to explain to him that the whole ideology of Bolshevism is Russian and not Jewish. He will not listen to you. His attitude is governed by a mass of inconsistencies. Like his Fascist colleagues in Italy, he has borrowed much from the administrative methods of Soviet Russia. The Hitler Youth is modelled on the Communist Youth of Stalin who first taught children to arm. The Berlin Gestapo is a replica of the Moscow Ogpu. But the Nazi will tell you in one breath that he is anti-Jewish because the Jew is a parasite and a profiteer. In the next he is away off on the charge of Socialism and Bolshevism which to him are almost synonymous terms. It is waste of time to point out to him that his attitude is wholly inconsistent or that the vast majority of Jews are neither profiteers nor Communists. In his eyes the Jew is guilty both ways. Was Karl Marx not a Jew? he asks you. He quotes the names of other Jewish writers on Socialism. Triumphantly he tells you that all the Socialist literature of the British Labour Party is written by Jews.

I have always admired the logic and reasoning power of the Jews. It is possible that in politics their logic has done them harm. I am a cynic about politics, which throughout the ages provide little more than a depressing record of passions and pendulums. In Germany the pendulum has not yet commenced to swing back, but passion is given a free rein. During my stay in Berlin there was a momentary lull in the more violent forms of cruelty against the unfortunate Jews. But if the voice of Streicher was temporarily hushed, it was still possible to buy on every bookstall the most scurrilous and pornographic anti-Semitic literature.

To-day, largely on account of Germany's attitude, anti-

Semitism has become one of the gravest problems in the civilised world. It is boiling under the surface in Poland, Rumania and Hungary. It is raising its ugly head in countries where it was previously unknown—in Italy, even in Yugoslavia—and the evidences of it are faintly discernible in Russia itself. It is being fomented by the clash of ideologies between the rival groups of Powers in Europe, and, unless its cessation is included as part of a general European appeasement, it is only too likely to spread before its fury exhausts itself. Incidentally, it would be interesting to know what Signor Mussolini has done with the medallion of Marx which in his Socialist days he always carried with him as a mascot and a charm.

There is another aspect of Anglo-German relations. I did not discuss it with Herr Silex, but I found among most Nazis a widespread contempt for democracy and a belief that France and, in a lesser degree, Britain were decadent. When the new army regulations, allowing the British soldier to wear mufti and to stay out late of nights, were published, the German cartoonists made merry. One cartoon showed a British Tommy lying in bed, while a smartly dressed maid brings him his morning tea and says: "The sergeant-major's compliments, Sir, and what time would you like to go on parade?"

On the other hand, I cannot say that I found any marked unfriendliness in the Nazi attitude towards Great Britain. Certain sections of the British public roused the full force of the Nazi ire. But the desire not to antagonise Great Britain to extremes was evident, and there was even a certain admiration for the experience and wisdom of the British type of statesman. If the days were gone for ever when German Ministers used to come to the British Embassy in the Wilhelmstrasse in order to consult Lord D'Abernon before they took a decision on any matter affecting foreign affairs, British diplomacy was still recognised as the one factor with which Germany had to reckon.

z

Lip-service, and perhaps more than lip-service, were paid to Mr. Chamberlain's efforts to promote European appeasement, and every word that he uttered on the German-Czech situation was read and studied in Berlin, with feelings either of relief or of apprehension. Nazis might profess to sneer at, and to question the motives of, the British rearmament campaign, but they followed its development with an interest which was the clearest proof that the strength of Britain entered more forcibly into Nazi calculations than the Nazis themselves pretended.

My most entertaining experience in Berlin was a visit to the Sportpalast to hear Dr. Goebbels speak. It was five years since I had last listened to his fiery oratory, and I wanted to see what progress this little demagogic wizard had made. His speech that evening marked the opening of the campaign for the plebiscite on Austria. Probably only Dr. Goebbels among Germans saw the inconsistency of the Fuehrer's removing Herr Schuschnigg, because he had dared to advocate a plebiscite, and then holding a Hitlerian plebiscite of his own. The little doctor did not neglect this obvious weakness entirely.

The democratic countries, he said, liked plebiscites. Well, Germany would give them one.

To me and, indeed, to the vast audience the most interesting part of his speech was his review of German diplomacy before and after Hitler. He began on a serious note. The tempo was slow. There was a withering contempt in his voice, as powerful as and more musical than, the Fuehrer's. Under the Republic Germany was weak. She grovelled, but she received nothing. Then came the Fuehrer. He went into the Rhineland—"and there was no war." He went into Spain "and there was no war." He went into Austria—"and there was no war." Each refrain was accompanied by quick staccato jerks of the right arm somewhat in the manner of Maklakoff, the great Russian orator of the former Duma, and with the last "and there was no war" the voice rose to

a shrill crescendo. The huge crowd, hypnotised by the oratory and delirious with delight, cheered itself hoarse. Dr.
Goebbels permitted himself a smile. His face reminds me
slightly of Borotra's, and on the rostrum he exhibits something of the same agility as the "bounding Basque" displays
on the tennis-court.

Then he went on with his speech. It was devoted to a
comparison between Germany under Hitler and Austria
under Schuschnigg. Since 1933 Germany had raised the total
number of persons employed from 11,500,000 to 19,000,000,
the consumption of meat had increased by 4 kilogrammes
per head of population, that of sugar by 5 kilogrammes, that
of wheat flour by 11 kilogrammes. During the same period
the consumption of meat in Austria had sunk by 44 per cent.,
that of sugar by 5 per cent., and that of wheat flour by 21 per
cent. From 1933 to 1937 the births in Germany rose from
97,000 to 1,276,000. In Austria they sank from 102,000
to 85,000. In 1937 the birth-rate in Berlin was 14 per
1000; in Vienna only 5.4 per 1000, the lowest rate in the
world.

I could not know if the figures were correct, but, as a
speech, it was an impressive performance. It confirmed another of the Fuehrer's dicta: "the spoken word is the sole
force capable of producing really great revolutions of sentiment." On the two occasions that I have heard Dr. Goebbels
speak, I have felt myself back in Moscow in the early days of
the Bolshevik revolution. Lenin would have found a job for
him, for the power of swaying the masses is in the little
German's blood.

He is also the greatest master of propaganda that the world
has ever seen. In this respect his power is almost limitless, and
his influence is not confined to his own country. You find
it popping up in nearly every foreign capital in the form of
broadcasts and of articles on the mal-treatment of German
minorities abroad, on the alleged myth of Czech democracy,
and on any subject whose ventilation may be expected to

facilitate the hammer-blows of Hitlerian diplomacy. Naturally, however, his power is strongest in Germany itself, and to-day the German people are allowed to know of the outside world only as much as he thinks fit for their consumption.

Here again Nazi-ism has learnt from Bolshevism, although Dr. Goebbels has far outstripped his Moscow teachers. Perhaps the most unfortunate characteristic of Nazi Germans is their deep-rooted belief that Germany lost the last war through the inefficiency of her propaganda. They have made up their mind that she will not fail in this respect in a future war.

Dr. Goebbels is dangerous both in himself and in the high office which he holds. He is more fanatical than his Fuehrer. From the point of view of pure intellect he has a better brain than any of his Nazi colleagues. Yet he has many enemies. Even in his own Party he is more respected than liked, and more than one Nazi story bears witness to his unpopularity.

The Nazis are in deadly earnest about big things. They are grim enough about little things which make foreign visitors laugh. They see nothing comic in the decree which lays down the music to be played at Nazi marriage services: Beethoven's *Creation Hymn*, Grieg's *Liebeslied*, Handel's *Largo*, which is the tune which Mr. Lloyd George wishes to be played at his funeral, the March from *Lohengrin*, and *Deutschland Ueber Alles*. Yet they are not entirely lacking in humour. They have their own jokes.

Britain and the United States have been flooded with anti-Nazi stories. Most of them are invented to besmirch the Nazi achievement and to illustrate the cruelty of the Nazi leaders. But every Nazi story sheds lustre on the wisdom of the Fuehrer. I give here two examples of Nazi stories which were popular during my last visit to Berlin.

The first takes the form of a riddle. What is the difference between Martin Luther, Hitler, Goebbels and Dr. Schacht?

The answer is:

> "Martin Luther said what he believed;
> Hitler believes what he says.
> Goebbels does not believe what he says;
> Schacht does not say what he believes."

The second story illustrates a talent which the Fuehrer shares with the late Vladimir Ilyitch Lenin: namely, his ability to hold himself aloof from Party wrangles and to keep his team in order without fuss and without any outward show of discipline. Dr. Schacht is on the point of making one of his periodical attempts to resign. He tries to see Herr Hitler, but the Fuehrer is an expert in keeping away from him people who may want to force his hand before he has made up his mind. After days of fruitless endeavour Dr. Schacht at last succeeds in button-holing his man. He begins to explain his grievances. But the Fuehrer cuts him short.

"I am sorry", he says, "but I am far too busy to be able to attend to these matters just now. Nevertheless, I'll give you a piece of advice. On your way home take the tramway and before you get into the car look at it carefully and see what is written on the front and on the back."

Dr. Schacht thinks that Herr Hitler is, indeed, mad but, impelled by an irresistible curiosity, he does what he has been told. He looks at the front of the car and reads the notice: "It is forbidden to speak to the Fuehrer (Driver)." At the back he finds another notice: "It is strongly forbidden to jump out of the car while it is moving."

Dr. Schacht takes the hint. He says no more about his resignation, and the story, told all over Germany, puts the Fuehrer's stock still higher up.

To what heights his popularity has soared I saw with my own eyes. One morning towards luncheon-time I found my way blocked by a huge crowd. The Viennese troops, now dressed in German uniforms, were leaving Berlin. As they passed the corner of the Wilhelmstrasse, the Fuehrer came on to a balcony to take the salute. The crowd became transfigured.

More than thirty years before, as a young student, I had stood in a similar crowd to watch the Kaiser and the King of Spain, accompanied by a glittering escort, ride down Unter den Linden. Then the uniforms had been brighter. But there was no doubt in my mind whether Kaiser or Fuehrer was the greater hero to his people. The balance of exalted enthusiasm was on the Fuehrer's side.

Herr Hitler may be like an erratic golfer in that his command of the unexpected is infinite. But he knows how to handle Germans, and to every class of German, and especially to German youth, he is as infallible as is the Pope to Catholics. The belief finds public expression in numerous catchwords such as "Hitler weather", "Hitler luck", and "Hitler instinct". The association of good weather and good luck with the divinity of the Fuehrer are merely further evidence of German romanticism. The belief in the Hitlerian instinct has a more solid foundation. Hitherto, it has proved itself to be remarkably sound. It is perhaps not too much to say that on its continued soundness depends the future peace of Europe.

CHAPTER TEN

IT IS A common-place that Nazi-ism is a youth movement. Its appeal is addressed to youth. It relies mainly on youth for its support. To judge Germany, therefore, without some personal knowledge of the young generation is equivalent to assessing the value of an army solely by its senior officers.

It is not easy for middle-age to penetrate the mind of youth. As far as mere external observation goes, my impression is that the young men and women in the new Germany are happy in mind and body and healthy in their outlook on life. They may be bewitched by Nazi doctrine. Certainly their hero-worship of the Fuehrer is almost fanatical. They may regard service in a labour camp as a nuisance, but they accept it willingly. They may ignore the atmosphere of repression which seemed to envelope me wherever I went. But they do not talk of war. Like the young Bolsheviks, they never question the wisdom of their leaders. Again like the young Bolsheviks, they believe that, sooner or later, all foreign youth will follow their example. But in their normal intercourse they are frank and friendly, and on the field of play they are good sportsmen.

I know that many British girls and boys who go to Germany are impressed by the healthy and friendly spirit of German youth. Munich, the finishing school of so many British society girls, has been a productive breeding-ground of British pro-Nazi-ism. My two nephews, both prominent athletes, spent two terms in Germany after leaving school. The German students, they told me, were remarkably good at field sports and gymnastics. They led healthy lives. They made a fetish of physical culture. But war, seldom if ever, entered into their conversation.

My two nephews enjoyed their time in Germany. My own son did not. I sent him to the university town where one of my nephews had lived. He came back an anti-Nazi.

He was irritated by the attempts of the young Nazi men to proselytise him. They had, he said, no ideas of their own. The only German that he found attractive and interesting was the widely-travelled head of the family with which he stayed.

These are two contradictory views of British youths.

As far as my own experiences are concerned, I was handicapped to some extent by the fact that I had been partly educated in Germany and by my prejudices in favour of the old system. But I had many opportunities of observing the wide cleavage between youth and middle-age in Germany. My friends in German diplomacy or in the German Government service could be divided into two categories. Those who were under forty embraced the Nazi faith with enthusiasm. The "over-forties" had not been able to readjust their minds so rapidly. Although they continued to serve the state, and to serve it loyally, they made many secret reservations in their acceptance of the Nazi creed.

Even more striking was the contrast between youth and age in the case of two German business friends, a father and son, whom I had known intimately for many years. The father was cautious in his criticisms. There were certain features in the Nazi programme which won his whole-hearted approval. He praised the restrictions on the multiple shops and the restoration of the "little man" to economic independence. But there were many things that he disliked and feared. He was a good German, but I should not consider him as more than a lukewarm supporter of the present régime.

The son, a fine, upstanding young man who spoke fluent English, was enchanted with the new Germany. It was his Germany. Now that everything had been put right and everyone was happy, why didn't I come more often? I must come in the summer and stay for a long time. Restrictions and war-dangers? There were no restrictions. General Goering had put down poaching. I should have fishing and shooting such as I had never had before. As for the danger of war, it was unthinkable. Nobody in Germany wanted war. There were some silly Czechs who were making trouble, but the Fuehrer would deal with them in his own time and in his own wisdom. But there would be no war. The Germans would not fight, and the Czechs couldn't.

He spoke in almost the same language as the tourist propaganda posters and advertisements of the German Information Bureau in London. "Do you want to renew your youth? Then come to Germany. You will find truth and friendship in personal contacts."

The willingness to be friends, at least with foreign Aryan youth, was evident. In some respects it was a reassuring sign. But in the education of German youth there were certain features which I found profoundly disturbing.

I had a long talk with a schoolmaster friend. He told me that in the schools and universities the standard of work had fallen. The minds of the boys and students were being distracted by other activities. To-day, every schoolboy learnt to signal, to read a chart, and to dig a trench. The work suffered. And not only the work of the schoolboys and students. With the elimination of the Jewish and anti-Nazi professors and teachers the quality of the teaching and research work had been greatly reduced.

My acquaintance was, admittedly, no Nazi enthusiast. But the truth of his statements was confirmed by proofs furnished by the Nazis themselves. While I was in Berlin, I bought a collection of the new Nazi text-books for schools and universities. The new histories threw a revealing light on Nazi methods of education.

Like all text-books now used in the German schools, they are written in accordance with the explicit instructions laid down in the handbook of the Reich and Prussian Ministry of Education. They therefore conform to one standard pattern.

The central date in Germany's new historical life is the 30th of January, 1933. Everything that happened in Germany before that date leads up to Adolf Hitler. Everything that has happened since 1933 is Adolf Hitler. The Great War is represented as a struggle of the Western democracies, typified by the Latin idea and the Anglo-Saxon conception of civilisation, against the spirit of Potsdam and the North-German conception. The causes of the war are the encirclement policy of the Allies and the ambitions of Serbia, "who fixed greedy eyes on Bosnia and Herzegovina". The German army, "alone against the world", is not defeated in the field. It is stabbed in the back by the Jews and Socialists in the rear. By order of the Ministry the heroism of the frontline soldier is to be taken as the foundation of the new national attitude.

These are perhaps natural tendencies. In their history textbooks all nations extol their victories and gloss over their failures.

It is the treatment of the Peace and the post-war period which makes one shudder and wonder where Germany is going. The Treaty of Versailles is condemned, again quite understandably, as the greatest betrayal in history. Much more serious is the spirit of hate and of revenge which pervades every page. The horrors of the French occupation of the Ruhr are perpetuated and magnified. In one history for the junior classes the following sentence is printed in distinctive leaded type: "The troops of the Occupation withdrew. They left 600 black bastards behind them. . . . Young German, remember the sufferings and the courage of your Rhineland compatriots!"

Nearly half of this particular text-book—and it is typical of the others—is devoted to the war and the post-war period. The lost territories, treated under the heading of "People Without Room", figure prominently in the list. The children are taught to be strong in order that these territories may soon be recovered. "We must go back to our old slogan: 'We will ride to the Eastland.' East Prussia has room enough; it is 'Room without People'."

In 1914 it was a sin for Serbians to seek to free their

countrymen in Bosnia and Herzegovina. To-day, it is the duty of every schoolmaster in Germany to instil into his charges the determination that not only the Sudeten Germans, but every German community living abroad must be incorporated in the Reich.

The glorification of racial superiority and of the armed might of National Socialism stands out on every page. The post-war period before Hitler is treated as Germany's "years of shame". Every German who has ever had a liberal idea is either neglected or vilified. Walther Rathenau, a patriot and one of the ablest Germans of his time, was murdered by the Nazis before they achieved power. He is honoured with a paragraph:

"At that time (the eve of the Armistice) a certain Walther Rathenau, who also played a part in the hour of Germany's fate, wrote the following shameful sentence: 'The history of the world would not have been worth writing if the German Kaiser had come riding in triumph into Berlin at the head of his victorious troops.' Could a German ever write like that? It was the *Jew* Rathenau, who a few years later was laid low by the avengers' bullets."

In accordance with the ministerial instructions the period from 1918 to 1932 has to be described as the attempt to force Western European ideas on Germany. During this period Catholicism has to be featured as the ally of the Marxist and Capitalist Internationals and Jewry as striving to establish world domination in Germany and in Russia. Germany has to be shown on the verge of Bolshevism. Then salvation comes to her in the person of Adolf Hitler. A new period opens with the apotheosis of the Fuehrer.

The heroes of the new history are not the generals, but the young men. Some are worthy heroes like the airmen Richthofen and Immelmann, the submarine commander Weddingen, and Leo Schlageter, the good-looking martyr of the Occupation period who was shot by the French for sabotage in the Ruhr.

Others, however, are of a more doubtful category. They include Horst Wessel, the composer of the song which ranks with *Deutschland Ueber Alles* as the Nazi national anthem. The son of a well-known Protestant preacher, he was a good-looking blond, who, left poorly off at the end of the war, led for several years a hand-to-mouth and disreputable existence. He had a job as a taxi-driver. But mostly he was known as a frequenter of low night-haunts. His mistress was a girl taken off the streets of Berlin. Then he was converted to Nazi-ism by Dr. Goebbels. He took over an S. A. troop and waged a semi-gangster war against the Communists. In the end the Reds got him. Eight of them entered his flat and shot him down in cold blood. Even Nazi supporters admit, although they dare not say so openly, that apart from his services to Nazi-ism Wessel was little better than a degenerate. But his martyrdom has washed away all the stain of a doubtful past, and to-day he is enshrined as the Rouget de Lisle of Nazi Germany.

Gone, too, are the old divisions of bourgeois who looked to Geneva, and of proletarian who fixed his eyes on Moscow. To-day, Germany is taught to regard itself as a united nation, and the chief precept of every German history is "Ein Volk, Ein Reich, Ein Fuehrer".

Even more significant of the mental fodder which is now being offered to German youth under National Socialism is the literary fare provided by the bookshops. I spent two afternoons in compiling a list of the books which, to the exclusion of almost all others, filled the front windows of the leading bookshops and the station bookstalls. I append it with a few comments. I have omitted the numerous works on various aspects of the National Socialist movement. They are, of course, available everywhere.

The list is divided into three categories: (*a*) Histories and war memoirs, (*b*) monographs and technical studies of war, and (*c*) books dealing with the German communities abroad and with German land-hunger.

(*a*). Clausewitz's and Treitschke's *Histories*. (These old friends are back in every window.)

Lives of Frederick the Great, Moltke, and *Nelson.* Jellicoe's *Memoirs* and Mr. Duff Cooper's *Haig.* (The German translation of *Haig* has had a large sale. It is read not because of its literary merits, but because it shows to Germans how nearly they came to winning the world war.)

Roman Heads. India's Security. Imperium Britannicum. Britain's Route to India. All-Islam: World Power of To-morrow. Japan in the World. Italy in the World (The interest in the weak points of the British Empire is significant.) Ernest Udet's *My Flying Life.*

(*b*). *Skagerack* (The Battle of Jutland: 300,000 copies sold). *Gibraltar. Suez. Tannenberg. The Hell of Gallipoli. Weather-Zones of World Policy. Politico-Economic Strategy. The German Soldier. Letters of the World-War. War Letters of Fallen Students.*

Technical Warfare. The War of the Future. War Without Pity.

(*c*). *People Without Room. All Waters of Bohemia flow towards Germany.*

On the Outposts for Germany. Wiete Wants to Go to Africa. (This last is a popular book, whose object is to persuade young German women to go to the former German colonies. The blurb has stamped on it in large letters the words: "Ninety-Five Per Cent. Get Married".)

These books, I repeat, were not taken from the back shelves. According to their display and to their sales, they were the most popular books in Berlin in the spring of 1938.

And no one will deny that they breathe the spirit of the Nazi official programme. Official Germany is dominated by war psychosis. While I was in Berlin, the Mexican Government expropriated the British and American oil properties in Mexico. The next day nearly all the Berlin newspapers carried a front-page article on "The Oil Trusts and War".

Nazis, therefore, can hardly blame foreigners if, as all foreigners do, they ask themselves the question: How long can a nation, taught on these principles and fed on this mental fare, be held back? The Fuehrer is responsible for Germany's education. Give a child a gun and he will want to use it.

And the nation was not only being taught. It was being trained and equipped as quickly as Nazi energy and Nazi drive could supply the uniforms, the guns, and the aeroplanes. When and where was this mad race going to end? In 1931 sixty nations of the world spent approximately £800,000,000 on armaments. By 1936 the same sixty countries were spending over £2,000,000,000—an increase of 150 per cent. in five years. Of these two billions Europe spent £1,750,000,000, or five-sixths of the world's total expenditure. And of the £1,750,000,000 Russia, Italy and Germany accounted for £1,300,000,000, or nearly 75 per cent.

These were the things which, in spite of all the pacific assurances given by the Nazi leaders, caused foreigners to be apprehensive, which induced shrewd French observers to write home to their friends: "tout va vers le conflit suprême entre le monde chrétien et le nouvel Islam; il ne nous manque que Charles Martel."[1] Was Nazi-ism a new Islam? It was not only the French who feared that it was. Englishmen and Americans—young diplomatists, young journalists, experienced business-men—came to live in Berlin. They came with open minds, prepared to believe the best and having already rejected as unworthy of credence the anti-Nazi stories published in their own country. And what happened? After a few months they were disillusioned, suspicious, anxious.

But I saw no sign of disillusionment or anxiety on the face of German Youth. It was true that it was almost shut off from contact with the outside world. But was it as intolerant as its masters were? Was it not curious and inquisitive like the youth of all countries?

---

[1] Everything is moving towards the supreme conflict between the Christian world and the new Islam; but we lack a Charles Martel.

During the summer of 1938 I saw one example of German youth accepting the evidence of its own eyes. A Nazi girl student came to stay with some friends of mine in Scotland. At first she was critical of all that she saw. Everything was better done in Germany than in Britain. The slums of Scotland made her shudder. Then her hosts took her to see the Glasgow Exhibition. By accident they almost brushed against the King and Queen, who were walking freely and unguarded among the people. The Nazi girl was amazed. In her own country she had been present at many Nazi manifestations, but she had never seen a Nazi leader who was not ringed by a bodyguard. She was impressed. Her conversation changed. She went back to Germany with at any rate one new idea in her mind.

I should like to think that there are many other young Germans like this Nazi girl who, when their vision has been broadened, will realise that there is something better to do with their lives than digging trenches and flying military aeroplanes.

Only a few months ago I spent an evening with one of the highest British officials in Palestine. He told me that the only hope of a peaceful solution of the Palestinian problem lay in the Arab and Jewish youth. The young Jews, he said, were showing signs of breaking away from their leaders. The young Arabs were no longer so subservient to their imams. If the British could keep the administrative machine running for a few more years, the young Jews and the young Arabs would make their own agreement and settle down together to the task of developing the country.

On most foreign visitors German youth makes a favourable impression, and I should like to believe that, with the passage of time, these healthy German girls and boys will see the folly of international enmity, and the illogicality of persecuting the foreign minority within their own territory and demanding better treatment for the German minorities abroad, and that they will then extend to their neighbours like the Czechs the same friendly hand which they now seem so willing to hold out to British youth.

It is perhaps a Utopian dream. Illogicality is not confined to Germans. In Britain and in other countries there are reactionaries who gloss over the cruelties of the Fascists and Nazis; there are Liberals and Socialists who shut their eyes to the greater savageries of Moscow. Humanitarianism has its party labels all over the world.

In particular, the future attitude of German youth is difficult to foretell. For propaganda is a new force in the world, and, when it is applied ruthlessly to the education of youth, its effects are incalculable. At present German youth accepts unquestioningly all the tenets of the Nazi faith: the illogicalities, the cruelties, the racial hatred, the burden of military service, and the claims on self-sacrifice, not only because it is told that these things are necessary, but mainly, I think, because its mind has been captured and fettered, almost from the cradle, by the German educational machine.

CHAPTER ELEVEN

AS MY STAY in Berlin drew near to its end, I began to try to crystallise my impressions. For ten years I had followed the development of the Nazi movement. I had striven conscientiously to free myself from prejudice. If I still retained my affection for my old German friends, I had also sought new acquaintances among the active members of the Nazi Party. Now the barometer of my emotions swayed between a deep depression and a cautious optimism.

It was easy to appraise the good parts of the Nazi programme. The achievement was there in ferro-concrete and cement, in the national consciousness of a new strength, and in the corporate energy of a nation bent to one will. In Germany you were either a Nazi or a pariah, but in every other respect social distinctions had been abolished. In Berlin I went twice to the theatre. The audience at the Opera reminded me more of the Big Theatre in Moscow than of Covent Garden. There was, too, something to admire in the Puritanism of the movement. The Fuehrer himself was a kind of Cromwell who, if he preached intolerance, also taught and practised self-denial, and his worshippers accepted his precept and followed his example. There was one fundamental difference between Nazi-ism and post-war Western democracy. In France and in Britain rich and poor alike expected something *from* the state, and grumbled when they did not get it. In Germany youth, at all events, was prepared to pull in its belt and to make sacrifices *for* the state.

Nor did I find it difficult to make allowances for German resentment of the Treaty of Versailles and the war guilt stigma. In a war or a civil war both sides are always right. I could appreciate Germany's passion for prestige. For fourteen years she had suffered bitter humiliation, until equality had become a national complex. And I could readily understand Germany's dislike of the Franco-Soviet Pact. It was a curious combination even to Western eyes, and to every German it looked suspiciously like a repetition of the former encirclement policy.

But there were other features of Nazi-ism which were more puzzling. To a friend of mine, who knows him perhaps better than any foreigner, Herr Hitler had said: "Nothing will induce me to go to war, but nothing will make me forego one jot of Germany's legitimate interests."

What were Germany's "legitimate interests"? Her trade with Central Europe and the Balkans was one interest. That was her legitimate sphere. Combined with Austria she took the preponderant share of the exports of these countries: 47 per cent. from Bulgaria, 41 per cent. from Hungary, 36 per cent. from Yugoslavia, 33 per cent. from Greece, and 27 per cent. from Rumania. It would be a folly as well as a crime for a combination of Powers to attempt to shut her out from developing her trade with these countries.

But was racial superiority a "legitimate interest"? When Germany insisted that we should recognise her as the leading Power on the Continent, did that mean that she was free to trample on "inferior" races? In Central Europe there were states of free peoples like the Czechoslovaks, the Rumanians, and the Yugoslavs, who had made remarkable progress since the war. These peoples wanted only peace in order to consolidate and extend the work of progress. Germany put guns before butter. And already she was talking in the language of guns to Czechoslovakia, the one new country in Central Europe whose form of Government conformed most closely to the ideals of democratic liberty. Germany could do what she liked inside her own frontiers. But was the carrying of the Nazi crusade into other countries to be accepted as a "legitimate interest"?

There was another aspect to this particular question. "Legitimate interests" are, or have been hitherto, a prerogative of the strong. They have a habit of growing with increasing strength. Germany's had not shrunk. They were not likely to shrink in the future. Pan-Germanism was in the ascendant as never before in history, and Herr Hitler was its god. What were the "legitimate interests" of a man who had openly proclaimed his hatred of "the motley collection of Greeks, Poles, Hungarians, Rumanians, Serbs and Croats" in Vienna and who declared that in defending himself against the Jews he was doing "the Lord's work"?

In March, 1938, the Fuehrer had declared to the world that within two years there would not be an unemployed man in Austria. He would fulfil his boast. Then he might say: "I have performed this miracle, but I am being hampered in its completion by impossible restrictions. I have to move goods from Carinthia to Hamburg. It is a crime that a great nation should be deprived of its natural outlet to the sea. I must have a port on the Adriatic!"

Would that be a "legitimate interest"? Another Great Power, similar to Germany in its form of government and in its outlook, would have to answer that question. We might say that it was no concern of ours. But if trouble ensued who knew where it would stop?

No honest man who asked himself these questions could help feeling apprehensive. His fears might be exaggerated. But optimism put a strain on commonsense.

During the past two years I had revisited more than a dozen European countries. In all but two I had found governments and peoples groaning under the burden of re-armament and living in the dread of war. Most of them were small nations. Some represented the highest form of civilisation in the modern world. All desired peace.

In the two other countries war was glorified as an ideal necessary for race preservation. The civil power had abdicated, and the administration was military in form if not in name.

Everywhere I had been, I had heard a mass of conflicting opinions. But in the small countries there were two points on which experienced men and women were in agreement.

In these countries there were few ideologists in the sense that they regarded the ultimate form of Europe's economic and spiritual life as a choice between Nazi-ism and Bolshevism. They refused to accept Nazi-ism as the champion of capitalism, or Bolshevism as the vanguard of a triumphant Socialism. They saw little difference in the administrative methods of the two systems. Hating both, they desired only to be left in peace to pursue their own saner course.

The other point—and here agreement was unanimous—concerned the maintenance of peace. In the smaller countries I met no minister, no public man, who did not believe that the key to European peace was to be found in an Anglo-German understanding, I met no man or woman who was not persuaded that, if war broke out anywhere in Europe, it would resolve itself into a final conflict between Britain and Germany.

Although this view was highly uncomfortable, I agreed with it. Germany was in the heart of Europe. There could be no freedom from anxiety in Western Europe so long as Germany remained outside the orbit of European co-operation.

I had, however, no illusions about the difficulty of achieving an Anglo-German understanding. The obstacles were almost insurmountable. There was a new Germany which we did not understand or which the Germans said we did not understand, and its destinies were in the hands of a man who had never been outside his own country. The break with the past was almost complete. You could see the continuity from Shakespeare to, say, Lord Halifax. You could trace none from Goethe to Hitler.

As for the British, it seemed to me that, in their attitude towards Germany, most people were too violently anti-Nazi or too blindly pro-Nazi.

Much as I admired his knowledge of Central European affairs, I could not agree with Mr. Wickham Steed, when he put "the proportion of German people who were in steady passive resistance to the Nazi rule" at not less than sixty per cent. The statement was not verifiable. It was a little like the father-to-the-thought wishes of the Russian *émigrés*, who for twenty years had steadily prophesied the collapse of Bolshevism within three months.

Still less could I swallow Major Yeats-Brown's assertion: "the young Germans are not being militarised; indeed, the opposite is true."

Here, too, the wish seemed to me to blind the judgment.

Nor could I find much comfort in the assurances of those distinguished British visitors who had had the privilege of meeting the Fuehrer socially in his mountain fastness. He was, they said, a man of peace. I hoped that it was true, although from that same mountain fastness he had sprung one or two surprises—surprises even to his own lieutenants—which were far from peaceful. When I asked highly-placed Germans who knew the Fuehrer's methods, they admitted that he was convinced that, provided Germany was strong enough, he could achieve all his aims piecemeal without war.

There was yet another fallacy that was very popular with British pro-Nazis: The Germans were our blood-brothers. An Englishman understood a German. He would never understand a Frenchman.

At the best this form of argument is only a half-truth. Personally I admit that I do not understand the French. They have the temerity to prefer Corneille and Racine to Shakespeare. To the Germans Shakespeare has long been a German and is already half-a-Nazi. I dislike French politics. I like individual Germans. I would rather have a German than a Frenchman as my companion on a fishing or shooting expedition.

But when I think of the cultural life of the two nations, my feelings are quite different. My mind goes back to Anjou, where I have spent the most peaceful months of my post-war life. I see the French peasant, thrifty, industrious, self-reliant.

He is an individualist, prizing his personal liberty and his personal equality above all the other gifts of life. He loves the soil and is prepared to defend it. But he hates war. He visualises it solely as an invasion of his country by a foreign aggressor. France is a nation of individualists trained in the civic virtues.

The virtues of the German are the warrior virtues. From birth he is taught that his strength is in the mailed fist, and that the destiny of his race is to follow the path of the Niebelungs. He is content and even proud to be an obscure unit in a great collective movement, and it is his passion for the corporate which leads so many German sympathisers in Britain to the doubtful conclusion that the exaltation of mailed strength in Germany is not dangerous "because Germans love playing at soldiers".

The British conception of life is closer to-day to the spirit of Anjou than to the spirit of Potsdam, and between British mentality and the mentality of Nazi Germany there is a gulf that will not be easily bridged.

I shall never forget the inaugural dinner of the Anglo-German Fellowship in London on December 5, 1935. The Fellowship had been formed in place of the former Anglo-German societies and clubs whose members were not in sympathy with Nazi-ism. Its main aim was to remove the misunderstandings between Britain and Nazi Germany. Membership therefore involved some sympathy with this praiseworthy object, and several important Nazis, including the Duke of Saxe-Coburg, made the journey from Berlin to London in order to attend the inaugural dinner.

In the chair was an ex-Minister of the Crown in the person of Lord Mount Temple. The goodwill was there. But the speeches were interminable, and long before the end everyone was irritated. While Herr von Tschammer und Osten, the Reich Sport Leader, was reading a dreary speech, the waiters filed into the room. The procession was headed by two chefs bearing a magnificent model in ice of an

Englishman and a German shaking hands under the flags of the two countries. This was too much for Commander C. B. Fry, that unique British genius who combines outstanding athletic prowess with a scholarship more brilliant than that of the late Lord Birkenhead and more profound than that of Sir John Simon. Although an admirer of Herr Hitler, the gallant commander could not resist the temptation of an epigram. "Ah," he said in an undertone louder than he intended, "*l'entente glaciale.*"

The blood brotherhood had broken down. At public dinners the flippant English are easily bored. The Germans are grimly serious.

I do not deny the value of racial relationships. But the value can be easily exaggerated. I do not believe that the blood-brotherhood theory forms a good approach to Anglo-American friendship. Still less do I believe that it constitutes the best basis for an Anglo-German understanding.

There are, I think, only two British foundations on which this understanding can be built. They are strength and tolerance.

We must be strong enough to make aggression by Germany impossible or tantamount to suicide. We cannot be wholly indifferent to the fate of Europe. If Europe is to be ruled by force, in the end we, too, shall have to bow to force.

We must be tolerant enough to promote by a combination of diplomatic action and firmness the economic and other readjustments necessary for the maintenance of peace and for the restoration of Germany's confidence in the efficacy of readjustment by negotiation. We must be tolerant to avoid alliances and *ententes* destined to create in the minds of other nations the feeling that they are being encircled by a hostile ring.

Our tolerance must go further. No man can spend, as I have spent, twenty-five years on the continent of Europe without realising the dangers to peace which come from violent nationalism. At the same time, in their impatience to create a World State the post-war internationalists are frequently as violent and as dangerous as the nationalists. Bellicosity and broken pledges are not the prerogative of dictatorships, and the history of democracies is rich in blood. We must learn to see the other fellow's point of view and to cultivate moderation.

To give a concrete example of sweet reason, I may quote the commendable attitude of Mr. Oliver Stanley who, in advocating tolerance as the best approach to understanding, said to me some months ago: "After all, every nation has broken its word at some time or other."

It is true that, by force of habit or, possibly, because Lord Halifax was also present, he hastened to add: "except ourselves perhaps."

But I see hope in that "perhaps". For the conduct of foreign affairs is or should be governed, not by what is ardently desired by one side, but by what is attainable by both sides. You cannot create a world state or even a modified League of Nations solely on democratic principles when more than half the population of Europe does not adhere to these principles. Democracies, like Fascist, Nazi and Bolshevik states, cannot have peace or any measure of appeasement solely on their own terms.

A policy of the attainable may seem unambitious and unsatisfying. But it has the virtue of realism. As a people the British, and especially the English, are a hundred years ahead of the rest of the world in political experience. Their governmental virtues are patience and forbearance. By the exercise of these qualities we can perhaps provide a relief to immediate tension and a breathing-space in which the Nazi revolution may modify itself. For in course of time all revolutions modify themselves.

The best-informed American in Berlin, a man who has spent many years of his life in Germany, told me recently that there would be no peace in Europe until the day when Herr Hitler drove, side by side with King George, to

Buckingham Palace. Well, British tolerance might try even this experiment.

But tolerance without strength is merely another form of surrender. We must be strong in ourselves and for ourselves. There is neither sense nor comfort in relying on unprofitable and unrealisable combinations. Only by our own strength can we win friends. Only by our own firmness can we hope to achieve any measure of European cooperation. The small nations of Europe wait on our firmness. The United States of America, the most powerful democracy in the world, will help a Europe that shows some sign of returning to common-sense. But, not unnaturally, America holds aloof from a Europe that always seems on the verge of war. The bond of blood will not persuade her to pick the British chestnuts out of the fire.

There was nothing new in this policy. It was in accordance with the best traditions of the past. It eschewed the dangers of alliances and guarantees. It recognised the value of non-intervention and the necessity of steering a middle course between the extremes of isolation and Utopian adventures. It commanded, I believed, as every foreign policy should command, the support of the majority of thinking people in Britain. It demanded armed strength, greater than we yet possessed, to put some check on violence and on the threats to peace, power sufficient to make Britain's word respected, and the requisite firmness to act resolutely when that word was flouted.

There was one question which I asked myself. Was Britain in a position to-day to put this policy, with all its implications, into effect?

I had only one doubt. Was our national will-power strong enough to make the necessary effort? Had freedom from invasion lulled us into a false sense of security? Or were our weaknesses only on the surface? Outwardly at all events, deep-cut divisions between wealth and poverty seemed to have undermined our unity. We devoted more time to pleasure, we had a higher standard of personal comfort, than any nation on the Continent. Had comfort and the love of pleasure sapped our energy?

Critics in England, I knew, always said that English people who lived abroad did not understand England. Perhaps this was true. There had been previous apathetic periods in our history. They seemed to follow naturally after great periods, as the listless, leaderless period of the Stuarts had followed the Elizabethan.

The foreigners who were always saying that Britain was decadent were expressing their wish rather than their belief. I remembered a conversation with a senior foreign diplomatist who has spent many years in London. He told me that when he first came to England he had only one friend, the *châtelaine* of a famous English house. His first visit was to her. She had recently had a child, and she led the Minister to the nursery to show him the baby.

"Ugly little brat, isn't it?" she said, with apparent indifference.

"It took me seven years," the Minister told me, "to understand that in that 'ugly little brat' there was more mother-love, pride of race, devotion, and capacity for sacrifice than in all the eloquent protestations of affection that I have heard from scores of women of other races."

English reserve, I know, covered a hidden strength of which few foreigners were conscious

At the same time there was, to me, something disturbing in the national unwillingness to face any form of thought that involved discomfort. There was even something unhealthy in our frequent use of the words "collective security". I knew that it gave to many foreigners, and not only European foreigners, the impression that we were trying to foist on others a burden which we ought to shoulder ourselves. For the biggest burden was ours. In a war we stood to lose more than any country in history. Even more unwholesome was the peace-at-any-price attitude of the "my money for my time" diners-out in London. Nations were like wolf-packs. When the strong grew feeble, they were pulled down.

I did not doubt our readiness to defend ourselves. What I sometimes questioned was our capacity for preparedness and our willingness to make, in time, those personal sacrifices which are the real strength of a nation. Violence of language was no substitute for national firmness. It merely convinced the dictator countries of the accuracy of General Goering's dictum: "the democracies talk, we act."

These were the thoughts which filled my mind during my last days in Berlin. Would they be the last days that I should ever spend in a city to which I owed much? I could not still my forebodings. I clung to every hope, to every promise. I made every allowance for the exuberance and violent language of dictators. I was not a stranger to the blood and fire of revolutions. But if I were to be honest to myself, I had to admit that my dominant emotion was one of profound anxiety.

On the eve of my departure I went to the British Embassy to say goodbye to Sir George Ogilvie Forbes. As I walked back to my hotel in the warmth of the mild spring evening, the sky behind the Brandenburger Tor was the colour of delicate rose-buds. Small fleecy clouds, tinged with pink, spread themselves like chariots across the horizon. The streets were almost empty. The chestnut-trees, a month in advance of their season, were already in bloom. For some time I stood at the corner of the Hermann Goeringstrasse admiring the scene. Presently the fleecy clouds smoothed themselves into flat stretches of yellow sand until the sky seemed like a lagoon with waves of mother-of-pearl washing the shores of amber islands.

I could not help contrasting this peaceful vista with all that I had seen during the past week: the mass of uniforms, the almost brutal earnestness of the Brown Shirts and of the black agents of the Gestapo, the huge new Air Ministry with its long grim fresco of bull-necked German generals on the front wall.

My last glimpse of Germany was at six in the morning at the last German station on the Dutch frontier. The long halt disturbed my sleep, and I rose up and opened the window. I heard the tramp of two thousand feet in unison. I looked out, and in the rain I saw a regiment of soldiers marching off to their morning exercises.

Nazi Germany was already at work.

INDEX

INDEX

2B

PRINTED IN GREAT BRITAIN
BY ROBERT MACLEHOSE AND CO. LTD.
THE UNIVERSITY PRESS, GLASGOW

EUROPE IN 1938

*The Red Circles indicate Towns
mentioned in the book*

Scale of miles

100   0   100   200   300   400   500

ATLANTIC OCEAN

NORTH SEA

SCOTLAND

Glasgow   Edinburgh

IRELAND

Dublin

WALES   ENGLAND

R. Thames   London

Esbj

Amsterdam   Groning
The Hague   Leukten   Gouda
HOLLAND   G
BELGIUM   Brussels
R. Rhine

Fl

R. Seine   Paris

Angers

FRANCE

Basle

Lausanne   Berne
Geneva   SWITZERLAND
Montreux
Stresa   Milan
Ve

ITAL

R. Ebro

PORTUGAL

Lisbon

SPAIN

Madrid

Barcelona

Valencia   MEDITERRANEAN

Ajaccio

R. Rhone

Sifton, Praed & Co., Ltd., London, S.W.I.